how the earth feels

dana luciano

ANIMA critical race studies otherwise
a series edited by mel y. chen, ezekiel j. dixon-román, and jasbir k. puar

how the earth feels

geological fantasy in the nineteenth-century united states

duke university press durham & london 2024

© 2024 Duke University Press
All rights reserved

Project Editor: Lisa Lawley
Designed by Aimee C. Harrison
Typeset in Portrait Text and Comma Base by
Westchester Publishing Services

Library of Congress Cataloging-in-Publication Data
Names: Luciano, Dana, author.
Title: How the earth feels : geological fantasy in the nineteenth-century United States / Dana Luciano.
Other titles: ANIMA (Duke University Press)
Description: Durham : Duke University Press, 2024. | Series: Anima: critical race studies otherwise | Includes bibliographical references and index.
Identifiers: LCCN 2023025629 (print)
LCCN 2023025630 (ebook)
ISBN 9781478025702 (paperback)
ISBN 9781478020967 (hardcover)
ISBN 9781478027843 (ebook)
Subjects: LCSH: Geology in literature. | Geology—Social aspects—United States—History—19th century. | Geology—United States—History—19th century. | American literature—History—19th century. | BISAC: NATURE / Environmental Conservation & Protection | HISTORY / Modern / 19th Century
Classification: LCC PS217.G56 L835 2024 (print) | LCC PS217.G56 (ebook) | DDC 810.9/36—dc23/eng/20231024
LC record available at https://lccn.loc.gov/2023025629
LC ebook record available at https://lccn.loc.gov/2023025630

Cover art: Frederic Edwin Church (1826–1900), *Cotopaxi*, 1862. Oil on canvas. Detroit Institute of Arts, USA. © Detroit Institute of Arts/Bridgeman Images.

FOR Z

contents

acknowledgments, ix

introduction. the "fashionable science," 1

1 **"the infinite go-before of the present"**
geological time, worldmaking, and race in the nineteenth century, 31

2 **unsettled ground**
indigenous prophecy, geological fantasy, and the new madrid earthquakes, 57

3 **romancing the trace**
ichnology, affect, matter, 87

4 **matters of spirit**
vibrant materiality and white femme geophilia, 114

5 **the natural history of freedom**
blackness, geomorphology, worldmaking, 137

coda. ishmael's anthropocene
geological fantasy in the twenty-first century, 171

notes, 181   bibliography, 211   index, 235

acknowledgments

It took a while to write this book, and I have accrued many debts in the meantime. My thanks to all those at Duke University Press who have worked to make its publication possible, especially my editor, Courtney Berger, and to my two anonymous readers, who made it stronger. I am also grateful to Emily Coccia for early research assistance and to Diana Molina for her help in preparing the manuscript. My research and writing were generously supported by the Huntington Library, the Society for the Humanities and the Atkinson Center for a Sustainable Future at Cornell University, Georgetown University, and Rutgers University.

My wonderful colleagues and students in the English and Women's, Gender, and Sexuality Studies departments at Rutgers University have helped me find my footing during the strangest of times. The list of those to whom I am indebted is so long that I will thank them here collectively rather than risk omitting anyone. It was hard to leave Georgetown University's Department of English after many years, and I will always cherish the wonderful colleagues I had there. The members of the DC Queer Studies reading group provided camaraderie as well as intellectual stimulation. Other friends who sustained me over the years in DC include Mandy Berry, Fiona Brideoake, Shyama Kuyver, Christina Handhart, Leon Lai, Rona Marech, Carla Marcantonio, Robert McRuer, Patrick O'Malley, Ricardo Ortíz, Amanda Phillips, Samantha Pinto, and Joshua Shannon. And a special shout-out to my partners in righteous crime, Jennifer James, Tita Chico, and Cheryl Spinner.

While at Georgetown I had the enormous good fortune to be part of a Sawyer Seminar, "Approaching the Anthropocene: Global Culture and Planetary

Change," funded by the Mellon Foundation. Thanks are due to my codirectors, Nathan Hensley and John O'Neill; to our fellows, Megan Dean, Meredith Denning, and Mabel Gergan; to Carma Fauntleroy, Patty Guzman, Karen Lautman, and Marielena Octavio for vital administrative support; and to the many fantastic speakers and seminar participants who made that year one of the richest periods of my professional life.

The earliest thinking about this book began during a year at the Huntington Library, where a wonderful cohort of fellows, especially Michele Navakas, helped me to explore its possible directions. Dear friends in LA, including Jennifer Doyle, Macarena Gómez-Barris, Jack Halberstam, Martin Harries, Virginia Jackson, Heather Lukes, and Molly McGarry made my time there a pleasure. A year at Cornell's Society for the Humanities helped me move the project toward something like its current form. I am grateful to my cohort there, especially Christine Bacareza Balance, Munia Bhaumik, Ann Cvetkovich, Amanda Jo Goldstein, and Saida Hodzic. Karen Jaime, Yael Kropsky, Gretchen Phillips, Camille Robcis, Shirley Samuels, and C. Riley Snorton helped to make Ithaca warmer.

Many venues have hosted talks on this material over the years. I am thankful for the attention and feedback of audiences at Wake Forest University, the Ludwig Forum for International Art, Kölnischer Kunstverein, Williams College, the Mark S. Bonham Centre for Sexual Diversity Studies at the University of Toronto, University of Richmond, Swiss Institute of Contemporary Art, University of Illinois Urbana-Champaign, Stone Walks, Capacious/Millersville University, the Futures of American Studies Institute at Dartmouth College, the University of California at Davis, Museum Brandhorst, Amherst College, Connecticut College, Queens College, the University of Maryland, Oakland University, SUNY Albany, Yale University, University of Toronto, the University of Southern California, the University of Wisconsin-Madison, Columbia University, the University of California-Berkeley, and Johns Hopkins University, as well as the American Studies Association and the Modern Language Association's annual conventions, the Herman Melville Society, and C19: The Society for Nineteenth-Century Americanists. Thanks, as well, to those who so generously hosted me in those spaces: Aimee Bahng, Elizabeth Maddock Dillon, Meredith Farmer, Jeff Insko, Jamie Jones, Susan Koshy, Elliot Krasnopoler, Tonio Kröner, Greta LaFleur, Bob Levine, Tobias Menely, Christopher Nealon, Michelle Neely, Emily Ogden, Katrin Pahl, Don Pease, Talia Schaeffer, Greg Seigworth, Dana Seitler, Jonathan Senchyne, Nathan Snaza, Cally Spooner, Stephanie Springgay, Jordan

Stein, Eric Sundquist, Karen Tongson, Sarah Truman, Martha Umphrey, and Tanjaa Widmann. I owe a particular debt to Nadja Argyropoulou, who invited me to join a group of artists and thinkers on Nisyros, where I gave a presentation about this work atop an active volcano—one of the high points (figuratively and literally) of my professional career.

Earlier versions of some of the material in this book were published in *ESQ, American Literature, J19, Transatlantica, American Quarterly*, the *Los Angeles Review of Books, Anthropocene Reading: Literary History in Geologic Times* (edited by Tobias Menely and Jesse Oak Taylor), and *Timelines of American Literature* (edited by Cody Marrs and Christopher Hager).

Many people have read or talked with me about this work over the years, and I am indebted to their insights. I am grateful to Gino Conti, who realized I was writing this book before I did. Thanks also to John Levi Barnard, Hester Blum, Jayna Brown, Mel Y. Chen, Peter Coviello, El Glasberg, Naomi Greyser, Jared Hickman, Zakiyyah Iman Jackson, Greta LaFleur, Stephanie LeMenager, Molly McGarry, Uri McMillan, Sarah Mesle, John Lardas Modern, Mark Rifkin, Cecile Rodeau, Pam Thurschwell, Kyla Wazana Tompkins, and Ivy G. Wilson. You all rock. (Sorry, I couldn't resist.)

This book was completed in the midst of a pandemic, and at a time of transition in my own life. I am especially grateful to Robin Bernstein, Brian Herrera, Patrick McKelvey, Kyla Schuller, and the members of the online work groups they led, for combatting isolation and providing accountability. Meredith McGill made my move to Rutgers possible. Stephanie Foote and Anthony Lioi, the best coeditors in the world, guided my entrance into the field of environmental humanities.

José Esteban Muñoz talked through many of the early ideas in this book. I miss his fierce intelligence and his joie de vivre. Lauren Berlant was a cherished mentor and beloved friend, and I will always feel a little bereft without her wit, brilliance, and care lighting my world.

The decade over which this book was written was a tumultuous and difficult one for me, and I could not have made it through without the support of dear friends. Mel Chen, Gino Conti, Elizabeth Freeman, Jody Greene, Jasbir Puar, Kyla Schuller, Dana Seitler, Jordan Stein, and Kyla Wazana Tompkins: thank you for being there. The ANAs make parenting easier and life brighter. Liz Tracey has been a *fidus achates*. Pam Thurschwell and Stephanie Foote buoy me up in an increasingly insane world. Pete Coviello is eternally my paisan. Kim Coles and Jennifer James are a daily source of cheer and care. Chris Nealon and Rob Hardies gave me a home when I very much needed one. My parents have always stood by me, even though they think what I do for a living is kind of strange. Very little would be possible without the ongoing support of my co-parent, Jenn Sturm. And to Z Luciano: it has been a privilege and a joy to see you grow. This book has stolen far too many hours away from you; my dedication is no recompense, but I hope you will accept it anyway.

introduction   the "fashionable science"

To the philosopher, geology is of incalculable value. No science digs deeper, few soar higher. Do you want a foundation for your philosophy, deep, abiding: here you may find it. For want of it, our so-called philosophies are castles of cards, erected today, blown down to-morrow. If history, written by the fallible finger of man, and extending over but two or three thousand years, is so important that men wisely spend a lifetime in its study, how much more important a history of events transpiring during countless ages, written by impartial historians, who have infallibly recorded the facts of the past! —William Denton, *Our Planet, Its Past and Future* (1868)

GEOLOGY IS NOT CONVENTIONALLY UNDERSTOOD as one of the "human sciences." Yet it has long possessed the ability to organize humans in relation to the worlds it describes. This has become clear in contemporary debates about the Anthropocene, a proposed new entry in the geochronological time chart that would recognize the planetary and durable impact of human geological agency.[1] In the two decades or so since the emergence of the term, the Anthropocene has provided many a thinker with the foundation for queries about what this epoch might reveal us to be, grounding speculation about what it means to be "geologically human."[2] But while the Anthropocene conversation is a recent development, the condition itself is nothing new; we have been geologically human for quite some time now. This is not merely true in a physical sense, with respect to the geologic matter dispersed through our bodies, such as the bones which, in Manuel de Landa's poetic formulation, "never forget [their] mineral origins."[3] It is also true economically, ideologically, and, as William Denton would have it, philosophically. Indeed, geology has actively entwined itself with not only *what* but also *who* we understand to be "human" ever since its emergence as a modern science in the late eighteenth century.

Denton, a British-born, US-based geologist and lecturer, was far from alone, in his day, in his enthusiasm for geology. By 1834, the *Knickerbocker*, an influential New York–based literary magazine, could call the study of the earth and its history "the fashionable science of the day."[4] Articles on the latest geological discoveries circulated in popular periodicals while geological cabinets, museum displays, and lectures attracted substantial public audiences eager to learn about the latest theories of the earth's formation, spread across a backdrop of countless eons. Curious arrangements of extinct megafauna and flora arrested readers with their uncanny appeal—alien to, and yet not entirely separable from, the world in which those readers lived. Fossils and other earthly matter appeared, in Ralph O'Connor's apt phrase, as "sublime relics of a legendary past" preserved in the rock record,

Figure I.1. Henry de la Beche, *Duria Antiquior* (1830). Source: Wikimedia Commons.

imbuing human history with a timescale that made room for thrillingly different forms of being.[5]

The novelty of the science lay not only in the bizarre life-forms and strange, now-vanished worlds it disclosed but also in its insistence on the sheer immensity of the planetary past itself, an insistence that constituted a wholly new understanding of time. By the start of the nineteenth century, geology had revised the scientific understanding of the scale of earth's history, asserting that it occupied not the six thousand years allotted in the Bible, but untold millions; as the Scottish scientist James Hutton affirmed in his 1788 "Theory of the Earth": "The result, therefore, of our present inquiry is, that we find no vestige of a beginning,—no prospect of an end."[6] Such observations left Hutton's contemporaries feeling "giddy [at] looking so far into the abyss of time."[7] The expanse of ages then referred to as the planet's "antiquity"— what we now know, in John McPhee's evocative term, as *deep time*—was both transfixing and unsettling, and its dizzying impact was not entirely dissipated by nineteenth-century geologists' dedication to filling in its outlines. Geological timescales mocked human achievements, collapsing the entirety of human history into a brief, insignificant moment. As Denton declared, "We speak of old English castles ... [and] the Pyramids of Egypt.... Yet what is the age of [these structures] compared with the age of the world? They are the veriest babes of time, the ephemera of a summer's day: they resemble the bubbles that float on Niagara's stream, glittering for an instant on its turbulent breast, then disappearing forever."[8] The earth's antiquity gave a new dimension to the traditional respect for the planet's unparalleled power to destroy. The excavation of the remains of Pompeii and Herculaneum, thriving cities buried by the massive explosion of Mount Vesuvius in 79 CE, kept before the eyes of eighteenth- and nineteenth-century audiences a reminder that the most cherished human constructions could be brought down in an instant.[9] The belief that such events were animated by supernatural forces intending to punish humans—an idea which still shadowed some popular Victorian representations of Pompeii—was sneered at by Hutton and other geologists, but their own emphasis on the daunting immensity of planetary time recalibrated the earth's ability to chastise human worlds. No longer did it need to *do* anything to check human self-importance; it could simply *be*.

The potential trauma caused by the new science's foundational claim— the hard-to-face fact of the planet's antiquity—was ameliorated in part by the geohistorical and cultural work that this claim enabled geology to accomplish. Nineteenth-century geologists set to work mapping the vastness of the planetary past in as much detail as possible. They frequently bragged of their considerable accomplishments in this respect, comparing themselves to European explorers such as Christopher Columbus and James Cook as they celebrated their "heroic" conquest of time. In publicly oriented geological writing, the seductive lure of bygone worlds was balanced by the salutary promise of planetary literacy. Children and adults alike were urged to learn to decode the language of the rocks, to become readers of what one text aimed at youth named "the great stone book of Nature."[10] When depicted as a form of literacy, geology took on a moral cast. The mastery of geological knowledge and the exercise of geological curiosity, whether viewing a cabinet or identifying rocks while on a walk in the country, were seen as positive aids to self-cultivation, the duty of the virtuous civilized subject. For many, the science was a highly practical area of study. Farmers, miners, architects, craftsmen, and others were exhorted to learn the basics of the science as a means of improving their livelihoods. And geology was also held to convey a spiritual message, despite its break with biblical time; as the French scientist Claude Antoine Rozet declared, "The study of the earth ... as of all other productions of nature, demonstrates at every step the existence of the Deity."[11] Samuel Metcalf, author of the 1834 *Knickerbocker* article, summing up the terms of its popularity, affirmed: "The wide extent of [geology's] applications—the lofty tone of its generalizations—the striking evidence which it affords of design and all-pervading benevolence, forcibly arrests the attention of every enlightened mind."[12]

Geology's ability to improve the modern subject is one of the ways in which the science colluded with biopower, Michel Foucault's term for the form of modern power exercised through the maximization or withdrawal of life, which came to flourish in the nineteenth century.[13] In Foucault's account of biopower's emergence, biology and statistics are the sciences that facilitate its administration. Yet contemporary theorists of biopower stress the flexibility of its targets, noting that it is not necessarily constrained by the borders of the human body or the form of the subject, or even by the notion of aliveness as we know it. As Jasbir K. Puar explains, "Societies of control [Gilles Deleuze's term for the extension of biopolitics into postmodern society] tweak and modulate bodies as matter."[14] *How the Earth Feels* explores some of the ways the body was situated as matter before the post-1950 period—a framing that opens the body to the geological gaze. From the nineteenth century onward, geology participated in the process of organizing bodies in relation to geological as well as biological substance. Despite its ostensible concern with nonhuman worlds, geology worked biopolitically to optimize the modern subject and to devivify those cast outside modernity.

The oscillation between the strange pleasures and creative possibilities offered by geological knowledge—the shivering alienation of geologic time and the captivating inhumanness of geologic matter—and the colonial structures and social hierarchies propped up by the geological timescale is the subject of this book. Geology, in the first half of the nineteenth century, was a new and exciting way of looking at the world. It was capable of endowing the most ordinary surroundings and the most common substances with awe-inspiring temporal heft and complexity. Its attention to the transformations of putatively inanimate matter across the eons suggested new understandings of agency. And as scientists began to fill in the outlines of a history of "past worlds" populated with weird, now-vanished creatures and vegetation, the science became a space to speculate about otherness. Geology's attention to the animacy of planetary matter over its long history offered new possibilities for understanding relationality and sexuality, contributed to the development of diffuse spiritual frameworks, and made possible new forms of speculation and resistance. At the same time, many of these imaginative projects were accompanied by a capacity to sediment colonial power and reserve the "humanity" that geology offset for a select subset of the species. In this introduction, I explain the cultural form that made these effects possible—geological fantasy—and examine some of the shapes it took both in the nineteenth century, when geology was first in vogue, and in our own moment, when it has become "fashionable" again. I'll consider the impact of geology's emphasis on the antiquity of the planet, how it undergirded the Euro/American conception of modernity, and how it structured colonial understandings of land and life. Finally, I will, in an overview of this book's archive, consider what makes the nineteenth-century United States a particularly apt site for an exploration of geological fantasy.

Geological Fantasy and Exomodernity

Central to my analysis in this book is the concept of geological fantasy. *Fantasy*, in my use of the term, does not signal an opposition to geological *fact*: it indexes, rather, a variety of ameliorative and creative formations that cluster around what are held to be the difficult truths geology teaches—truths that are founded upon the undeniable-yet-inassimilable realities of deep time and species extinction. These new realities made it possible to think innovatively about the relationships between humans and the world around them. But the alienation-effect assigned to them was central to the cultural meaning of the science. The planet's antiquity was widely hailed as a concept relatively easy to grasp but profoundly hard to cope with. Hutton's colleague John Playfair, in a reflection now reproduced more often than is Hutton's own writing, described the challenge of viewing, with Hutton as guide, the Siccar Point "unconformity" (a formation in which two noncontinuous rock strata index a missing span of time—in the case of Siccar Point, about 80 million years). "On us who saw these phenomena for the first time," he reflected, "the impression will not easily be forgotten.... The mind seemed to grow giddy by looking so far into the abyss of time; and while we listened with earnestness and admiration to the philosopher who was now unfolding to us the order and series of these wonderful events, we became sensible how much farther reason may sometimes go than imagination can venture to follow."[15]

What I am calling geological fantasy emerges from the persistent positing of such chasms—the hole in the earth filled with time, the division in the observers unable to wrap their minds around it—as gaps foundational both to geology as a modern science and, in a sense, to modernity itself. To call it "fantasy" does not mean that it takes the side of the imagination against reason, but that it shuttles between those two poles, eroding that division even as it insists upon it in the name of science. My understanding of geological fantasy builds on Lauren Berlant's iterations of the concept of fantasy, which they uses to gesture not only toward "ideologies that create falsely disinterested representations of the world" but, crucially, toward "the unconscious continuities we project that allow us to trust the world enough to test it and change ourselves and it."[16] Fantasy, in the latter sense, is a thing we develop as a bridge to the world, something we need in order to be able to feel ourselves in relation to that world and to operate within it. Geological fantasy works precisely in this way: it turns an object depicted as an inhospitably indifferent planet into a world, or worlds, we can work with. Insofar as geology was (and continues to be) depicted as the site of hard truths about the planet's indifference to the human, geological fantasy, especially at a time when those hard truths presented themselves as newly glimpsed realities, operates as a cultural site where modes of connection between the figures supposedly estranged by geology, *planet* and *human*, could be proposed. Geological fantasy thus exemplifies—indeed, literalizes—Berlant's description of fantasy as "the means by which people hoard idealizing theories and tableaux about how they and the world 'add up to something.'"[17] Despite Playfair's assertion, imagination catches up to geology's hard facts one way or another; any damage done by the earth's "giddying" power to diminish the human is ameliorated or activated otherwise in stories that bring the planet and the human back together somehow.

The impact of the planet's immense antiquity on human hubris is often figured as the annihilation of the species itself in the revelation of its ephemerality, its relative unimportance in view of the long history of the planet. McPhee, the twentieth-century writer who coined the term *deep time*, illustrates it precisely by imagining the disappearance of the human: "With your arms spread wide... to indicate all time on earth, look at one hand with its line of life.... [I]n a single stroke with a medium-grained nail file you could eradicate human history."[18] Yet the sheer persistence of that obliterative comparison in geological writing has sponsored a constellation of fantasies that effectively reestablish the humanity the comparison was said to erase. Indeed, the very assumption that the two were inherently opposed brought a new, modern version of the human to the fore: one that was fundamentally self-obsessed and consequently a little anxious when that obsession was exposed as such. The inassimilable temporal otherness geology introduced to the present scaffolded that figure in the form we might, adapting a concept from Mark McGurl, call *exomodernity*. Considering the persistence of literary-critical and philosophical appeals to deep time as a conduit to the world that "lies beyond or outside style," McGurl proposes the term *exomodernism* to designate the self-ironizing gesture that undercuts a designated period's stabilizing narratives, shadowing them with hallucinated "glimpses... of the unincorporated remainder."[19] Gestures toward the geological outside have been with us since the late eighteenth century, destabilizing modernity and its record of human achievements so reliably that they constitute a mode of stability in themselves. Just as an exoskeleton encases the body of an animal, exomodernity encircles the life—or, more precisely, the liveliness—of modernity. Planetary time stands as the outside to Man: something that exceeds him in its immensity and unknowability but also something through which he can constitute himself, through his unflinching recognition of this fact and its implications for his investigation and quantification of the earth's history. Exomodernity, in the sense I intend the term, takes the form of Man pressing up against a geologically informed limit, a boundary that at once refutes his expansiveness and, in doing so, provides a structure that supports his growth.

On this view, the oscillation between appeals to the planetary past as the site of Man's undoing and as a scaffolding for his achievements functions as a kind of *fort/da* game with geological time. Freud's description of this game in *Beyond the Pleasure Principle* illuminates the role of unpleasure in the formation of the self. An infantile pastime meant to manage the trauma induced by the child's inability to control their world, the fort/da game consists of casting something standing in for the self's foundation (symbolized, for the child, by the mother) away from the self (*fort*, the German word for *gone*), then bringing it back (*da*, German for *here*). The anxiety of the self's potential undoing, in this sense, is deliberately excited in order to be soothed; the game operates as a phantasmatic structure used to stabilize the subject's sense of themselves in relation to the world. From this perspective, we can comprehend geology's alternations as a fort/da game around the stability of modernity, threatening it in order to confirm or transform it. The heft of geological time, the power of planetary forces, the vastness and variability of the globe, the fragility and impermanence of life-forms, dependent as they were on particular ecologies—the very foundations of geological knowledge—became the material for endless rounds of geological fantasy that sometimes operated to shore up and extend the existence of Man, sometimes to direct it otherwise.

The aesthetic appeal that the science possessed helped to fuel these rounds. Modes of fantasy issuing from, within, and through the geologic operated across numerous genres, including popular and professional scientific writing; fiction, nonfiction, poetry, and politics, the visual arts, and the natural-historical museum. All of these were recruited for the dissemination of geological knowledge in the nineteenth century. In his impressive study *The Earth on Show*, O'Connor documents geologists' efforts to gain acceptance for the new science, often manifested in an immersive and spectacular geopedagogy—dramatic storytelling, vivid illustration, engaging displays and panoramas. In the English geologist William Buckland's phrase, geologists should seek to bring their audiences into "immediate contact with events of immeasurably distant periods, as with the affairs of yesterday"; through such dramatic methods, skeptical audiences would be converted and enticed to learn more.[20] This inclination to spectacle, I propose, was also linked to the very dilemma the science posited as its own: the near-incomprehensibility of the time spans it invoked.[21] Amplifying the attractions of geology was a way of managing its inhuman subtractions, of coping with its insistence on the "giddying... abyss of time" and other manifestations of the planet's magnitude and might. "Imagination," which was, in Playfair's view, less willing to plumb the fathomless depths of the planetary past, would in fact be central to geology's popularity. Imagination brought the embodied subject into the drama of alien landscapes and bizarre life-forms, what Brian Noble calls the "otherworld-making" techniques of geological storytelling.[22] William Denton's description of the newly formed earth, for instance, invites his audience to "uproll the curtain that unnumbered ages have dropped, and view the wondrous scene. Before us spreads a fiery ocean, bounded only by a fiery sky: its lightning-capped billows heave heavily under the influence of sun and moon; and now, as if mad, they leap in fury to the ruddy clouds that lower above them. Hissings, seething, boiling like a huge cauldron, while dense vapours rise continually from its surface, it presents to us a picture that none but a demon could truly paint."[23] The arresting theatricality of Denton's portrayal of the Precambrian era models the ideal of "immediate contact," as the wild, fiery fury of the scene imbues the earth with affect that transmits itself to an audience transfixed before the spectacle. Such methods engaged the body as a geological instrument, carrying audiences to worlds almost unimaginably strange, setting them down in bizarrely lively landscapes, inviting them to feel their way into the earth's past.[24]

Geologic fantasy was not only a matter of estrangement and novelty, though. It also inclined toward the sedimentation of familiar social forms and relations, the shoring-up of those forms surrounding the idealized Western subject.[25] Rational objectivity and empirical observation, watchwords for nineteenth-century scientists, controlled the play of the unfamiliar. In the first of a series of articles on the early history of the North American continent which appeared in the *Atlantic Monthly* in 1863, Harvard geologist Louis Agassiz explained this balance: "I am aware that many of the inferences, drawn from what is called the 'geological record,' may seem to be works of the imagination. In a certain sense this is true,—for imagination, chastened by correct observation, is our best guide in the study of Nature. We are too apt to associate the exercise of this faculty with works of fiction, while it is in fact the keenest detective of truth."[26] The ability to speculate beyond the visible, to draw connections not immediately obvious, was understood as the mark of an enlightened mind; this capacity, as Adelene Buckland has shown, was identified by Darwin and other nineteenth-century scientists as what distinguished the civilized from so-called primitive peoples unable to transcend their own time and space.[27] At the same time, relying too much on the imagination was also a danger; the imaginative drama of geologic otherworld-making needed always to be tempered by an orientation toward "truth" rather than fancy. Geologists insisted on the value of systematic and direct engagement with the intricacies of the natural world. This approach, they claimed, established their superiority to their scientific forerunners, who, failing to base their conclusions on empirical evidence from the "rock record," had constructed their planetary histories mainly through speculation. Science, modern geologists insisted, required not "dream[s], formed on ... poetic fiction[s]," as Hutton wrote of the work of his seventeenth-century predecessor Thomas Burnet, but observation and objectivity; these alone could rationalize and order the geological past.[28]

In the wake of Georges Cuvier's decisive argument for the reality of species extinction, the fossil record became a primary means of organizing geochronology.[29] Early debates about whether primary agency in the formation of the world belonged to aqueous or igneous agents—positions known as the Neptunist or Wernerian and the Vulcanist or Huttonian systems, respectively—gave way, by the 1820s, to the labor of filling in the sequence geologists referred to as the "rock record." And while that record disclosed creatures that appeared bizarre and sometimes frightening to modern audiences, effects that were often played up in geological spectacle, scientists nevertheless insisted on the fundamental orderliness of the worlds that geology chronicled. Noting the alarm an iguanodon might create if it suddenly appeared in an English forest, Edward Hitchcock, the Massachusetts state geologist and Congregationalist minister whose work is examined in chapter 3 of this book, hastened to assure readers that the creature, in the proper prehistoric context, was not at all strange; though it might be "very natural to feel [geology] is the history of monsters … further examination rectifies our mistake, and we recognize [extinct animals] as parts of one great system."[30] The geohistorical succession of lifeworlds was held to reflect steady, directed progress as well as reassuring order. In the first half of the nineteenth century, most prominent geologists (the British scientist Charles Lyell was a noteworthy exception) held that the rock record clearly demonstrated steady improvement in the organization and sophistication of life. Echoing the tenor of much popular geological writing, Denton confidently assured his audiences that "Progress is the law of our globe, as geology abundantly testifies." A merely human view of history, limited to a handful of decades, might overlook that fact, he added, but "sweeping over the ages of the mighty past, and contrasting its early appearances with those widely succeeding, we can doubt no longer."[31] The belief in improvement was used to support the claim that the long history of the earth could ultimately be viewed as a directed event: a slow, steady preparation for its tenancy by humans, the pinnacle of evolution. This claim essentially reversed the argument that deep time obliterated the works of man by depicting the accomplishment of those works as deep time's ultimate rationale. The planet's antiquity was not only redeemed but rendered a positive resource in this account insofar as human history, far from being diminished by the vastness of the planetary past, had been its destination all along, and the long wait had ultimately improved it.

As Denton affirmed, "The tree was growing whose fruit should be humanity; and the ages were necessary to knit its giant trunk and perfect its branches."[32]

This faith in progress was linked, in Western Europe and the United States, to the devotion to reason and hard work associated with the sciences but also, for many, to the moderated and scientifically verifiable faith in God that continued to guide much scientific writing and to shape beliefs through the first half of the nineteenth century.[33] The convictions of natural theology—the belief that the presence of God revealed itself in the workings of the physical world—structured the way the science came to bridge the abyss between deep time and the human, as Peter J. Bowler contends: "By 1830, it was firmly accepted in responsible geological circles that divine providence was manifested in the physical world not through continual miracles but in the original design of the system itself."[34] As Bowler points out, it was natural theology, and not the evidence of the fossil record, that shaped geologists' view of earth's history as directed. The conviction that the earth had evolved for humans was laden with spiritual as well as moral significance. Hitchcock, for instance, was able to trace a seamless path from his geological research to his religious instruction in a series of lectures titled *The Religion of Geology and Its Connected Sciences*. Despite their dismissal of the biblically guided 6,000-year history of the earth, geology was not purged of religion in the nineteenth century. Instead, it reimagined a belief in the divine as the inevitable corollary to the observation and contemplation of such a complex, yet orderly world.

The alignment of reason and faith indicates the science's participation in the history of secularism as some scholars have recently come to understand it: not as the development of a religion-free polity but as the management of belief to appear compatible with a modernizing world. Geology, in this view, provided a form of secular discipline, access to what Emily Ogden, glossing Talal Asad, describes as "a set of prescriptions for those who . . . 'aim at modernity.'"[35] As the target of belief management, "modernity" is not so much a historical period or an achieved fact as an optimizing ideal tied to self-governance, which the sciences, geology among them, sought to support. Geology was celebrated as an educational tool uniquely suited for the production of refined, productive, and healthy individuals in a democratic society. The science was not only attractive to the "fashionable" classes; it was promoted across racial and class lines as an accessible as well as improving subject. An article recommending the construction of "Family Cabinets of Nature and Art" was printed in the *Colored American*, a New York–based African American weekly paper, in 1841.[36] The article, authored by Josiah

Holbrook, founder of the Universal Lyceum movement promoting popular education for adults as well as children, detailed the making of household cabinets of geological and other natural specimens. These, Holbrook insisted, would provide "amusement... raise the character and the usefulness of schools... diffuse knowledge over the globe... increase wealth... improve morals... [and] promote religion."[37] Moreover, the amusement associated with the project, Holbrook stressed, was hygienic, as young people would eschew frivolous, expensive, or immoral pursuits for the healthful attraction of a walk to procure geological specimens. In such contexts, geology presented itself as a democratizing as well as universally appealing subject; insofar as its materials were easily accessible, the advantages it conferred were available to all who wished to "aim at modernity."

The association of geology with reason, faith, and productivity alternated and often coexisted with breathless indulgence in dramatic visions of prehistoric otherworlds. Both genres of geological fantasy played into the maintenance of a modernity that, despite its supposed diminishment by the planet's antiquity, could not have existed without it.

Geological Fantasy in the Anthropocene

The proliferation of geological fantasy in the nineteenth century reflected the world-changing impact of the new science's foundational tenets. Nineteenth-century geology rapidly invented a radically new understanding of the earth, remapping the human relationship to the planet and proposing unforeseen possibilities for living thereon. In tandem with its reconceptualization of planetary history, geology put forth novel understandings of embodiment in relation to geological matter as well as an unsettling new genre of death in the scaled-up finality of species extinction. The fashion for geology indexed the science's success not only in describing the earth but in making it mean anew.

A similar transformation of planetary meanings is recurring in our own time—a moment when anthropogenic climate change has once again altered our understanding of the connections between humans and planetary systems, when global environmental and climate crisis makes time feel both intensified and foreshortened, when species extinction appears not as an aspect of the geohistorical past but as part of the texture of daily life. Geology, accordingly, is once again trending. By the end of this century's first decade, it was difficult to miss what Elizabeth Ellsworth and Jamie Kruse describe as "an increasingly widespread turn toward the geologic as source of explanation, motivation, and inspiration for ... responses to conditions of our present moment."[38] The Anthropocene debate has brought reporting on geological concerns back to the pages of popular journals, while the question of what it would mean, in light of the proposed epoch, to be, in philosopher David Wood's phrase, "geologically human" preoccupies numerous artists and academics.[39] In terms of the Anthropocene, which I discuss in this book's coda, the question evokes consideration of planetary trajectories of environmental harm, of how to correlate impact and cause in the mapping of the present (as) crisis. But what Ellsworth and Kruse identify as a "geologic turn" has surpassed the confines of this debate. This "turn"—which, in light of the science's nineteenth-century popularity, is very much a *return*—is both the inspiration for and ultimate target of this book's analysis. Especially in light of the sense of urgency that surrounds this return, I want to ask: how does the resurgence of geologic fantasy in the twenty-first century compare to its initial emergence in the nineteenth? Given the presumptive *new*ness of our situation, how new are the forms of "explanation, motivation, and inspiration" that geology has delivered? What genres of fantasy have remained with us over the past two centuries? Though for the majority of this book I will concentrate on nineteenth-century antecedents to the present—the "geologic turn" 1.0—I want, here, to briefly consider some of the long-standing patterns that have come to mark this recent return in the hope of illuminating some of these questions.

Most noteworthy, and most predictable, has been the reiteration of the inassimilable nature of deep time. The Anthropocene's potential intervention into the geochronological chart keeps the enormity of the planetary past persistently in view, and its challenges are frequently highlighted. A 2011 article in the *Scientific American* hypothesizes that "the human brain may not be hardwired to comprehend the billions of years of history that have shaped the modern environment"—an assertion that essentially updates Playfair's description of the gap between reason and the imagination into cognitive-science terms.[40] Admittedly, the difficulty of deep time can't quite be said to have *returned* in the present, insofar as it never really left: recall, for instance, John McPhee's nail-file comparison or Steven Jay Gould's 1987 account of the "great temporal limitation imposed by geology on human self-importance."[41] But of late it has been recruited for new uses. "The Anthropocene," Dipesh Chakrabarty asserts, "requires us to think on the two vastly different scales of time that Earth history and world history respectively involve.... [I]f we do not take into account Earth-history processes that outscale our very human sense of time, we do not quite see the depth of the predicament that confronts humans today."[42] The intellectual difficulty of deep time is refracted, here, into the existential depth of our current predicament, employing the exomodern in the service of the epochal.

Within the humanities, geology's renewed appeal has been evident in the diffuse set of critical developments some have called the "nonhuman turn," a rebellion against the allegedly anthropocentric limits of humanist thinking. The urgency with which these developments have been framed is conveyed in Richard Grusin's introduction to a 2015 collection on the topic, where he asserts that "almost every problem of note that we face in the twenty-first century involves engagement with nonhumans," including the Anthropocene.[43] The impact of geological fantasy within this "turn" is especially noteworthy in its early years, when it served as the foundation for a number of claims. The science frequently operates as a conduit to ontology, as geologic matter, especially the fossil, indexing the heft of planetary time, points beyond the epistemologies that, like the humans who generate them, are ultimately ephemeral. Speculative realist Quentin Meillassoux's meditation on the arche-fossil, for instance, calls upon geology to counter what he calls "correlationism," the belief that "we [humans] only ever have access to the correlation between thinking and being."[44] The arche-fossil is technically not a fossil, but a trace of energy from the beginning of time, for which the antiquity of petrified geologic matter serves as a kind of metonym. Object-oriented philosopher Timothy Morton likewise deploys the fossil—in this case, the dinosaur fossil—as an introduction to hyperobjects, things that affect us profoundly even though they elude our conception. For Morton, the birth of modern geology, proxied by Mary Anning's momentous 1823 discovery of a Plesiosaurus skeleton, is the historical condition of possibility for the hyperobject insofar as it marks the time-bending moment where "vast non-human spatial and temporal magnitudes" could manifest physically within human lifeworlds.[45] As at once an index of deep time and a token of extinction, the fossil is also the conduit to a "petrifying" future, one in which humans, too, may exist on the earth only as mineral formations buried within the geological stratum that modern infrastructure will have become.[46] Geologic matter pulls time away from human perception, inducing what Morton describes as temporal undulation, a kind of uncanny time in which we can never be fully at home.

In these contexts, geological time does what it has always done—it checks the "human hubris," in new materialist philosopher Jane Bennett's terms, that is the common target of object-oriented and other anthrodecentric thought.⁴⁷ This move appears so often that McGurl wryly designates this body of work "the new cultural geology," using its quest to "position culture in a time-frame large enough to crack open the carapace of human self-concern" as the basis of his account of exomodernism.⁴⁸ As suggested by the frequency with which the Anthropocene is mentioned, the stakes of that disruption are assumed to be, at least in part, environmental: the introduction of an ecocentric rather than narcissistically anthropocentric view of the world and, as per Chakrabarty, the proper framing of the existential crisis facing the species today.⁴⁹ Yet aggressively bashing deep time against the merely human may actually be counterproductive as far as inspiring environmental action goes. Geologist Marcia Bjornerud contends that this all-too-familiar opposition "suggests a degree of insignificance and disempowerment that not only is psychologically alienating but also allows us to ignore the magnitude of our effects on the planet."⁵⁰ Elizabeth Povinelli makes a related point about Meillassoux's arche-fossil; part of its appeal, she argues, is its ability to deflect attention from present-tense concerns by "mobiliz[ing an] intense self-involvement with things that existed before we got here, things that cannot demand accountability from us."⁵¹ The presumed political innocence of the geologic allows it to shelter us from a present in which we are implicated in ever-more-intricate webs of responsibility and obligation. The capacity to distract us from those webs also serves to mask the reductive version of the human that Euro/American geology has long upheld. As Zakiyyah Iman Jackson points out in a powerful response to the nonhuman turn, such critiques of anthropocentrism misrepresent the figure they seek to decenter insofar as they privilege a specific genre of the human that postcolonial theorist Sylvia Wynter would identify as Man—a self-avowedly rational, bounded, and forward-moving entity of Euro/American descent—overrepresenting himself as if he were the Human in toto. (Indeed, as I discuss in more detail below, geological fantasy has played a role in developing and sustaining that figure.) In this sense, Jackson argues, much so-called posthumanist thought actively reproduces the overrepresentation of Man in its "sidestep[ping of] the analytical challenges posed by the categories of race, colonialism, and slavery"—ongoing structures that are subsumed into the overall diminishment of human history by deep time.⁵²

The turn to geological time that marks the "new cultural geology" generates forms of time markedly different from Chakrabarty's deployment of the Anthropocene as a call to a dual historiography. The latter works to integrate and thereby to reenergize planetary and global history—maintaining a focus, through the lens of the planetary, on such issues as the currently disproportionate impacts of climate change on the global South. The ontological bent of the former recruits the geological toward a more-than-historical sense of the past, a kind of suprahistoricity that often carries notably marvelous, even mystical, undertones. The impact of designating something a hyperobject, for instance, seems to render interacting with it "fascinating, disturbing, problematic, and wondrous." Writing of fossil fuels, Morton asserts that "oil is the result of some dark, secret collusion between rocks and algae and plankton millions and millions of years in the past. When you look at oil you're looking at the past."[53] Geologic matter, here, opens up a time that cannot be mapped onto any conventional timescale insofar as it shimmers across and between epochs. At other points, it becomes a means of escaping from time itself. The encounter between a paleontologist and a fossilized dinosaur footprint becomes, for Morton, an instance of "realist magic"; the scientist "coexists with the dinosaur and the ancient mud in a nontemporal configuration space.... It's as if this level of reality is a vast mesh of crisscrossing lines, marks, symbols, hieroglyphics, riddles, songs, poems and stories."[54] The speculative dimension of geological thought is here employed to invite the reader into a world within, yet beyond, the known one, a realm of mysterious signs to be decoded—the reading of an alternative rock record, in which the distinction between the rock and the human is compellingly unclear.

The mystical dimension of this more-than-historical geology expands on the moral clarity ascribed to this process of reading by nineteenth-century advocates of the science. Accessing this level of reality seems to have a moral, or at least an ethical, import in object-oriented thought insofar as it demonstrates one of the key tenets of this body of work: that objects are "not just lumps of dullness."[55] The activation of objects curtails human self-importance and elevates the significance of the nonhuman world, moves that may have environmental and social impacts—although much of the nonhuman turn, especially object-oriented thought, is not oriented toward "politics" in any conventional sense. Unlike Chakrabarty's dual planetary/global focus, though, the encounter with mystical-geological strata bypasses global historical measures; Morton's gaze at the "dark, secret collusion" between the nonhuman agents at the origin of "oil" sidesteps such factors as the human labor that turns oil into fuel or the mass land conquest powered by the petroleum industry. In this sense, the secret history of Mesozoic algae pits the planetary *against* the global, overshadowing other stories oil might be made to tell.[56] The bypassing of such histories is not simply an effect of this mode of thought—it appears, at times, to be part of the point, as swift dismissals of historical materialist thought as static and insufficient appear frequently in this body of work.⁵⁷ The avoidance of "correlationist" or anthropocentric historiography, which would block the effort to establish more authentic relations with the object-world, draws once again on geology's presumed political innocence.

A somewhat different mode of geological fantasy operates within recent vitalist and new materialist thought. For new materialists, as Diana Coole and Samantha Frost explain, "materiality is always something more than 'mere' matter: an excess, force, vitality, relationality, or difference that renders matter active, self-creative, productive, unpredictable."⁵⁸ The mind-bending impact of the geological timescale is less central to this body of thought; rather, a focus on geological processes opens perspectives on the active materiality Coole and Frost emphasize. When cited at all, the earth's age tends to operate, as it does for Deleuze and Guattari, as a window to the perpetual flux of all matter: "The hardest rocks become soft and fluid matter on the geological time scale."⁵⁹ This flux guides Manuel de Landa's approach to "reality" as a "single *matter-energy* undergoing phase transitions of various kinds"; from this perspective, he can craft a geologic historiography which highlights those "dynamical elements (energy, flow, nonlinear causality) that [humans] have in common with rocks and mountains and other nonliving historical structures."⁶⁰ Similarly, Jane Bennett's "geo-affect" enables us to catch the vibe of what she terms vibrant matter, which might point toward an "expanded political economy," while Kathryn Yusoff's "geologic life" opens a corporeal dialogue with the inhuman, developing an awareness of how the "mineralogical dimension of human composition" impacts social, economic, and political life.⁶¹ Such encounters with geologic forces and planetary matter abandon the rational, distanced objectivity upheld by nineteenth-century geology; instead, they enfold it alongside humans into what Karen Barad describes as "the world's differential becoming."⁶²

The activation of geologic time through matter and material processes in the new materialisms undoes what Bjornerud identifies as the potentially alienating effect of deep time. Geologic vibrancy alters the status of the human by drawing it closer and animating it differently, an ethical move that is often explicitly environmental, although it too seeks to transform what "politics" means and how it operates. Attention to what gets swept along in the flow of the rocks, though, reveals the limits of vitalist and new materialist efforts to reconceive the human. In *The Transit of Empire*, Jodi Byrd (Chickasaw) tracks the twinning of settler-colonial and Orientalist thought in Deleuzoguattarian figurations of the "Indian." Deleuze and Guattari, whose work is central to much new materialist thought, employ the "Indian" as a deterritorializing figure; yet this positioning follows the pattern Byrd identifies as a transit through a "paradigmatic Indianness" deployed to facilitate US imperial desires. In *A Thousand Plateaus*, Deleuze and Guattari decorate fantasies of the "rhizomatic [American] West" with the idea of "Indians without ancestry," ultimately declaring that "America... put its Orient in the West."[63] That observation enfolds these "Indians" with residents of the Asian subcontinent, who are elsewhere used by Deleuze to figure a different approach to the unconscious, drawing on "more dynamic models: from the drifting of continents to the migrations of peoples." Contrasting Indian and Egyptian burial sites, he contends, "the Indians pass into the thickness of the rocks themselves, where the aesthetic form [is identified with] the creation of paths without memory, all the memory of the world remaining in the material."[64] The "rocks" seem to be a reference to Hindu burial caves, yet the Orientalized "Indians without ancestry" from the American West, situated outside biological descent, also resonate geologically. The move toward a nonrepresentational philosophy, pursuing the possibility of difference through material processes, locates "Indians" alongside the "drift of continents," outside human history. In this sense, as Byrd notes, Deleuzoguattarian thought becomes an "ontological trap" reifying colonial discourse: "What we imagine to be outside of and rupturing to the state, through Deleuze, already depends on a paradigmatic Indianness that arises from colonial discourses justifying expropriation of lands through removals and genocide."[65]

Deleuze's lithified Indian, as I demonstrate in this book, has a long history within colonial and geological thought. But this is not the only way in which Indigeneity gets absorbed into ontology. Zoe Todd (Métis), in a critique of actor-network theorist Bruno Latour, whose concept of distributed agency plays a part in much new materialist work, points out that such models resemble, but do not cite or consider, Indigenous thought. In this sense, she contends, the "ontological turn" sustains the colonizing function of the Western academy as a whole.[66] As Todd argues, "The colonial moment has not passed.... So it is so important to think, deeply, about how the Ontological Turn—with its breathless 'realisations' that animals, the climate, water, 'atmospheres' and non-human presences like ancestors and spirits are sentient and possess agency, that 'nature' and 'culture', 'human' and 'animal' may not be so separate after all—is itself perpetuating the exploitation of Indigenous peoples."[67] This breathlessness, tied to the aforementioned sense of urgency, reveals the "nonhuman turn" to be engaged in something similar to what Jean O'Brien (White Earth Ojibwe) describes as the settler practice of "firsting," the space-clearing claim that settlers were the first peoples to construct a meaningful social order in a given location.[68] In this sense, scholarship animated by the desire to respond to planetary crisis remains implicated, Todd asserts, in "ongoing colonial realities throughout the globe."[69]

The geologic inflection of much new materialist thought is, in this light, a particular concern, not simply because of the science's long history of involvement in colonialism but also because of its desire to remain in responsive dialogue with the earth. In Ellsworth and Kruse's description of the "turn toward the geologic as source of explanation, motivation, and inspiration," the "geologic" is not a gestural and vague relation to the planet as an abstracted whole; rather, it attaches thought to more specific, often located geologic processes and materials and to the relationships that can be established with and through these.[70] The cluster of desires animating this call to dialogue seems, in this light, to be reaching toward something like the structure Leanne Betasamosake Simpson (Michi Saagiig Nishnaabeg) and Glen Sean Coulthard (Yellowknives Dene) describe as "land as pedagogy," which Coulthard glosses as an approach to land as "an ontological framework for understanding relationships—a consideration of *what the land as system of reciprocal relations and obligations* can teach us about living our lives in relation to one another and the natural world in nondominating and nonexploitative terms."[71] The geologically inflected search for "explanation, motivation, and inspiration" can be understood, I believe, as a quest for similar knowledge. But this framework is problematic in at least two respects. The first is the erasure of Indigenous sovereignty: the "geologic" in this context is another form of space-clearing that overwrites specific Indigenous relationships to land, which are bound up with modes of governance and sociality, in favor of a general invocation of the human in relation to the planetary actualized through specific sites.[72] Even as the geologic transcends such merely human forms as citizenship, it retains the shape of the "settler common sense" that Mark Rifkin describes: not a "conscious repudiation of identity" so much as a "structure of feeling and set of routine orientations...that arise from and propel the extension of claims to Native lands and dismissal of Native polities."[73] The second problem is the related erasure of Indigenous intellectual and social labor. As a theory of force rather than work, the geologic renders invisible the necessity of directed energy in the maintaining of such systems.[74] Geology threatens, in this sense, to take the place of "nature" as it features in Romantic invocations of Indigenous life. As Mishuana Goeman asserts, "These sorts of telling make possible settler narratives that elide the very hard work it takes to make healthy and responsible communities, communities that take into account not only the human but nonhuman."[75] The "modes of collective placemaking and governance" that are, as Rifkin points out, central to Indigenous sovereignty dissolve into a generalized vibrancy that turns *place* into the *space* where matter inter/acts.[76] While vitalist and new materialist geologies may be able to show humans what we "have in common with rocks and mountains," as well as with nonhuman biotic forms, it is less clear what "geologic life" might have to say about the terms on which to live that commonality.[77]

Bennett describes new materialism's "uncanny task" as "see[ing] what happens . . . if the 'call' from things is taken seriously."[78] I would argue that the forms of attention developed in response to that call—the effort to attend to the vitality of matter in new materialism, geologic and otherwise—have been most successful thus far in the development of a revitalized critical sensorium, a reorganizing of the senses beyond the limitations of the Aristotelian model.[79] This kind of work remains crucial, as the rehabilitation of the sensorium and its modes of apprehending knowledge are necessary for comprehending and responding to a transformed ecology. At the same time, as Jayna Brown asserts, "materialist studies need to attend to the ways in which systems of inequality are embedded in our understandings of that materiality and the processes by which scholars theorize it."[80] Some recent projects have managed to take up the geologic while maintaining this kind of attention. Tiffany Lethabo King's *The Black Shoals: Offshore Formations of Black and Native Studies*, discussed in chapter 5 in this book, establishes a geological form, the shoal, as the shifting foundation for a sustained dialogue between Black and Indigenous feminisms, while E Cram's *Violent Inheritance: Sexuality, Land, and Energy in Making the North American West* develops the concept of "land lines" as a means of tracking the convergences of sexuality, energy, infrastructure, and colonial violence on western land.[81] Without this type of reckoning, materialisms fueled by geological fantasy tend to absorb "difference" into materiality without providing an account of the forms of power that stratify it.

The assumed political innocence of geology, as a science of the non- and prehuman world, meant that it largely escaped the kind of critical interrogation that biology and other sciences received in the last decades of the twentieth century. Yusoff's recent critique of what she terms *White geology* begins to remedy this oversight, making visible how the science has operated as "a racialized optic razed on the earth."[82] *How the Earth Feels* takes up this work, using the complementary terms *settler geology* and, following Sylvia Wynter, *geology of Man* [overrepresented as the Human], to more precisely identify the historical forms that whiteness has taken. Any return to the geologic, I argue, needs to develop a stronger sense of the long history of geologic fantasy, including its participation in projects of dispossession. Geological fantasy, as we will see, does not only read past worlds out of the rock record; it has sought, as well, to sediment the social hierarchies of the present.

Geology as Biopower (and Beyond)

Both the conviction that geology was good for individuals and the stories about extinction and evolution projected onto the geochronological record reflected the collusion of the science with the establishment and maintenance of modern biopower. Biopower, Foucault explains, is concerned with regulating the meanings, behaviors, and effects of bodies in line with "the right of the social body to ensure, maintain, or develop its life."[83] Despite geology's ostensible concern with nonlife, I argue, the liveliness of geological fantasy binds the science to the possibilities attached to life on both social and individual levels. Biopower builds upon the reconstitution of bodies in relation to land and organizes the racialization of death across deep time—two strategies for the exomodern management of the geological "wound" projected in the enormity of the planet's age.

Unpacking the entwinement of geology with biopower, Elizabeth Povinelli asserts that the analysis of global modernity is incomplete without an understanding of what she calls *geontopower*.[84] Geontopower is not simply an alternative to or substitute for biopower, but a mode of power that subtends it by demarcating "the difference between the lively and the inert"—a distinction that is particularly salient in settler-colonial contexts.[85] As we have seen, geology undergirded the life of the modern Western subject: it strengthened his mind and improved his circumstances; it positioned him as sufficiently secular to prioritize scientific empiricism over biblical literalism but also sufficiently devout to praise the deity by (literally) grounding his faith in the material world; it rendered him healthful and manly, yet also erudite and "fashionable." In this light, geology's optimization of the subject was bound up with the cultivation of whiteness, defined positively by means of these qualities and in contrast to the putative inertia, backwardness, and postanimacy that geological fantasy helped ascribe to racialized others through its hold upon material space—land—as well as geochronological time.

In Euro/American natural history and geology, land is approached as a knowable, classifiable object. The scientific gaze developed to gather that knowledge aligns with what Macarena Gómez-Barris calls the "extractive view," which "render[s] land as for the taking."[86] The earth sciences participated in the maximization of land's potential, not only as an object of study but as a source of productivity and profit, well before the emergence of modern geology as a temporal science at the end of the eighteenth century. The modern colonial "genre of the human" that Wynter designates Man overrepresented as the human initially predicated its claim to humanity on the asserted superiority of European rationality, held up as justification for colonial administration. That claim, importantly, remade colonized land alongside colonized bodies, physically and conceptually transforming the terrain—Wynter nods to the "ongoing expropriation of New World lands and ... the instituting of the large-scale slave plantation system"—alongside the displacement and forcible re-emplacement of Indigenous and African people thereon.[87] Settlers viewed New World lands and peoples alike as unproductive and unworthy without partition, development, cultivation, and governance. As they facilitated that transformation, the physical sciences, including mineralogy, geography, and natural history, played a central role in this dimension of colonial expansion, supporting the development of Man both materially, as they contributed new techniques to facilitate the accumulation and extraction of resources, and ideologically, as they consolidated a vision of land as inert, alienable, and wholly knowable, which made its expropriation and exploitation possible.

The division between rationality and irrationality, for Wynter, was most often expressed as one between the civilized citizen and the animalized savage. Mineral and vegetal associations, I propose, operated in tandem with animalization. European natural historians maintained that both Africa and the Americas were "newer" landmasses than Europe; hence, as Katherine McKittrick observes, people attached to those lands were assumed to be less sophisticated. Indigenous people of the Americas were often lithified in the process of being dispossessed. The acceleration of silver mining in South America through the application of European scientific techniques and the mita system of enforced Indigenous labor operated in precisely this way; as the Conde de Lemos, the newly appointed Viceroy of Peru, declared in a 1667 letter about the brutality of South American silver mines, "The rocks of Potosí ... are bathed with the blood of Indians, and ... if the money which is extracted from them is squeezed, more blood than silver would flow."[88] The terms of de Lemos's liberal protest hardened over the centuries into settler-geological common sense, though with less sympathy. Henry Rowe Schoolcraft, an American geologist discussed in chapter 2 in this book, complained, while on an 1820 exploratory voyage up the Mississippi River, of his Winnebago guides, who were not as helpful in finding local ore deposits as he had hoped, that "[they] look to the eyes of civilization as if they themselves had faces of stone, and hearts of adamant."[89] Black bodies were also reinscribed in relation to reconfigured colonial lands, particularly in the installation of the plantation system. What McKittrick terms "plantation geographies," oriented toward "black placelessness and constraint," tethered Africans brought to the New World to the land they worked.[90] The plantation, McKittrick observes, "became the location where black peoples were 'planted' in the Americas—not as members of society but as commodities that would bolster crop economies."[91] Such plantings sometimes gave rise to conceptions of what Monique Allewaert calls "ecological personhood," a vital mode of being that straddled (what we understand as) biotic life, objects, and landforms, in opposition to the European preoccupation with classification and quantification.[92] But the insistent foreclosures of the plantation economy also generated what Katherine Adams identifies as "dirt determinism," a fixed alignment of Black bodies and the soil they worked.[93]

The forcible remaking of land and bodies as extractible quantities stands as an early example of Povinelli's geontopower in its quest to overwrite and displace Indigenous and Black understandings of land, which maintained livelier, more reciprocal relationships to place. Such relationships—visible in forms like Simpson's "land as pedagogy" and McKittrick's "alternative mapping processes"—comprehend the earth's surface as a site that participates in the ongoingness of life, intimately and sensually bound up with humans as well as nonhuman life.[94] In its violent reinvention of Indigenous land and Black bodies as property, though, settler modernity depicted such frameworks as misrecognitions of the crucial distinction between life and nonlife, between (active) members of the modern world and (inert) raw material to be used for its benefit.

It would be the massiveness of the geological timescale, however, that would make possible the specific mode of life—the "life of the species"—through which biopolitics operates, with extinction, the massified and hyperfinal genre of death that geological time makes visible, standing as the ultimate threat to life on a species level. Wynter's account of New World colonization tracks the expansion of its genres of the human from the primarily spatial forms discussed thus far to the temporal ones that emerged along with the reorganization of the sciences in the nineteenth century around newly developmental paradigms. Biology and anthropology have been the fields most closely associated with the colonial administration of time. But geology, which owed its very existence to the invention of a new, paradoxically modernizing form of time—the antiquity of the planet—also played a key role. As we have seen, the ability to recognize and properly respond to the vastness of geological time was held up as a sign of civilized status, another mark of intellectual "liveness" conforming to the ethnographic and biopolitical distinction between the forward-thinking and the "backward." Geologists were particularly fond of contrasting their own modern way of understanding the material world to Indigenous beliefs. Schoolcraft's 1822 report on a fossilized tree announced itself as the scientific analysis of an object "which has heretofore only served to excite the wonder, and exercise the superstition, of the Indian tribes."[95] What O'Brien would describe as an act of "firsting" feeds into Schoolcraft's assessment of the inertia of Indigenous understandings of the object, which failed to contribute the knowledge needed for both scientific and economic development. That assessment ties into the concomitant practice of "lasting," which O'Brien explains as the assignment of a temporalized construction of race which held that "Indians can never be modern because they can never be the subjects of change, only its victims"—a case Schoolcraft would elsewhere make as he insisted on the incompatibility of Indigeneity and civilization.[96]

The trope of Indigenous extinction followed on this insistence, resulting from "the coupling of the insistence of stasis for Indians with notions of blood," which, when confronted with the inexorable modernity that settlers were etching into the land, catalyzed a process of imagined degeneracy culminating in predictions of imminent extinction.[97] Geologically inflected depictions of Indigenous people as extinct played up the radical otherness, distance, and difference from the present imputed to Indigeneity; they suggested that not only Indigenous people but also their lifeworlds—the "great systems" to which they belonged—had also vanished, to be replaced, in the teleological sequence of (geo)history, by systems within which settlers could make themselves at home, temporally as well as spatially. The extinction trope, Kyla Schuller points out, materializes Coulthard's description of settler colonialism as "territorially acquisitive in perpetuity."[98] As geological fantasy, the trope of Indigenous extinction remade land for the support of settlers, imagining not just polities but entire ecologies designed to promote the growth of settlements.

In casting Indigeneity outside of and anterior to the realm of the human, the extinction trope revised it into the form that Wynter, following Jacob Pandian, identifies as the "fossil other." Definitively established as an index of species extinction by Georges Cuvier at the outset of the nineteenth century, fossils served as both support and counterpoint for evolutionary theories of life's development. The fossil other designated those "archaic, stunted, undeveloped forms" of the human that fell off from the flow of life and were preserved unchanged as relics of other, now-surpassed worlds.[99] As a figure that turned land into time, space into race, geos into bios, the fossil other is an especially good index of the relay between biopower and geontopower. Tying together their oppositions between life/death and animacy/inertia, respectively, it comprehends Indigenous peoples as *post-animate,* associating them with a logic of species that played into the politics of racialization, lending itself to the state project of revising Indigenous sovereignty into racial identity.[100] The fossil other's uncanny post-animacy inverts the racialized living death whose ongoing production is central to what Achille Mbembe designates the necropolitical dimension of global modernity, its "creation of death-worlds," such as the plantation and the postcolony.[101] These racialized worlds operate in suspended time, outside-within the modern, constituting the contemporaneous but noncontemporary racialized counterpart to the exteriorized Indigenous populations imagined as already extinct. Adams's "dirt determinism," drawing on the plantation's alignment of Black bodies and soil, the most geologically recent and agriculturally active layer of the planet's surface, indexes this temporal suspension. Like dirt, the living-dead flesh of the colonized is at once productive and a potential contaminant, recalling the death-dealing function that Foucault, in his discussion of race as an axis of biopower, linked to depictions of the racial other as "threat to the species." Even as Indigenous lifeworlds were aligned with prior extinctions, signaling an imminent pastness, the modern racialized other was said to threaten the possibility of a future extinction and, hence, needed to be managed, contained, or even eradicated.

As practices and concepts, the earth sciences have been bound up with the establishment and maintenance of colonization and racialization, which should be understood, as Byrd emphasizes, as "concomitant global systems that secure white dominance through time, property, and notions of self."[102] As practical sciences, mineralogy and geology guided (and continue to organize) the material and conceptual reinvention of Indigenous lands and consequent destruction of Indigenous land-based modes of relation and governance. As a temporal science, geology supported the necropolitical transformation of African bodies forced to labor on these reinvented lands as well as the imagined fossilization of Indigeneity. And as a fashionable science, it worked to optimize the historical form of whiteness that Wynter and Foucault both identify as Man, who carries forward the "life of the species." As it both plays into and, in its facilitation of land partition, exceeds biopower, geological fantasy is bound up with a vision of modernity, and of Man, literally and figuratively grounded in colonialism.

Geological Fantasy in the Antebellum United States

How the Earth Feels examines texts from and/or about the United States from roughly 1800 to 1870, a period that saw the high point of the science's popularity. My focus on the antebellum United States complements existing scholarship that addresses on the postbellum geological imaginary. Much of this scholarship highlights the coincidence of geology and continued westward expansion after the Civil War: the major geological surveys led by Clarence King, Ferdinand Hayden, John Wesley Powell, and George Wheeler; the sensationalized "bone wars" between two rival paleontologists, Edward Drinker Cope and Othneil Charles Marsh; and the rise of the national obsession with dinosaurs, resulting in part from the work of these two men.[103] Postbellum geological surveys have received far more historical and critical attention than their antebellum counterparts, in part because they were accompanied by photographers whose images captured (and continue to enchant) the public eye. Yet the visual language operating in those images—the expansive spaces standing in for deep time as well as their relentless relegation of the Indigenous residents of those lands to the past—drew upon themes and concepts that were already established, as I show, in antebellum geological fantasy. In the same way, dinosaurs, which became the most popular representatives of the geologic past in the United States near the end of the century, stepped out onto terrain that had been prepared for them in the antebellum period, even as they manifested a more ferocious conception of US imperialism.[104]

The book's focus on the United States highlights its status as an especially good case study for geological fantasy. American scientists, as we will see in chapter 1, framed the North American continent as an exceptional geological exemplar, pronouncing it more instructive and more interesting than Old World landmasses. But the United States does, in fact, provide an exemplary illustration of one common form of geological fantasy: the imbrication of geology and nationalism. Long before the formation of the United States Geological Survey (USGS) in 1879, geology helped to coordinate state power and American national affect with respect to conquered and annexed lands. Geologists accompanied most of the exploratory missions launched by the

United States over the course of the nineteenth century. Their purpose was largely pragmatic: the identification and mapping of mineral deposits and other information pertaining to what Schoolcraft, one of those surveyors, termed "national and domestic purposes."[105] Yet their writing about those lands and their travels thereon also fueled public interest in the geologic past. As Thomas Allen notes, the ability to "imagine [American] land as a repository of time—ages of time stretching unfathomably far into the depths of the earth" satisfied the perceived need for a national history sharply distinguished from that of Europe.[106] Geologic nationalism also served the purpose of land conquest, annexation, and settlement by providing a deep history that white settlers could orient toward their own arrival. The biopolitical dimension of settlement, the remaking of kinship, sexuality, and reproduction toward domestic-familial modes, was accompanied by a geo-phantasmatic reconstruction of the earth, one that imagined the continent as progressing toward the establishment of those modes. This fantasy served to justify the idea of land ownership as the foundation of the American household even as practical geology's mapping of the land according to "resources" facilitated the possibility of extraction.[107]

The archive for *How the Earth Feels* includes both formal scientific publications and popular geological writing as well as newspaper and magazine articles, poetry, oratory, fiction, and the visual arts—all common sites for the circulation of geological information in both pragmatic and speculative guises. I pay particular attention to the aesthetic dimension of these writings because this is where geological fantasy most often takes hold. I have deliberately sought, in these pages, to expand the handful of canonical writers whose work tends to be highlighted in studies of the influence of geology on nineteenth-century authors (Ralph Waldo Emerson, Henry David Thoreau, Herman Melville), both because those writers have already been ably addressed in this context by Branka Arsić, Eduardo Cadava, and many others, and because their writings exemplify only a portion of the wide range of forms geological fantasy took in this period.[108] I am especially indebted to two fine books that examine geological time in the nineteenth-century United States: Wai Chee Dimock's *Through Other Continents: American Literature across Deep Time* and the geological chapters of Allen's *A Republic in Time: Temporality and Social Imagination in Nineteenth-Century America*. Dimock's and Allen's analyses of how nineteenth-century writers wrestled with the problem of geological time, which primarily address transcendentalist writers, make possible my own exploration of geological fantasy by other writers and my consideration of how geological time intersects with biopower in settler-colonial and racialized contexts. I also owe a great deal to the work of cultural historians focusing on British geology in this period, including Adelene Buckland, Ralph O'Connor, and Noah Heringman. Heringman's account of what he terms "aesthetic geology" has been especially useful in my discussion of nineteenth-century American geological fantasy insofar as he attends to the interplay of the sublime alterity of rock, in the British Romantic imagination, with "economic geology," the part played by the science in the development and capitalization of land. My attention to settler colonialism and to the ways geological fantasy operated in relation to those genres of the human that took form in the Americas builds on this insight.

This book progresses from an initial overview of dominant forms taken by nineteenth-century geological fantasy to four chapters organized around case studies. Chapter 1, "'The Infinite Go-Before of the Present': Geological Time, Worldmaking, and Race in the Nineteenth Century," explores a range of geological texts from Europe and North America as they navigate the meanings of the planet's antiquity, turning it into a form of cultural capital for overrepresented Man. Dwelling on the centrality of Cuvier to Foucault's understanding of life, I excavate the occluded role of geological fantasy in modern biopower, then turn to the way writers focused on the United States engaged with this figure as a means of establishing both territorial dominion and racial hierarchy across the continent. The genre I term "manifest geology" nationalized and racialized geochronology, tying together the deep past and the American future. Yet geology also sponsored critical departures from this genre. In a closing consideration of James Fenimore Cooper's adventure novel *The Crater, or, Vulcan's Peak: A Tale of the Pacific* (1847), I show how the recalibration of geology's time could be used to question its foundations.

Chapters 2 and 3 highlight fantasies that took shape around regional geological events whose paces diverged: Indigenous and settler responses to a series of earthquakes in the central Mississippi Valley area in 1811–12, along with the extinction fantasies sedimented in their aftermath, and settler scientific and poetic writing about fossilized footprints identified in the Connecticut Valley in the mid-1830s. Chapter 2, "Unsettled Ground: Indigenous Prophecy, Geological Fantasy, and the New Madrid Earthquakes," begins by considering the nongeological analyses of the earthquakes developed by Indigenous people in the region, which regarded them as an anticolonial activation of the earth, and by settlers, whose religious and sensational responses to the quakes were enfolded into narratives of US national benevolence used to further white settlement and Indigenous displacement. From there, it goes on to document the absorption of Indigenous analyses of the quake into the oft-repeated settler romance of "Tecumseh's prophecy," which provided (and continues to provide) a form of national-geological catharsis, even as geological investigation of the quakes and their effects abetted Indigenous removal by imagining them in the mode of the fossil other. Chapter 3, "Romancing the Trace: Ichnology, Affect, Matter," examines scientific writing, sermons, and poetry about the fossil tracks, which were initially identified as the traces of long-extinct birds. Focusing in particular on writing by the Massachusetts state geologist Edward Hitchcock and the Romantic poet Henry Wadsworth Longfellow, I show how the tracks both continued and partially unsettled the work of settler geological fantasy seen in the previous chapters. Two opposing takes on human agency imprinted on the tracks emphasize at once its limits and its endurance in ways that make them available for alternate political purposes, including the condemnation of chattel slavery.

Chapters 4 and 5 focus on what I term "minor geologies": located clusters of fantasy that operate apart from, and often against, the geology of overrepresented Man. Here I consider two such locations—the experimental queering of the white feminine body and the geologic forms of freedom envisioned by Black male antislavery writers. My intent is not to provide a broad overview of nineteenth-century minor geologies—a project that scholars have begun to take up—or to catalog the many forms they might take.[109] Rather, in selecting these specific sites of analysis, I want to highlight the unevenness that so often marks fantasies of geologic dissolution and reconstruction. In each chapter, the writers I address draw brilliantly on the other-than-human possibilities geology offers but never fully detach from the forms associated with Man, maintaining investments in whiteness and masculinity, respectively. Chapter 4, "Matters of Spirit: Vibrant Materiality and White Femme Geophilia," focuses on how the supposedly porous bodies of white women intersected with stratigraphic and speculative explorations of the planet's past. I point to parallels between contemporary new materialist attention to the energetic nature of matter and to nineteenth-century reflections on something like the spirit of geological matter—though a spirit that, in this chapter's decidedly unconventional examples, markedly departs from the Christian inflection employed by writers considered in earlier chapters. The first example addressed is a series of geological experiments conducted by Elizabeth M. Foote Denton and Annie Denton Cridge, William Denton's wife and sister, who claimed the ability to sense the past experiences of geological matter and other objects. The second case is Harriet Prescott Spofford's 1860 short story "The Amber Gods," whose unusual narrator, Giorgione Willoughby, a young white woman from a wealthy family, uses amber—"fossil gum"—to access the geological past, a site where she can invent new ways of being and new erotic possibilities. In both cases, the porosity of the white feminine body stops short of unsettling its whiteness; while white femme geophilia departs markedly from the masculinism of much nineteenth-century geological fantasy, it inclines toward the replication of antebellum American racial hierarchies.

Chapter 5, "The Natural History of Freedom: Blackness, Geomorphology, Worldmaking," continues the examination, begun at the end of chapter 3, of how geological fantasy might be organized in opposition to chattel slavery and antiblackness in the United States by focusing on the uptake of geological tropes and analyses in writing by African American men at midcentury. Drawing on Britt Rusert's analysis of "fugitive science," I consider how fugitive and speculative geology drew on the aesthetic and historical dimensions of the science, exploring its potential for resisting slavery and for generating alternative forms of African American humanity. Some of these emerge from citations of volcanism by Frederick Douglass and J. Sella Martin, who framed it both as a figure of Black heroic leadership and as the site of geologies and ecologies suggesting genres of the human other than possessive individualism. The chapter also considers James McCune Smith's geological theories of race and Black worldmaking. McCune Smith, as I show, deftly employed geology both to counter white-supremacist theories of biological fixity and to imagine modes of Black social life that alternately reflected and departed from the conventional association of geology with "progress." In both cases, though, the omission of any consideration of gender diminishes the potential of these creative responses to the conditions of Black life.

In a brief closing Coda, "Ishmael's Anthropocene: Geological Fantasy in the Twenty-First Century," I address the Anthropocene proposal as the dominant form of contemporary geological fantasy. As the proto-Anthropocenic musings of Ishmael, the narrator of Herman Melville's 1851 novel *Moby-Dick*, demonstrate common responses to the epochal proposal draw on phantasmatic structures that reach back to the nineteenth century, reproducing some of the affects and genres associated with overrepresented Man. In place of the same old story, I contend, the present crisis requires not the "geology of mankind"—a term sometimes used synonymously with Anthropocene—but a geology *against* Man, one that can manifest geology's otherworld-making capacity responsively within our own.

"the infinite go-before of the present"

1

geological time, worldmaking, and race
in the nineteenth century

RALPH WALDO EMERSON'S description of language as "fossil poetry" is perhaps, for scholars of nineteenth-century American literature, the best-known instance of geologic fantasy. The phrase, which appears in Emerson's 1844 essay "The Poet," competes with several others—"the archives of history," "the tomb of the muses"—illustrating the once-vital, now lost origins of our everyday speech. Yet it is the geologic catachresis of "fossil poetry," unexpectedly yoking two disciplines that today would not even be found in the same building at most universities, that continues to compel. The passage in which the phrase appears reads: "The etymologist finds the deadest word to have been once a brilliant picture. Language is fossil poetry. As the limestone of the continent consists of infinite masses of the shells of animalcules, so language is made up of images, or tropes, which now, in their secondary use, have long ceased to remind us of their poetic origin."[1] "Fossil poetry" compels because it brings language back to life—or, rather, brings the reader back to the moment of its origin. By the time Emerson wrote, fossils had been firmly established as remnants of worlds that were no longer, monuments to the finality of species extinction. Yet for Emerson, the fossil trope paradoxically enlivens its subject; poetry and geology alike become vehicles for time travel, enabling nineteenth-century subjects to return to those worlds. Several decades later, Walt Whitman would also connect language and geology in an essay on American slang.[2] Slang, he argued, revives the unruly origins of language in the intimacies of common use. These origins could be traced by the "science of language," which "has large and close analogies in geological science, with its ceaseless evolution, its fossils, and its numberless submerged layers and hidden strata, the infinite go-before of the present."[3] Philology uncovers the thickness and wildness of language just as geology illuminates the motion, the "ceaseless evolution" of that which may, to us, seem motionless, inert.[4] The fossil, for Whitman, is the conveyor of a time that is more than time: numberless and infinite, and hence immensely generative.

The sensuality of geology in these two poetic invocations results, in part, from its freshness. The science was, for nineteenth-century Americans, a startling innovation, the source of "novel and unexpected truths . . . overturn[ing] so many pre-conceived opinions," as Samuel Metcalf declared in the pages of the *Knickerbocker*.[5] This oft-cited capacity to defamiliarize was central to geology's appeal. Emerson and Whitman seized upon it as poetry's ally in reorienting the space and time of everyday life.[6] For Emerson, an active understanding of geological time as pulsing through human history, not simply the locus of stored-up treasures of a long-lost past, could also denaturalize histories of exploitation, as he does in his 1860 essay "Fate." Ironically imitating the natural-historical framework favored by scientific racists, Emerson declares that "the steadiness with which victory adheres to one tribe, and defeat to another, is as uniform as the superposition of strata."[7] He goes on to emphasize the violence expended in such "victories": "The German and Irish millions, like the Negro, have a great deal of guano in their destiny. They are ferried over the Atlantic, and carted over America, to ditch and to drudge, to make corn cheap, and then to lie down prematurely to make a spot of green grass on the prairie."[8] Emerson's reference to guano—fertilizer made from fossilized deposits of seabird excrement mined from Pacific and Caribbean islands—situates the substance, commonly used to bring depleted soils back to life, in the context of death, aligning it with people who, imported to serve the establishment of an Anglo-American nation, become part of the soil in what this chapter will illuminate as a biopolitics of sedimentation.[9] The depiction of subjugated groups as fertilizer for American fields highlights, in Tao Leigh Goffe's apt phrase, "dehumanization as foundational to the United States."[10] The continuity, in "Fate," of geological and national history uses the inhuman agency of the former to underscore the inhumanity of the latter.

Emerson's use of geology to interrogate those foundations went against the grain of the narratives the science was most often employed to uphold. Geology's association with a modern, civilized, and, in the United States, distinctly Anglo-American whiteness held to be the apex of planetary development worked in tandem with the reconstruction of New World lands as profoundly historical, potentially productive space in which the future of that whiteness could unfold. This chapter highlights this operation, examining how nineteenth-century fascination with the radical rupture that the discovery of the planet's antiquity was said to constitute—its diminishment of humanity on a species level—paradoxically became the *terra firma* under the feet of the figure of Man. As geology began, in Georges Cuvier's evocative phrase, to "burst the limits of time," planetary history was gathered up and arranged as cultural capital. Geology made visible long-vanished worlds that were at once deeply appealing in their alienness and deeply flattering to those whom the science designated as their rightful heirs. This perspective on the past enabled US-based writers to construct planetary histories and accounts of the land that enabled US settlers to naturalize their presence across the North American continent. At the same time, the science retained the capacity to mobilize the planetary power it represented critically, so that the "interruptions of material history," to use Stephanie LeMenager's phrase, could still be positioned against the excesses of the nation.[11]

"Time!—Time!—Time!": Earth's Antiquity and Geological Modernity

It was time that made geology into the science that would become "fashionable" in antebellum America: time, and a great deal of it. With the massive influx of planetary time that came to define it as a science, geology became a resource for the telling of compelling stories about the strange histories of the planet. These positioned unfamiliar concepts within such recognizable forms and genres as the drama of discovery, which narrated the unexpected appearance of an almost inconceivably ancient planet against the limited time frames that had hitherto bounded European geognostic thought, and tales of exploration and conquest. William Whewell's 1839 presidential address to the Geological Society of Britain, for instance, hailed early nineteenth-century geochronologists as conquerors of a new world: "The great geological theorizers of the past belong to the Fabulous Period of the science; but I consider the eminent men by whom I am surrounded as the Heroic Age of Geology. They have slain its monsters and cleared its wildernesses; and founded here and there a great metropolis, the queen of future empires."[12] Whewell's elaborate praise for his epic generation mingles the language of legend with that of the geological space-clearing that both narratively evoked and practically facilitated colonial conquest and settlement. Louis Agassiz carried the same trope across the ocean as, outlining the geology of the American continent in the pages of the *Atlantic Monthly* twenty-four years later, he predicted the grand achievements of his successors: "We shall have our geological explorers and discoverers in the lands and seas of past times, as we have had in the present,—our Columbuses, our Captain Cooks, our Livingstones in geology as we have had in geography."[13]

The exploration trope, which depicted scientists from Europe and the United States as consolidating control over the earth's past alongside those powers' extension of their dominion over its surface, projected a number of idealizing qualities upon those who carried it out. First among these was bravery. Defying biblical teachings about the relative brevity of the earth's past was said to require a certain fortitude—although British and American geologists sought to balance this with a respectful deference to the Christian God.[14] The science also demanded courageous leadership in confronting the difficult truths it taught. Two oft-repeated passages about the late eighteenth-century discovery of the planet's "high antiquity," credited to Scottish scientist James Hutton, show why geology was said to require heroism instead of, say, assiduity. The first underscores the sheer enormity of geological time: Hutton concluded his *Theory of the Earth* (1795) by declaring that he could find "no vestige of a beginning—no prospect of an end" to the story of the planet. The second, embodied in John Playfair's famous response to Hutton's work—that it made the mind grow "giddy by looking so far into the abyss of time"—emphasizes its near-incomprehensibility. Numerous writers in the geological canon reiterated this pattern, citing not just the immense antiquity of the planet but also the dizzying difficulty of confronting that fact. An 1827 study of the geology of central France by the volcanologist George Poulett Scrope points to the gap between rational conjecture and imaginative conception: "The periods which to our narrow apprehension, and compared with our ephemeral existence, appear of incalculable duration, are in all probability but trifles in the calendar of Nature. It is Geology that, above all other sciences, makes us acquainted with this important, though humiliating fact.... The leading idea which is present in all our researches ... the sound which to the ear of the student of Nature seems continually echoed from every part of her works, is—Time!—Time!—Time!"[15] As the heft of planetary time became the keynote of geological thought, writers gestured repeatedly to the burden it placed on human understanding, the "humiliating" knowledge that the science forced modern subjects to confront. The contrast between "our ephemeral existence" and the timescale that could account for planetary phenomena dealt a blow to human self-regard—humbling at best, shattering at worst. For the British scientist Charles Lyell, one of the most influential geological thinkers of the nineteenth century, geology could actually hurt: "The imagination was first fatigued and overpowered by endeavouring to conceive of the immensity of time required for the annihilation of whole continents.... Such views of the immensity of past time, like those unfolded by the Newtonian philosophy in regard to space, were too vast to awaken ideas of sublimity unmixed with a painful sense of our incapacity to conceive a plan of such infinite extent."[16] Pointing to the limitedness of current geological knowledge—the rocks then classified as primary, he observed, were probably relatively recent by planetary standards—Lyell declared that this "immensity of time" offered geologists "no resting place" as they thought through the implications of numerous, perhaps numberless, worlds before all knowledge.[17]

Even as they underscored the hazards of pondering the planet's antiquity, geologists developed a set of themes that could mitigate these by reconciling this new understanding with extant habits of thought. Prominent among these was the assertion that good Christians ought already to be accustomed to such humility. Scrope reminded his readers, in a footnote to the passage cited above, that "there are many minds that would not for an instance doubt the God of Nature to have existed *from all eternity*, yet would reject as preposterous the idea of going back a million of years in the History of *His Works*. Yet what are a million, or a million million, of solar years as to an Eternity?"[18] Geologists' insistence on the antiquity of geological phenomena could be aligned with the longer tradition of submission to divine omnipotence; sacred time could pave the way for geological time, rendering it not only comprehensible but morally useful. Scientists frequently informed their readers that Nature did, in fact, have a plan, that planetary time was not really an abyss but a series, however enormous, of discoverable processes that testified to the Creator's benevolence. Geologically ancient objects, Agassiz affirmed, should be "of deeper interest to men than the relics of their own age, for these things tell more directly of the thoughts and creative acts of God."[19]

The insistence on the legibility of the processes that had taken place in the earth's past also promised the restoration of a degree of human pride. The age of the planet might be difficult to grasp, but it opened new possibilities for scholars bold enough to recognize it. By working diligently through the "leading idea," Time, modern geologists hoped to draw a more accurate picture of the history of the planet than the wild speculations they attributed to their predecessors' need to cram into a few dozen centuries events that had taken millions of years. More time, that is, would mean better history. Martin Rudwick, a historian of geology, maintains that it is this revision of its historiographic capacity, rather than the "discovery" of deep time per se, that should be regarded as the decisive event in the science's modernization: modern geology is not simply a temporal science, but above all a historical one.[20] This framework changes how the science's history itself might be narrated. If a founding figure is required, that part should be played not by Hutton, Rudwick suggests, but by Georges Cuvier, the French anatomist who posited a decisive argument for species extinction. The fact of extinction enabled Cuvier and his followers to use fossils to organize the abyss of geological time into a knowable sequence punctuated by the appearance and disappearance of specific life-forms. Though Cuvier is not primarily remembered as a geologist, the preface to his masterwork *Ossumens Fossiles* (1812) identified "the ancient history of the earth" as "the ultimate goal toward which all [my] research is leading."[21] Cuvier declared his own discoveries a major step forward; empirical study of the fossil record would enable scientists following in his footsteps to "burst the limits of time," tracking the history of life before the present and elevating their entire species in the process: "Man, to whom has been accorded only an instant on earth, would have the glory of reconstructing the history of the thousands of centuries that preceded his existence, and of the thousands of beings that have not been his contemporaries."[22] In this account, geochronology compensates for the diminishing impact of the planet's age; human presence on the planet might be a recent phenomenon, but geology could provide knowledge no species had hitherto attained, justifying the fascination of "enlightened men" with the planetary past.[23]

The exchange outlined in this passage—the celebration of geohistorical knowledge as ameliorating the damage of deep time—is, I contend, central to geology's account of its contributions to modernity. The new devotion to reason, dedication, and empirical observation, advocates insisted, disenchanted the science, rendering it compatible with secularism. It also overcame merely affective responses—giddiness, pain, humiliation—to the fact of time's immensity, now positioned as an ultimately empowering one. The rapid progress of stratigraphy, the subdiscipline devoted to organizing the earth's history, consolidated this story, offering comfort to those who might feel stranded in the depths of geological time. Developed by the British geologist and civil engineer William Smith, stratigraphy built upon the emergent knowledge of fauna sequencing gleaned from research into the fossil record. By correlating new discoveries with extant chronologies and systematizing the principles for organizing that knowledge, stratigraphers promised to make the earth legible, useful, and meaningful. The introduction to Smith's 1817 manual reiterated the pattern of humiliation and consolation; though the "immensity" of the fossil record might strike many as incomprehensible, Smith declared, studying it illuminated what he called "the great unerring cause": "In this, as in every other part of the creation, there seems to have been one grand line of succession, a wonderful series of organization proceeding in the same train towards perfection."[24] Stratigraphy, that is, not only uncovered the history of the planet but also revealed it to be a story of directed progress.

This story permitted Smith to design his system around an argument for the moral as well as religious implications of geology, one that came to characterize writing about the science throughout the nineteenth century: the claim that knowledge of the earth could make one a better man. The study of fossils, Smith observed, was a healthful source of amusement and self-cultivation, beneficial to young and old alike. Country gentlemen and their families would find more profit in hunting fossils than hunting game: "one squanders time and property, the other improves the mind and may afterwards extend such infant knowledge to the improvement of the estates he may enjoy."[25] A grasp of natural history, moreover, was a duty owed both to the world and to the self; ignorance of that history constituted an "insult to nature ... [whose] productions ... are superior to the finest [human] workmanship" as well as an "insult to the understanding" with which nature had endowed humans.[26] Organized stratigraphically, the earth's past supported the labor of genteel self-cultivation.

While education was seen as a means of self-betterment in general, geology was said to possess certain advantages by virtue of its relationship to space and time. From the earliest stages of New World colonization onward, knowledge of the earth was applied to the project of its domestication, transforming it into ordered terrain that could be turned into capital, with "improvements" maximizing profitability. The evolution of geology into a historical science generated spiritual and cultural capital as well. In the hands of British and US writers, planetary time, as it shored up the figure of Man, generated a distinctly Anglo-American version of bourgeois whiteness: properly Christian yet sufficiently secular and rational; adventurous and manly in a well-mannered way; devoted primarily to Truth, though not averse to profit. Whewell's 1839 address predicted that geology's Heroic Age would be followed by a "Historical Period" in which geology would settle into its newly conquered time-spaces, "carry[ing] her vigilance into every province of her territory, and extend[ing] her dominion over the earth, till it becomes, far more truly than any before, a universal empire."[27] Imagining planetary time as global space to be converted into History (the capitalization signaling its status as cultural capital), Whewell and his colleagues followed the pattern that Sylvia Wynter describes, ranging from space to time as the measure of Man. The secular manliness associated with geological empire-building is both an intellectual and a physical quality; compatible with—indeed, obligated to—a proper degree of Christian devotion, it appears as secular in Ogden's framework insofar it involves the management of belief rather than the withdrawal of religion. As Ogden points out, though, belief management is a gendered practice in which excesses of belief were frequently assigned to women.[28] This was also true of geology; as the science's conquest of the earth's past rationalized the chaos associated with the murky abyss of time, it was said to dispel the feminized "fancies" of earlier geohistorians. The genders installed through secular belief management, Peter Coviello notes, are also always racialized, and geochronologists who understood themselves as following in the footsteps of European explorers, bringing the light of modernity to regions where darkness had reigned, were no exception here either.[29]

Some of Whewell's contemporaries were not quite so confident about their ability to subdue the immensity of the planetary past. Lyell, now remembered as the century's most important geological thinker, remained skeptical. In the midst of his widely read three-volume overview, *Principles of Geology* (1830–33), Lyell asserted that despite the diligent efforts of modern scientists to fill in its outlines, the wound inflicted by deep time—the "painful sense of our incapacity"—would remain open because of the fossil record's incompleteness. Given both the contingency surrounding the conditions of fossilization, which privilege marine over mammalian and other land-based species, and the manifold events that might have erased fossil deposits or rendered them inaccessible to human observation, the full history of the earth was beyond human reach. In her nuanced study of nineteenth-century British geological narrative, Adelene Buckland positions Lyell's view as a geopoetic counterperspective: "if the geologic record was so muted and fragmentary, geologists could never hope to know the pattern or shape of earth history, epic, progressive, or otherwise."[30] In light of the massive holes in time that geologists could never hope to fill, the nineteenth-century quest for scientific self-understanding—the "glory of reconstructing" earth's history—seemed like a game of chance played in deep time. Geology, in this view, could never fully compensate for the trauma of the planet's antiquity; it would continue confronting the modern world as the site of its own perpetual dispossession.

The frequency of appeals to deep-temporal dislocation in our own time makes sense in light of Lyell's centrality to latter-day historians, as his cautionary stance now overshadows the confident predictions that characterized many of his less-remembered contemporaries. Yet Lyell's status as the most important geological thinker of the mid-nineteenth century was, as Rudwick points out, belatedly conferred; during his own lifetime, the debate between his steady-state theory, which eschewed celebratory narratives of improvement as well as fantasies of completion, and his rivals' progressive framing of earth history was not as conclusive.[31] Though Lyell's work was widely read and admired both within and beyond geological circles, his reminders of the gaps in the fossil record did not prevent other nineteenth-century geologists from telling the story of the earth in directed, even teleological, terms. Indeed, as Peter J. Bowler documents, they often did so in full awareness that this was not a story the fossil record could fully support. Instead, they leaned on the natural-theological inference that the design of earth's systems expressed the benevolent intentions of the deity, who was slowly but surely preparing the earth for human habitation.[32] The fact that each geological era was suited for the habitation of the living creatures specific to it confirmed this benevolence in their accounts.

The geophantasmatic contention that geology documented the progress, not simply the history, of the earth became a kind of common sense by the middle of the nineteenth century, used to support a number of systems of thought. The Spiritualist Andrew Jackson Davis placed the science's discoveries literally at the foundation of his explication of nature's "divine Revelations," asserting that its accounts of the successive development of earth's layers and of the interlocking relations of matter also provided the growth and infinite duration of the spirit.[33] The phrenologist J. Stanley Grimes, in his system of "phreno-geology," affirmed that the history of the earth paralleled and predicted the development of the human mind, which he organized into various faculties hierarchized according to their contributions to civilization."[34] As the progress of the earth became the basis for spiritual and psychological assessments of the rise of human civilization, it was also used to ground racial hierarchies. The popular orator and entrepreneur George Francis Train mapped his antiblackness stratigraphically, declaring, "Geology shows us the different strata of the earth; ethnology teaches us the different strata of man; the negro is the *paleozoic.*"[35]

Lyell's emphasis on the enigmatic condition of the planetary past exemplifies but one pole of the fort/da game geology played with deep time. Many of his colleagues, and those they influenced, followed the game through. The dizzying age of the planet was rediscovered, again and again, in order to be ameliorated; it functioned as an existential problem that called meaningful intellectual and spiritual histories of the earth into being. As a solution for deep-temporal trauma, the project of reconstructing the earth's history linked geology to the ongoing labor of civilization and modernization; not only was the earth's past knowable and directed, it also ordered the human social world. The immensity of geological time, as it contributed to the advancement of those who understood it, provided infinite space to inscribe the developing figure of Man.

Cuvier, Geochronology, and Biopower

The connection of geochronology to progress, and that of the study of the science to self-enhancement, are some of the ways the science entwined with biopower. As Foucault outlines it, though, biopower operates on both individual and mass levels. The planetary past supported the latter mode as well; along with the aforementioned techniques, which we might recognize as geologic discipline, geologic knowledge, especially the idea of species extinction, also sponsored forms of fantasy that lent themselves to the biopolitical control of populations. Cuvier himself plays a key role in Foucault's theorization of biopower, although his presence, and that of geology as a whole, is withdrawn from the concept's initial explication in *The History of Sexuality, Volume 1*. Underscoring biopower's temporal dimension, Foucault asserts that it was bound up with "Western Man's emergent understanding of what it meant to be a living species in a living world."[36] In his consideration of this new understanding of "life," Foucault gestures apophatically to his earlier thinking on the subject in *The Order of Things: An Archaeology of the Human Sciences*. That book's Eurocentric account of the figure Foucault calls "Man," whose arrival signals, for him, the emergence of the modern episteme around the turn of the nineteenth century, assigns a decisive role to the development of modern biology. If the discovery of the planet's antiquity constituted the rupture that modernized geology, the parallel event in biology, according to Foucault, was Cuvier's work on comparative anatomy, which confirmed species extinction.[37] From Cuvier onward, he argues, "Life" became a proliferating and elusive force, organizing the internal coherence of living forms and rendering them dependent on external conditions. The modern understanding of life is fundamentally discontinuous: "the living being wraps itself in its own existence," bound together both by anatomical and physiological mechanisms and by its interaction with its environment—"all that surrounds [the living being]...the air it breathes, the water it drinks, the food it absorbs."[38] Life, that is, is dependent on what we can recognize as *lifeworlds*. This is the cause of its disjointedness, insofar as lifeworlds, when seen from a geological perspective, appear and disappear across the fossil record. Hence, instead of illustrating a directed "continuity of time," fossils, as indices of the life-forms to which they had "once really belonged," revealed time's brokenness.[39] Foucault works hard to align Cuvier with this account of discontinuity. He argues away Cuvier's disbelief in evolution and assigns the progressive understanding of nature's development to the earlier Classical period although, as Bowler demonstrates, it outlasted Cuvier by several decades at least.[40] What seems to be decisive, for Foucault, is Cuvier's confirmation of species extinction and, hence, of lost lifeworlds, which map a history of life traversed by death, both on the level of the organism and of nature itself.

The Foucault of *The Order of Things* overestimated Man's instability, a blind spot generated by his chronic inattention to the dynamics of colonialism. Wynter's more precise account of the simultaneous development and interdependence of Euro/American science and New World colonization shows how Man, overrepresented as the Human, supports himself by drawing life, figuratively and materially, from othered populations. Foucault's later thinking about biopower arguably made more room for these dynamics, though it remained limited by its inconsistent and still Eurocentric attention to them. The discontinuity of *bios*—life's perpetual imperilment—forms the core of his analysis of modern racism. In a series of lectures at the Collège de France delivered in 1975 and 1976, later published under the title "*Society Must Be Defended*," Foucault asserts that it is the "subdivision of species into races" that enables racism to take hold, and that it functions as "primarily a way of introducing a break into the domain of life that is under power's control: the break between what must live and what must die."[41] The conviction that society must progress demands that life be oriented to forward movement. Individuals and populations said to threaten that movement can thus be depicted as endangering life on the species level. The administration of racialized death draws upon repressed anxieties over human extinction; as Mary Mader glosses, "Justifications for state killing phrased in the terms of threats to future lives may ignite unacknowledged existential concerns for the unthought longevity—and brevity—of human genealogical relations."[42] In promoting the "life of the species" in time as positive value, then, biopower at once solicits and sublimates the accompanying thought of extinction. All species, in time, go extinct, but biopower infinitely defers that eventuality through the production of peoples marked for death in order to allow Man-as-the-species to go forward.

Nineteenth-century geology's involvement in the formation of bio- and necropolitics becomes clear at this juncture. If Cuvier's conception of *life* lies at the root of modern biopower, his confirmation, via the fossil, of species extinction inscribes that conception into the history of the earth itself.[43] The geological timescale, with its vast secular understanding of time, is also necessary to the formation of the modern episteme in this account; Foucault asserts that the "discontinuity of living forms [in the guise of extinction] made it possible to conceive of a great temporal current"—geological time—which "replace[d] natural history with a 'history' of nature."[44] Biopower, in Foucault's thinking, is undergirded by concepts—the earth's antiquity and species extinction—central to the development of geochronology. In this sense, geochronology itself can be seen to function biopolitically. Despite the looming threat of species extinction and the diminishing power of the geological timescale, the growth of Man, like the development of the planet, was charted in an orderly fashion by those nineteenth-century geologists who claimed the planet had developed for his benefit. The order imposed on both geo- and human history differs from Foucault's emphasis on Life's discontinuity; the latter privileges the Darwinian model of evolution, which, like the Lyellian understanding of planetary history on which it partially drew, departs from the linear-developmental accounts embraced by many other nineteenth-century scientists. But Darwin's "victory" was conferred retrospectively; the more continuous models supported by Lamarckian thought, as Kyla Schuller has shown, continued to shape both scientific and popular understandings of evolution throughout the nineteenth century, particularly in the United States.[45] Cuvier himself underscored the possibility of sequential mapping in geochronology: "There is a collection of facts . . . and a series of epochs anterior to the present time, the order of which can be verified without uncertainty, although the duration of the intervals between them cannot be defined with precision. They are so many points that will serve to give measure and direction to this ancient chronology."[46] Even if the duration of geological time remained unquantifiable, the earth's past, Cuvier contended, was nevertheless discernible; it could be deciphered and ordered "without uncertainty." Index fossils, remnants correlated to different epochs in the deep past on the basis of their disappearance from the rock record, were the "points" that provided "measure and direction," despite the disruptions extinction created in the flow of life. Extinction thus contributed to the ability to know the planet's history, enabling Man to affirm his place on earth: if life was perpetually disrupted by death, death also served to orient life in its movement forward in time. The fossil record became a relay between the knowable and the unfathomable, between vitality and stilled life, between biopower and exomodernity, traversing these on both individual and collective levels.

Those relays are evident in the trope through which geology assisted biopower in taking hold of Indigenous bodies. As I have observed, knowledge of the earth's composition formed part of the geographic displacement of Indigenous peoples, as justification for the agricultural and extractive "development" that settler colonialism depicted as the proper use of land. Geochronology was employed as a means of extending this displacement. Geology's historical turn tied into the figure Jacob Pandian names the "fossil other": the human other rendered inert by the fantasized application of geological time. Indigenous people, preemptively represented as "extinct," were the primary targets of this mode. The Indigenous extinction trope did not at first resonate in a geological register; it was in common use at least since the time of the American Revolution, when the question of species extinction was still a matter of debate.[47] But after the question was settled in the early nineteenth century, the term *extinct* began to resonate with the authority of science in imbricated geo- and sociohistorical accounts of expropriated lands. The second volume of Lyell's *Principles of Geology* cites the displacement of Indigenous people in the United States and Australia to explain the role of habitat change in species extinction:

> A faint image of the certain doom of a species less fitted to struggle with some new condition in a region which it previously inhabited, and where it has to contend with a more vigorous species, is presented by the extirpation [localized extinction] of savage tribes of men by the advancing colony of some civilized nation.... Few future events are more certain than the speedy extermination of the Indians of North America and the savages of New Holland in the course of a few centuries, when these tribes will be remembered only in poetry and tradition.[48]

Lyell's comparison, representing colonization as a natural and inevitable process, uses Indigenous people to mark settler-national time, consigning them to the future anterior as he envisions an epoch when they *will have been*. At that point, he predicts, settler legends of Indigenous people will, in essence, enclose them as fossils of modernity, pointing future historians back toward their now-vanished worlds. Lyell uses the comparison to illustrate his contention that habitat change causes extinction, which is therefore a gradual and dispersed process. This claim, in turn, demonstrates Lyell's larger point: that such processes can only be apprehended through a correct understanding of the earth's antiquity. The comparison thus aligns settler-national and deep geological time, using Indigenous people as the bridge between the two.

As the geological correlative to the broader settler fantasy of "vanishing" Indigeneity, the imagined fossilization of Indigenous people deadened their relationship to their lands and assigned them the status of animalized bodily forms—specimens of anatomy and physiology rather than participants in social worlds. Seen in this light, the mineralization envisioned in the extinction trope operated as a precursor to biologized racialization. "Race," as a category administered by science and the state, was applied to Indigenous people in North America unevenly and relatively belatedly, arriving on the heels of the theft of land sovereignty and the disruption of kinship relations; removed from the relations that structure and sustain Indigenous worlds, Indigeneity would be redefined by the state as "Indian blood," a hereditary characteristic inhering in the body.[49] Insofar as that theft and disruption were abetted by their figuration as "fossil other," geology played a role in the state's conversion of Indigenous people into biological beings, subjects of biopower in the sense Foucault outlined.[50] In stabilizing the lifeworld of Man, the Indigenous-extinction trope became one of the conventions of exomodernity.

Extinction was not the only form of death-against-life that geochronology was invoked to support. As Mbembe's description of colonized and racialized populations as "living dead" suggests, death operates in numerous temporal registers within modernity, including the ascription of fixity to racialized populations held to be incapable of development. And though they ostensibly focused on nonliving matter, geological and paleontological claims became part of the evolutionary arguments posited by racial biologists. Some geologists, like Lyell, approached the early history of the human race reluctantly or not at all, but Cuvier and others regarded it as part of the science's purview. Cuvier even used human records to supplement the "rock record" in his quest to illuminate the most recent planetary catastrophe, which he, like many others, believed to have been a global deluge that would have brought about a "renewal" of all human societies: "Nature everywhere... tells us that the present order of things does not reach back very far. And—what is indeed remarkable—mankind everywhere speaks to us like nature."[51] The deluge provides Cuvier with the opportunity to develop theories about the relationship between geological events and human difference. Against "our [European] present knowledge and civilization," which he traces to Egypt and Phoenicia, he defines East Asians as "another race... so different from us that it is tempting to believe that their ancestors and ours escaped from the great catastrophe on two different shores."[52] Africans receive even worse abuse; he declares them "degraded" and bestial, complains that they have "nowhere preserved either annals or traditions" that would benefit his research, and finally returns to his catastrophic theory for an explanation, though in the end he finds it equivocal: "all [their] characters show clearly that [they] escaped from the great catastrophe at another point than the Caucasian and Altaic races, from which [they] had perhaps been separated long before that catastrophe took place."[53] Mankind here is made to speak like nature, with racial difference at once confirming the deluge and standing apart from it.

Cuvier's use of planetary catastrophe to prop up his theories of racial development, and vice versa, contradicts the long-standing presumption of geology's political innocence. This is a presumption that, as I argued in this book's introduction, persists today; indeed, we can see it in operation in Martin Rudwick's editorial attempt to set Cuvier's contributions to geochronology apart from the history of scientific racism, within which Cuvier (who, after the death of Sara Baartman, a Khokhoi woman brought to Europe and exhibited in England and France, notoriously dissected her body) is also a significant figure.[54] Rudwick asserts that his volume on Cuvier's geological writing is not concerned, "except indirectly and in passing, with [Cuvier's] work on the human sciences," and that it therefore "has no bearing on arguments over his position in relation to such modern concepts as racism and sexism."[55] A footnote to the passage maligning Africans continues in this vein, commenting that "Cuvier's opinions, however distasteful to modern sensibilities, are those of his time and place" and claiming (inaccurately) that his assessment of race against catastrophe "did not assume the intrinsic superiority of the Caucasians."[56] As Samantha Pinto aptly observes, Rudwick "insists on a narrative separation that can keep natural history 'natural' by excising it from the histories of colonialism, enslavement, and anti-blackness that generate the very grounds of its emergence."[57] The assertion of geological innocence here rests on two claims: that Caucasians were not "intrinsically" privileged in Cuvier's theory of racial development, an argument seemingly predicated on the belief that racism can only result from biological essentialism; and that geological theorizing can be separated from merely personal "opinions," which result from a particular historical moment.[58] Geochronology, that is, remains untainted by Cuvier's merely historical white supremacy. However, the very possibility of geochronology is bound up with white supremacy in Cuvier's correlation of human and natural-historical evidence. His assertion that "mankind everywhere speaks to us like nature" did not mean mankind spoke everywhere the same; in his assessment, mankind was as stratified as the rock record, and both could only be "read" properly by literate Europeans.

Not all geologists shared Cuvier's racial vitriol, but geology was a popular support for writers who sought to establish racial fixity and hierarchy. William Usher, who contributed the chapter on "Geology and Paleontology, in Connection with Human Origins" to the infamous compendium *Types of Mankind: Or, Ethnological Researches* (1854), based on the work of racial craniologist Samuel Morton, drew on the research of contemporary geologists, including Louis Agassiz, to argue that fossilized human remains provided evidence of racial fixity stretching back to prehistoric times.[59] "Fixity" was an aspect of polygenetic thinking; the contention, allegedly backed up by differences observable in human fossils, that the races had remained essentially unchanged over vast spans of time was spun into an argument for the multiple, geographically diffused origins of races whose varying cranial structures (again supposedly evident in fossils) signaled gradations of intellectual and moral strengths. Like Cuvier's deluge, the fossil record was also made to bespeak white supremacy. Louis Agassiz, another contributor to Morton's book, adopted Morton's views on polygenesis and the immutability of species shortly after moving to the United States.[60] His swipes at Darwinian theory in the *Atlantic Monthly* series and elsewhere might have been motivated by this specific conviction as much as his general disbelief in evolution, insofar as Darwin was confident that his understanding of evolution would definitively disprove polygenesis. The depth of Agassiz's racism may actually have won Darwin some converts. Charles Lyell, who resisted evolution until late in his career, wrote to a colleague in 1860: "I admit that Agassiz's last publication moved me far into Darwin's camp, or the Lamarckian point of view, because when he suggests the origin of every human race to a separate, independent act of creation—and when this is not enough, he creates whole nations simultaneously, each individual separately 'from earth, air and water' as Hooker put it—these miracles do not appeal to me."[61] Though nineteenth-century racial science appealed most heavily to biology and zoology, its attempt to root its ideas deep in the history of the earth by means of geological and paleontological claims undermines the contention that geology, because of its ostensible focus on nonhuman matters and prehuman times, stands inherently apart from politics. The centrality of Cuvier's work to the understanding of "life" that supports biopower—which, despite Foucault's own neglect of race, has become a key rubric for the analysis of modern racism—suggests how deeply early geochronological thought was imbricated with race. Geology was not innocent of nineteenth-century protoracial and racial biopolitics; rather, it provided them with a planetary infrastructure.

Manifest Geologies

American writers turned geology into a technology of settlement both practically and phantasmatically. As white settlers occupied Indigenous lands, mapping and extracting natural and mineral resources and populating them according to US ethno-racial hierarchies, their territorial claims were supplemented by geohistorical ones. Geologizing the continent was a way for settlers to make themselves at home on lands where they had no social history. "Americanness" became a geologic as well as a civic property as the United States took hold of the continent, surface *and* bedrock. As Thomas Allen observes, the geological lens provided the new nation with a way to differentiate its lands, and its relationship to those lands, as distinct from "unsuitable European models. Geology gave the American land a history and, through both scientific study and artistic representation, gave the people a felt connection to that history."[62] North American geology provided Louis Agassiz with an opportunity to proclaim the superiority of his adopted homeland, at least as far as the rock record went. Leading off his *Atlantic Monthly* series with an article titled "America the Old World," Agassiz suggested that the United States would become the center of scientific as well as civic progress: "the American continent offers facilities to the geologist denied to him in the so-called Old World."[63] The continent's recent arrival to "culture and civilization," he declared, was balanced by its status as the first land to emerge from the waters: "while Europe was only represented by islands rising here and there above the seas, America already stretched an unbroken line of land from Nova Scotia to the far West."[64] Long disparaged for its lack of cultural history, the United States could finally look down on Europeans for something. James D. Dana likewise affirmed that the geology of North America was purer, and hence more instructive, than that of Europe. In his *Manual of Geology*, published the same year as Agassiz's *Atlantic* series, Dana declared that because it was a "simple isolated specimen of a continent," the North American strata delineated "the laws of progress...undisturbed by the conflicting movements of other lands."[65]

As the United States established dominion in the wake of other colonial claims, the "felt connection" to the land generated through geological fantasy erased previous histories not only by dispossessing Indigenous people but also by purifying the whiteness it sought to establish on that land. The British geologist David Ansted's *Gold-Seeker's Manual*, published the year after the United

States annexed the northern half of Mexico, ties both projects of erasure to an extractive agenda. The book, which directed most of its attention to the North American west coast in response to the recent discovery of gold in California, declared the region's geology and topography well-suited to the needs of "civilized men ... especially of the Anglo-Saxon race, whether on this or the other side of the Atlantic."[66] The Spaniards, who had previously claimed the region, had, he lamented, made little of the superior land, but now that it had "fallen into the hands of a race certainly as much inclined to make the most of its natural advantages as any people in the world ... [it] will ... at least, have justice done it."[67] "Justice," for Ansted, equaled extraction and agriculture; rich terrain, in his view, deserved to be developed toward maximal profitability. Rather than sink Anglo-American presence into the ground through geochronological fantasy, Ansted directed the geological gaze to the future, guiding Anglo/American settlers in the project of etching themselves materially into the land by showing them where to mine and farm.

Other writers would take up the task of Americanizing the deep-temporal history of California, dramatizing just how long the land had been waiting for (Anglo) America to show up and carry its legacies forward. Settler geology interweaved physical knowledge of the continent with the Anglo-American biological-reproductive imaginary, projecting settler populations into the future and displacing Indigenous land tenancy and kinship practices.[68] Land was depicted as a kind of natural inheritance formed over deep time, shaping and nourishing the reproduction of whiteness materially and affectively.[69] An enthusiastic speech given by the scientist and physician Charles F. Winslow before the California State Assembly in 1854, four years after the region became the thirty-first American state, exemplifies this genre of geological fantasy. Invited by the assembly to deliver a lecture on agriculture, Winslow decided to take a broader historical view, waxing geological as he chronicled what he called "the preparation of the Earth for the Intellectual Races": "What a long chain of great events is stretched between us and the infancy of the earth—between its present surface, so fertile and productive, and that bare, uninhabitable rock which was first uplifted from the bosom of the primeval seas! How long the epochs devoted to the accomplishment of that wonderful scheme,—the fertilization of the soil, and its preparation for the advent of the human race!"[70] Tracking this history stratigraphically, from the lowest strata to its "present surface," Winslow dwells on what each stage contributed to be carried forward through the ages, ultimately to serve human needs; the Carboniferous, for instance, was built on the decayed marine life that preceded it and left vegetal remains that "laid down the inexhaustible beds of... coal which are now so necessary for the comfort of man, and so advantageous... in developing the resources of the world, and in enlarging the limits of human knowledge and power."[71] The late arrival of Man to earth is not evidence of his insignificance but of divine favor—an intentional delay until the surface of the earth had been properly prepared for them. Human history follows geochronology in a long-scale sedimentation of whiteness: Asia, where Winslow locates the origins of "primeval society," represents the "slate beds and limestones of the primitive seas"; Greece plays the part of the Carboniferous period, depositing fuel for later civilizations to use; the emergence of Christianity and of science, spearheaded by the "rapid advancement of the white race," signals "a sort of tertiary age in the history of the moral world"; and the Spanish, French, and British empires stand in for the now-extinct reptiles and mammals which once populated North America.[72] All of these, he insists, existed to "prepare the way for the great American epoch,—the last stratum in the successive developments of human society."[73]

California, in particular, is destined to carry the nation, and hence humanity, into the future: "Cast your eye over the physical geography of the western slope of the North American continent, and behold this comely region of the earth! God... has reserved it until the present age, to give a fresh and more vigorous impulse to the development of human society. It holds the same relation to the old nations and to old forms of civilization, as does the modern geological age to all that preceded it."[74] Winslow's perspective places agriculture above extraction as the motor of settler development. Gold, accordingly, is of little interest; the future will come, instead, from a different area of the geological past—the decomposed bones of mastodon and ichthyosauri, which fertilize the soil. Settler geology values land for its ability to stimulate "the physical, intellectual, and moral growth of human society" in tandem.[75] Physical growth is tended by fertile soil and useful mineral deposits; the intriguing stories told by the rock record, as it documents the history of the earth, serve intellectual development; and the beauty of the land stimulates aesthetic and spiritual evolution—including, evidently, the production of gender differentiation: agriculture, Winslow notes, is a manly pursuit, while the flowers that California grew in profusion nurture the "deep, humble, chaste, and sweet spirit of the cultivated woman."[76] The sexual division of the soil's cultivating influences materializes the fantasy of the land as the inheritance of white Americans, connecting the geologic past to the reproductive family and interlinking the future of whiteness and the future of the planet.

As they inscribe the Anglo-American into the terrain, Ansted's topographical overview and Winslow's deep-historical account both supplant California's

Indigenous tribes, though in different ways. Winslow's contention that the "great American epoch" will be built upon the traces of "decayed nations— the Oriental, Egyptian, Grecian, Roman, and Saracenic"—omits both Africans and Indigenous Americans from his transcontinental, transhistorical sweep, establishing his account as a stratigraphy of whiteness.[77] Ansted, in contrast, acknowledges the Indigenous as well as white populations of northern California in a brief ethnographic overview drawn from Sebastian Biscayno, a seventeenth-century Spanish explorer, and Alexander von Humboldt, who never visited the region and himself got the information secondhand. He declares that "the natives of this part of the American coast are described as being a quiet and even industrious race."[78] The surprise indexed in the adverb *even* reflects a general disbelief in Indigenous industriousness, although he notes that their ability to dress stag skins "might become a very considerable branch of commerce."[79] Beyond this, he confines his consideration to estimates of the number of Indigenous men involved in gold prospecting.

Ansted confidently predicted that the discovery of gold in California would lead to rapid development of coastal land and a bustling Pacific trade, with ships carrying white people to "shores which, till now, have rarely seen any... except those of Spanish blood." But the Gold Rush and its aftermath would be devastating to the Indigenous population of California. Not only did the sudden and massive influx of white prospectors and settlers cause widespread starvation and illness, but white gold prospectors and miners, viewing Indigenous people as competitors, killed an estimated 9,000 to 16,000 of them in the quarter-century after the rush began. In their first session, the newly formed US State of California's legislature passed the ironically named Act for the Government and Protection of Indians, which permitted Indigenous children and adults to be pressed into long-term indenture to white settlers; at least 10,000 Indigenous people were forced into labor in the decade that followed.[80] Despite this actively genocidal campaign, Peter Burnett, the state's first governor, in his initial State of the State address to the legislature, slid into the language of natural history when discussing the status of the Indigenous population: "That a war of extermination will continue to be waged between the races until the Indian race becomes extinct must be expected. While we cannot anticipate this result but with painful regret, the inevitable destiny of the race is beyond the power or wisdom of man to avert."[81] The power of the Indigenous-extinction trope in the settler imaginary is evidenced in Burnett's depiction of what he acknowledged to be an active "war of extermination" as nevertheless a natural and unavoidable process, something "beyond the wisdom or power of man."[82] Three years before Winslow would stand before the same legislature narrating the deep-temporal history of whiteness, California's governor claimed the ability to write the region's geologic future, promising one more extinction to crown the fossiliferous strata that Winslow would call upon to fuel and feed the state. As they clustered around the creation of a new state, scientists and legislators demonstrated the extent to which nationalism could be understood as the sedimentation of white Americanness. Geology and geological fantasy worked in tandem to overwrite the annexed land of California as a space filled with settler time.

"Historical and Geological Incidents": Cooper's *The Crater*

Nineteenth-century writers who emphasized geology's diminishment of human history also liked to proclaim its superiority to human creativity. In *The Wonders of Geology*, Samuel Goodrich declared, "There is nothing in history—nay, even in poetry or romance—so startling and so wonderful, as the incontestable facts disclosed by geology."[83] An 1836 article in the *North American Review* pronounced the narratives contained in the rock record "so interesting, that the most splendid fictions of the human imagination sink into insignificance when compared with [them]."[84] By the time James Fenimore Cooper published his 1847 adventure novel *The Crater, or, Vulcan's Peak: A Tale of the Pacific*, he may have felt the need to supplement the story with science. The novel's preface takes for granted its readers' interest in the kind of "historical and geological incidents" that fill its pages.[85] But the novel's relationship to then-current geological theory and its deployment of geological fantasy are too complex to be explained by a simple wish to capitalize upon public interest in the science. Cooper's novel is often read as a straightforward endorsement of nineteenth-century Lyellian theory, which it draws upon to portray the (literal) rise and fall of the Pacific archipelago on which the action takes place, a process it parallels to the metaphorical rise and fall of empire. Yet while it embraces the kind of practical geological knowledge employed to expand the American colonial project, its relationship to theories of the earth's formation is somewhat more ambivalent. Even as it restores geological knowledge to the familiar role of rebuking human hubris, diverging from the confident alignment of planetary and national history endorsed by thinkers like Winslow, it also interrogates the fashionable science's own hubristic tendencies. In tandem with its concern over the excesses of contemporary American life, the novel's skepticism about the direction of contemporary geological theory inverts the logic of manifest geology: instead of mutually confirming histories, both geology and America, if left unchecked, threaten to become parallel manifestations of arrogance.

The Crater narrates the story of a colony established by a band of expatriate Americans on a South Pacific island, focalized by the life of its founder, the American-born Mark Woolston. Woolston is marooned on an uncharted reef island along with a shipmate, Bob Betts, who is soon swept away in a storm. Woolston manages to survive alone for some months, until one day, after a massive earthquake, he is astonished to find that the small reef island has increased in size considerably while a larger island has become newly visible nearby. This island, crowned by a two-thousand-foot mountain which he names Vulcan's Peak, turns out to be a verdant paradise. After Woolston is miraculously rescued by Betts, the two men bring a small group of Americans to the archipelago and establish a colony with Woolston as governor. Within a few years, the colony becomes a thriving community, increased by the arrival of numerous American expatriates. Things eventually go downhill, as the greed of new arrivals sends trade and new settlement spiraling out of control. After Woolston is voted out of office, he, Betts, and their families embark on a short visit to the United States, but on their return, they discover to their horror that the archipelago has sunk entirely into the ocean, leaving no survivors and no trace save the rocky, guano-covered tip of Vulcan's Peak, which pokes out of the water to mark the spot where the colony formerly stood.

The sudden, dramatic surfacing and sinking of the archipelago, evidently the "geological incidents" promised in the preface, provide the backdrop against which Cooper could compress his rise-and-fall narrative into the span of a single lifetime. But it is the everyday rhythms of practical geology on which the plot initially depends; it is both the means of Woolston and Betts's initial survival on the reef island and, later, the conduit to the colony's success. Betts's familiarity with the use of guano, which abounds on the rocks surrounding the reef, enables the men to create tillable soil out of "the otherwise barren deposit of the volcano."[86] The soil allows them to plant crops for their survival; later in the novel, it also serves as a site for the implantation of national fantasy, as the rich, fertile land of the larger island—produced, Woolston conjectures, by the "vast deposit of very ancient guano" that covers the tip of Vulcan's Peak washing down into the soil when it rains—fuels the ambition of the colonists.[87] As John Levi Barnard points out, the dynamics of empire surround the use of guano from the start.[88] Upon the introduction of the substance, the narrator references it as an "article which is now ... extensively known," a confident solicitation of readerly knowledge which reflects the novel's publication in the early years of what Jennifer James identifies as nineteenth-century America's "guano-mania."[89] Guano's efficacy as fertilizer, James observes, meant that it quickly became an "unlikely symbol of economic and earthy renewal within disparate mid-nineteenth century 'utopian' ideologies."[90] Its importance in *The Crater* reflects this utopian promise. Once he learns of its usefulness, guano fills Woolston with hope—"From the hour when he found muck, and sea-weed, and guano, he felt assured of the means of subsistence"—and his optimism, in turn, sustains the colonial project, which attracts disgruntled Americans who sought the chance to begin again.[91] But if guano's promise guided utopian fantasies like those of *The Crater*'s colonists, it was also, as James and Goffe point out, connected with histories of labor exploitation and imperial conquest.[92] The novel indexes these in the subplot concerning people Cooper identifies only as "Kannakas," Indigenous residents of a nearby group of coral islands. (The word, derived from the Hawaiian word for "person," was used in the nineteenth-century United States and the British Empire as a derogatory term referencing Pacific Islanders, most often Hawaiians or Melanesians, who were employed by colonists as indentured workers.) After defeating the islanders in war, the colonists take a hundred of their young men captive—"hostages for the good behavior of their parents"—and use them as a cheap and plentiful source of labor, a force the narrator describes as a "sort of Irish for [the] colony."[93] They are put to work breaking down the rocky base of the islands to enable the colony's further development. In the end, though, they manage to avoid the fate of those Emerson referred to as the "guano-races of mankind," whose very lives are made into fertilizer for the growth of the nation. After Woolston is deposed and leaves the island, the colonists overwork the islanders and refuse to pay them. In response, they return en masse to their own islands and are, accordingly, spared the colony's catastrophic fall.

Against the ordinariness of practical geology as it grounds the expansive fantasies and material degradations of colonization, the drama of the land's providential appearance and devastating disappearance reads as something out of romance. But while the novel's catastrophic ending provoked one nineteenth-century critic to denounce it as "preposterous," the sudden surfacing of land in the ocean as the result of a seismic event was not unknown in Cooper's lifetime.[94] One such case was the rise and fall of Graham Island, a landmass resulting from the 1831 eruption of an undersea volcano in the Mediterranean, which sank within a few months' time. Graham Island was the subject of both political and geological controversy in its brief tenure above the waves; it was claimed by Britain, France, and Sicily, each of which gave it different names, and it was cited by Charles Lyell and others in a debate about the nature of volcanoes.[95] (It is likely that Cooper, like many of his contemporaries, read at least some of Lyell's writing; the events that shape the novel's plot correspond in some respects to Lyell's description of volcanic islands and to his account of a Chilean earthquake that raised low-lying land several feet above sea level.)[96] The brief history of Graham Island provides *The Crater*'s seemingly fantastic narrative with the authority of geological realism, borne out when Woolston, who has been exposed to the sciences at school, manages to account for the archipelago's sudden appearance in geologically plausible terms, reasoning that the volcano's subterranean explosion had cracked open the seafloor, generating enough steam to force quantities of rock and land to the surface, which enlarged the reef island and elevated the larger verdant island, which had previously lain below view.

While most critics have assumed that Cooper's narrative endorses Lyell's theories, the novel is more equivocal on this point. Indeed, the narrator immediately moves to undermine the authority of Woolston's seismic theory, remarking that it "may have been true, in whole or in part, or it may have been altogether erroneous. Such speculations seldom turn out to be minutely accurate. So many unknown causes exist in so many forms, as to render precise estimates of their effects, in cases of physical phenomena, almost as uncertain as those which follow similar attempts at an analysis of human motives and human conduct."[97] The depiction of geology as a speculative and imprecise science calls into question the novel's classification as "above all a 'scientific' narrative" by its modern editor, Thomas Philbrick.[98] Instead of embracing modern science, the novel declares itself agnostic. The analogy between geology and the analysis of human motives further undermines the authority of the former, since, as the narrator goes on to explain, motive analysis isn't analysis at all; people generally just project their own thinking onto others. Though the discussion isn't brought back around to the question of geological theories, the analogy suggests the possibility that geology, too, may be a location for human self-projection.

The narrator's skepticism about geology's accuracy might serve to remind the reader that alongside the preface's promise of "historical and geological incidents," a seeming guarantee that the novel will be founded on truth, Cooper has also declared such a foundation unimportant: "Truth is not absolutely necessary to the illustration of a principle, the imaginary sometimes doing that office quite as effectually as the actual."[99] What matters most, he affirms, is that Americans discern a "timely warning in the events here recorded," permitting the republic to remain in God's favor.[100] Whether geological truth can be brought in line with the moral truth that Cooper prioritizes here is left unanswered. The moral so often derived from the geologic—the rebuke delivered to human ambition by the massiveness of geological time and the indifference of geological matter—offers itself as one possible candidate near the novel's close, in an allusion to Thomas Cole's celebrated series of paintings, "The Course of Empire," completed between 1833 and 1836. The paintings narrate the gradual rise and decline of a civilization against a stable geological point of reference: the rocky hill that appears consistently in the background, bearing indifferent witness to each successive stage. Cooper greatly admired "The Course of Empire"; in a reflection on Cole's work, he described it as "landscape painting raised to a level with the heroic."[101] The paintings' appearance in the novel comes as Woolston recognizes the guano-covered tip of Vulcan's Peak peering above the waves, the only visible remnant of the colony; it is said to resemble "that sublime rock . . . in Coles' series of noble landscapes that is called 'The March [sic] of Empire'; ever the same amid the changes of time, and civilization, and decay."[102] The rock's durability underscores the ephemerality of the human scenes that surround it—scenes whose importance vanishes, like the colony itself, against the heft of the geologic.

But if this observation presents itself as a useful lesson, it is not quite a "timely warning"; as a familiar moral corollary to natural law, it is, like the rock itself, ever-present, not an intervention into a potential crisis. The warning itself appears a couple of pages after the allusion to Cole, as the "chastened" Woolston reflects on the wayward growth of the colony, where capitalism had begun to spiral out of control and the proliferation of newspapermen, lawyers, and sectarian clergymen created an atmosphere much like the American mainland. An overconfidence in "self," the narrator declares, led the colonists to forget about "that divine hand which alone can unite the elements of worlds as they float in gasses, equally from His mysterious laboratory, and scatter them again into thin air when the works of His hand cease to find favor in his view."[103] This theological turn suggests that the "rise and fall" of the colony should be read not as nineteenth-century geologists would understand it, or Cole's painting would depict it—as an event governed by the laws of nature—but as the direct effect of a deity who varies those laws to His purposes. Cooper's theo-geology conforms to an earlier, nonsecular model; bypassing nineteenth-century natural theology, which viewed the laws of nature as regular and predictable, established by a benevolent God, it embraced the kind of science that the historian and clergyman Thomas Prince described in a sermon preached after an earthquake that rocked Boston in 1727. Prince spent part of the sermon reviewing "those natural Causes, whose operations are known to us all," embracing a then-current theory that earthquakes were caused by the expansion of subterranean gases. Still, he warned, "What we call the Laws of Nature are only the usual Methods in which he is pleased to Work in the World.... [God] can shake the Earth out of Her Place in a moment without any Instruments; for He needs them not, nor is confined to them."[104]

It remains unclear, in the end, whether Cooper intended the reader to side with the version of natural law evidenced in Cole's painting and Woolston's modern, secular theory of the island's collapse or with the narrator's account of the collapse as the deliberate and chastening work of the deity. Indeed, the tension between the two theories may be part of the point. The novel's skepticism, that is, is not an outright dismissal of geology—nor, for that matter, does it oppose the American project itself. Rather, the novel takes aim at the self-centered forms both had taken on, conforming to Cooper's dismay over the excesses of American democracy and his concern about the speed, though not the fact, of US expansion. The narrator complains that modern scientists, like the colonists, mistake their own purposes for those of the divine: "Thrice happy would it be for the man of science, could he ever thus hold his powers in subjection to the great object for which they were brought into existence."[105] Cooper's admiration for individualism and progress were moderated by a critique of the self-centeredness that threatened to undermine the "great American epoch." But that critique would not, in the end, shake Man or his science out of place.

The alignment of geology and global conquest by figures like Whewell and Agassiz has had a lasting impact on the image of the science; indeed, one late twentieth-century history of the field describes the progress of nineteenth-century geology as a story of "those who subdued the planet through curiosity."[106] The "heroism" of such figures could convert the terrifying expanse of geological time itself into a natural resource, something that could be mapped and mined to fuel progress. Geological fantasy was not inevitably oriented toward conquest, of course, as subsequent chapters of this study will show. But the ease with which it was turned toward land expropriation and biopolitics generates doubt about the romantic insistence on its more-than-human magnitude. Geology "carries us back 'through the dark posterns of time long elapsed,'" Metcalf declared, "and speaks to us in a language more magnificent than that of men."[107] Yet despite this magnificence, the science could still be made to speak the language of Man.

unsettled ground 2

indigenous prophecy, geological fantasy,
and the new madrid earthquakes

A STORY ABOUT THE NEW MADRID EARTHQUAKES of 1811–12 centers on the fate of an "Indian" man, of unspecified tribal affiliation, who was swallowed by the earth and then spit out again. Such an event might have been physically possible. Timothy Flint, an evangelical Christian writer, describing the landscape some seven years after the quakes had ceased, declared: "The chasms in the earth ... were of an extent to swallow up not only men, but houses, 'down quick into the pit.'"[1] Flint's description combines topography with biblical prophecy, referencing Moses' promise of God's punishment for those who rebelled against him.[2] The reference draws upon a long-established spiritual view of earthquakes as instruments of divine chastisement, one that, as we saw in chapter 1, was not wholly displaced by the modernization of geology. Christians, however, were not the only ones who read the quakes as divine messages. The New Madrid earthquake series coincided with and intensified an ongoing Indigenous revival movement that linked cultural renewal with anticolonial resistance. This context is reflected in the tale about the Indian man pulled underground. As the story, recounted in the *Lexington Reporter*, goes: "seven Indians were swallowed up; one of them escaped; he says he was taken into the ground the depth of two trees in length; that the water came under him and threw him out again—he had to wade & swim 4 miles before he reached dry land. The Indian says the Shawanoe Prophet has caused the Earthquake, to destroy the whites."[3]

The largest earthquake series in recorded North American history, the New Madrid quakes tossed up a great deal of matter. Beginning on December 16, 1811, with a shaker estimated at between 7.2 and 8.2 on the modern Richter scale, the earthquakes continued through the following spring, numbering over 1,800 in total. They were centered in an area the United States called the Louisiana Territory, in a region now shared between southeastern Missouri and northeastern Arkansas, although the largest ones were felt over a million square miles. They destroyed huge tracts of forest and permanently altered the course of rivers; local legend held that during the worst quakes, the Mississippi River flowed backward. The riverbank town of New Madrid, for which both the earthquakes and the fault later designated as their cause would be named, was all but destroyed by months of shaking and flooding.[4]

Perhaps surprisingly, given its magnitude, the New Madrid earthquake series has left little in the way of cultural memory. The exception is a rewrite of the prophecy cited by the Indian pulled underground. During the period of the quakes, accounts of the tremors as messages encouraging a return to tradition and as events designed to drive settlers from the land traveled through the region, supported by the pan-Indigenous spiritual revitalization movement led by Tenskwatawa (the "Shawanoe [Shawnee] Prophet" referenced in the report) and his brother Tecumseh, leader of an allied pan-tribal military confederacy. Contrary to the ruptures Flint emphasized, this reading understood the quakes as a *reorientation* of that land, correcting the far greater disruption posed by settler occupation. Many of the region's Christian settlers also read the quakes as prophetic messages, retribution for the sinful life settlers led on the US frontier, and church attendance spiked each time the tremors intensified. But settlers' sermons about the quakes as signs of the biblical End Times gave way, after the shaking subsided, to secular-nationalist messianism as the US federal government, celebrating its own benevolence, provided land grants to quake-displaced settlers, which helped to consolidate US control over the region.[5] Meanwhile, the lack of assistance provided to the already displaced Cherokee, Shawnee, and Delaware communities along the banks of the St. Francis and White rivers and elsewhere in the region forced many to move farther west.

The displacement of Indigenous people and augmentation of the settler population as a consequence of state "benevolence" mark the New Madrid earthquake series as an instance of what we might call disaster settler colonialism.[6] But the ability to profit from catastrophe extended beyond the political opportunism surrounding the New Madrid Federal Relief Act, as the nation went on to organize the quakes' meanings in line with its own purposes. As they consolidated their occupation of the Mississippi Valley region, US settlers also appropriated Indigenous interpretations of the earthquake, embedded in a Romantic narrative about the Shawnee leader Tecumseh. This rendition of the earthquake prophecy has lasted for nearly two centuries, resurfacing most recently in scientific and environmental publications. Nineteenth-century geological writers also noted Indigenous accounts of the earthquakes, though these citations tended less to romanticize them than to perpetuate an imagined connection of Indigenous people to rocks and fossils. Even as geologists naturalized settler presence on the land by claiming both its material contents and its geological history as objects of modern scientific knowledge, they aligned Indigenous communities with that deep history, erasing them from the present tense. The geological aspect of New Madrid's disaster-colonialist aftermath offers a particularly compelling illustration of how geology has functioned, conceptually as well as pragmatically, in support of what Glen Sean Coulthard (Yellowknives Dene) identifies as the territorializing drive of settler colonialism by using its apprehension of the earth to erase Indigenous relationships to the land.[7]

Indigenous, evangelical Christian and settler-nationalist accounts all positioned the earthquakes in relation to a catastrophic rupture in time, though they located that catastrophe differently. Evangelical Christians saw it as long foretold, viewing the quakes as a form of scriptural fulfillment intended to halt secular time altogether. From the US nationalist perspective, the disaster was seismic, a geological revelation of human powerlessness. Scientific theories about the earthquakes' cause varied widely, but the state did not need a specific cause to authorize its secular-messianic remedy. Federal intervention sought to restore the region to the linear and future-oriented time of the nation, while Romantic history and geochronology supplemented the inscription of settler time on the land by identifying Indigenous people with cultural and geological pasts. Indigenous interpretations connected the quakes, in contrast, to the ongoing rupture that colonization instantiated. In contrast, interpretations of the quakes like Tenskwatawa's addressed them less as disaster than disaster response. Circulated through the pan-Indigenous revival, such accounts synthesized earthly history, tradition, and modernity, revising creation stories through recent events as they sought to revitalize Indigenous connections to the land and make Indigenous futures possible again.

The contrast that structures my inquiry in this chapter is ultimately not between "scientific" and "nonscientific," or "spiritual" and "secular," assessments of the New Madrid quake series, contrasts that implicitly position Indigenous and settler Christian views as antiquated or premodern. Rather, what I want to explore is the way these assessments bring into focus varying depictions of the relationship between humans and the earth's past, present, and future. Accounts of the quakes as anticolonial comprehended them within broader circuits. For all their violence and terror, they responded to the still greater violence of occupation, which disrupted Indigenous relations to the land; acting alongside humans, they might succeed in reasserting those interrupted histories. Prophecy-based understandings of the earthquakes, in this sense, identified them as sources of energy and invitations to connect, similar to the resurgent, relational modes of knowing that Leanne Betasamosake Simpson (Michi Saagiig Nishnaabeg) terms "land as pedagogy," which require active and reciprocal relations to land.[8] Geologically informed views, in contrast, held the quakes formally apart from human action or history: as natural disasters, they revealed only the planet's profound indifference to human affairs. This formal separation was, however, undermined by settler-colonial deployments of geological fantasy, which reaffirmed the importance of the human—or rather, of Man overrepresented as such—in the face of, and often, paradoxically, by means of, geology's revelation of human insignificance in relation to the power and vast age of the earth.[9] Indigenous people, viewed as the "fossil other," were identified *as* earth, undirected and post-animate, sources for knowledge-gathering that would project settlers alone into the future.[10] Geology, on this view, has abetted colonization in two ways: not only by guiding and supporting the extractive practices—from New World mining to global petrocapitalism—driving it but also by cultivating a geochronology of populations that undermined Indigenous relations to the land by identifying them, in turn, with premodern "superstition" and with the prehistoric time associated with earthly matter.

This chapter opens by considering various Indigenous interpretations of the earthquakes, including those that aligned the tremors with Indigenous resistance to the encroachments of white settlers. From there, it turns to white settler writing about the quakes, highlighting spiritual as well as sensational/affective accounts. But, as I demonstrate, it would ultimately be US nationalism that, drawing on and redirecting earthquake affect, consolidated the meaning and purpose of the quakes for whites. Once settlers could regard themselves as having survived—indeed, triumphed over—the convulsions, they moved on to the work of appropriating Indigenous claims about them, folding these into both historical and mineralogical/geological accounts of the earthquake period. The conclusion to this chapter shows how settler fantasies about Indigenous people consolidated through geological writing about the earthquakes remain with us to this day.

Turning Over the Land: Earthquakes as Anticolonial Resistance

The story with which this chapter opened is perhaps the first printed account of a prophecy-based interpretation of the quakes cited in Creek, Osage, Chickasaw, and Cherokee communities. The contention that the earthquakes would reverse white settlement, circulated along the pathways of an ongoing pan-Indigenous spiritual movement kindled several years earlier, after Tenskwatawa, who would become known as the "Shawnee Prophet," experienced a series of visions calling for Indigenous people to unite around traditional teachings and practices. In its most common iteration, the prophecy held that the quakes would rid the land of white settlers in recompense for an embrace of Indigenous tradition and the abandonment of settler lifeways. From their beginnings in December 1811—a month after US forces burned down the pan-Indigenous settlement at Prophetstown, Indiana, in response to settler demands—the ongoing earthquakes caused widespread alarm among Indigenous people in the region, catalyzing debate about their cause and implications. The un-settling interpretation worked both to quell fears and to confirm commitment to the renewal movement that was already underway. In this sense, it operated, as Gregory Dowd writes of that movement as a whole, as an innovative response to the "catastrophe of colonialism."[11]

The Kispoko Shawnee brothers Tecumseh and Tenskwatawa stood at the center of this movement. It began after a healer then known as Lalawethika experienced a series of visions, beginning in April 1805, which promised salvation for Indigenous people who returned to tradition, relinquishing settler technologies and practices. Renamed Tenskwatawa, meaning "Open Door," the visionary called for an end to intertribal violence and an embrace of communal life, forswearing the desire for wealth and property that, he argued, had infested Shawnee society as a result of settler influence. The promise of revitalization was attractive. As historian R. David Edmunds (Cherokee) observes, the erosion of Shawnee social and economic systems by US encroachments on their land had left Shawnee society in disarray by the early nineteenth century.[12] Nevertheless, Shawnee leaders condemned Tenskwatawa, as did the leaders of most other tribes; some would later argue that the earthquakes were intended to reveal him as a false prophet.[13] Still, the movement swelled with converts from a number of regional tribes who were disillusioned by their leaders' sale of lands to the United States. In 1808, Tenskwatawa and his brother Tecumseh, a warrior distinguished in late eighteenth-century Shawnee struggles against US encroachments, founded the village of Prophetstown near present-day Lafayette, Indiana. Tecumseh sought to build a pan-tribal political and military confederacy to protect Indigenous land, which, he argued, belonged to all Indigenous people in common and therefore could not be sold or surrendered by individual tribal leaders.[14]

The understanding of Indigenous land as held in common was supported by a vision Tenskwatawa experienced in 1806, which resembles the later earthquake prophecy in its rendition of earthly turmoil as a response to settler encroachment. The vision centered on an encounter with "a great ugly crab that had crawled from the sea, its claws full of mud and seaweed." The Master of Life informed Tenskwatawa that the crab had come from Boston, bringing some of that land with it; he promised that if Indigenous people abide by tradition, the crab will "overturn the land, so that the white people will be covered and you alone shall inhabit the land."[15] These lands, the Master of Life asserted, "were not made for" whites, who had originated in the scum created by an ocean storm.[16] Alongside this origin story, the figure of the crab points toward Anishnabeeg and Haudenosaunee creation narratives that feature earth-divers—a water animal or bird who dives into the primordial waters and brings up the mud beneath, forming land and giving humans and other creatures a place to live. Vanessa Watts (Mohawk/Anishnaabe) points out that such accounts of creation exemplify "Indigenous place-thought," an orientation toward the world in which place founds the possibility of thought and agency.[17] That connectedness to place is conjoined to an expansive conception of time. Distinct from the Christian origin story, which unfolds as a singular event that founds a linear time line, Indigenous creation stories reflect what Shawnee philosopher Thomas M. Norton-Smith describes as "a world that is creative, animate, dynamic, purposeful, and unfinished."[18] Tenskwatawa's vision incorporates this dynamism, reaching across tribal traditions to construct a pan-Indigenous narrative in which the promised overturning of the land by the crab renews the earth's genesis, even as the creature's origin in Boston connects it to the comparatively recent history of European presence in North America. The promise that the crab will "overturn the land" is, in this context, more than an echo of the earlier creation narrative. As Mishuana Goeman argues, creation stories establish relations between Indigenous people and the land, but historical change demands that narratives mapping these relations likewise evolve.[19] The crab prophecy appears as one such remapping: a syncretic reconstruction comprehending the deep and ongoing history of the earth alongside the recent history of colonization and resistance.

Edmunds argues that Tecumseh's insistence that the land "belonged" to Indigenous people reflects a partial adaptation of Euro/American notions of land ownership.[20] Yet Tenskwatawa's vision suggests that land tenancy might be regarded less as possession than habitation, a relationship between humans, nonhuman creatures, and the land itself. The promise to "turn over the earth" is intended to provoke a return to practices that are predicated in part on that relationship. The earth would not be turned over *to* Indigenous people, but turned over *along with* their actions, reaffirming forms of knowledge and relation incommensurable with those maintained by settlers. This sort of alliance with the land has been central to Indigenous resistance. As Coulthard explains, "The theory and practice of Indigenous anticolonialism ... is best understood as a struggle primarily inspired by and oriented around *the question of land*—a struggle not only *for* land in the material sense, but also deeply informed by *what the land as system of reciprocal relations and obligations* can teach us about living our lives in relation to one another and the natural world in nondominating and nonexploitative terms."[21] Colonization displaces that system of relations and obligations, replacing it with a static conception of land as property. Tenskwatawa's observation that the whites had "poison'd the land" and his condemnation of their wasteful practices, such as hunting deer for their skins alone, underscores the difference between this mode of land tenancy and the extractive approach to land as potential property installed under European and American occupation.[22]

While Tenskwatawa's crab vision depicted the former as a return to tradition, the mutual responsiveness it depicts should not be understood as one of those "romanticized visions" that Goeman describes as "equat[ing] Native body to land."[23] In her explication of a Haudenosaunee framework that "center[s] Indigenous conceptions of land as connected, rather than land as disaggregate parcels at various European-conceived scales," Goeman emphasizes that this is a critical framework, a response to the incursions of the settler state, highlighting the "very hard work" it takes to establish and sustain such connections.[24] Part of the work the crab vision helped to sustain was the labor of alliance-building around the federation's conception of Indigenous land as not only connected but held-in-common. As Tecumseh explained: "The way, and the only way to check and stop this evil [settler land encroachment] is for all the red men to unite in claiming a common and equal right to the land ... for it never was divided, but belongs to all, for the use of each."[25] The promise, in the crab vision, that only Indigenous people ("you alone") would inhabit the land positions collective Indigenous land tenancy in incommensurable opposition to what Robert Nichols terms settlers' "transformation of the earth into a proprietary grid," a transformation that settler geographic and geologic surveys would help to accomplish.[26]

The kind of pan-Indigeneity envisioned in Tenskwatawa and Tecumseh's confederation posed a challenge to traditional tribal governance. Leaders of a number of tribes sent a collective message to the Prophet in 1810 accusing him of influencing young men to actions "contrary to the customs of the nations to which they belong," and William Harrison, then governor of the Indiana Territory, dismissively declared that such an idea could never succeed.[27] Still, the combined spiritual and political power of the movement was viewed with alarm by settlers. Earthquake prophecies added to this alarm. A June 1812 letter to the *Louisiana Gazette* asserted that growing tensions between white settlers and neighboring Chickasaws and Creeks could be traced directly to the earthquakes' fulfilment of a prophecy. Based on a report from a Chickasaw envoy, the letter warned that "the Prophet [Tenskwatawa?] previously to the Battle of the Wabash told the Indians if they would [illegible] him against the Whites, he [would speak] to the Great Spirit, and [illegible] of his great displeasure at their [disobedience], the [Earth?] should be [unusually?] agitated and convulsed and threatened immediate [dissolution?]. This statement gaining ground they believe the Prophet, for their disobedience caused the frequent shakings of the Earth experienced during the last winter."[28] The version of the earthquake prophecy cited in this report interprets them as punishment for Indigenous people who failed to support the movement; in this sense, they echo another early prophecy which, according to Jonathan Hancock, might also be said to predict the quakes. In the winter of 1807–08, Tenskwatawa, affirming that the Master of Life possessed the "power to change the course of nature," asserted that in four years' time, "all the unbelievers shall be utterly destroyed."[29] Even so, by the time of the earthquakes, settlers viewed themselves as the prophecy's ultimate targets, as reflected in the *Louisiana Gazette*'s declaration that "the Chickasaws with the assistance of their neighbors . . . are meditating an energetic and destructive blow on the Whites."[30] The writer goes on to cite the envoy's belief that "even the deep foundations of Nature tremble at [the Prophet's] command," adding ominously that "[t]he Chickasaws say that something great will be done when the [tremors?] grow larger."[31] Reports like this, citing widespread belief in the Prophet's devastating agency, suggest significant concern about the continued power of the pan-Indigenous movement. Hancock points out that the appeal of earthquake prophecies had a role in maintaining that power, helping to regain Indigenous support for that movement in the wake of the November 1811 Battle of Tippecanoe. Faith in Tenskwatawa's power waned after his petitions to the Master of Life failed to protect Indigenous forces, but as the June 1812 report confirms, settler anxiety about the movement was still active the following spring, in tandem with newspaper reports of various versions of the prophecy.³²

While prophecies attributed to Tenskwatawa invariably endowed the earthquakes with an antisettlement function, interpretations among the Cherokee were more wide-ranging. John Gambold, a Moravian missionary in Cherokee County, Georgia, complained in a March 1812 letter that "even the lies of the Shawanee prophets are being circulated this far."³³ Yet Cherokee people also developed their own understandings of the quakes' significance. Some of these reflected increasing division over the question of assimilation and accommodation versus resistance to colonial pressure in the decades before the Indian Removal Act of 1830. The Georgia Moravians recorded a report from Peggy Vann, a Cherokee woman aligned with the mission, the day after the first of the quakes: "Our Peggy, who was at neighboring Indians today on business, could not describe in what consternation she found the poor people everywhere. Some of them attributed the event to conjurors and some of them to a great snake that must have crawled under their house, and some of them to the weakness of the earth which, because of its great age, would soon fall in."³⁴ As Vann indicates, multiple theories about the quakes circulated right from the start. One of these was structural weakening due to the earth's "great age." Another entry in the mission diary quotes Chief Bead Eye, on a visit to the mission, who observed that "the earth is very old" and asked the missionaries "would it soon fall apart?"³⁵ This contention, situating the quakes in an apocalyptic frame, rendered human agency irrelevant. If the earth was falling apart because of its antiquity, humans had done nothing to cause the situation, nor could they do anything to change it. The theory that the earthquake had been caused by a "great snake," in contrast, made room for the earthquakes' connection to human behavior. Hancock notes that this theory aligned with a view of snakes as "ubiquitous and fundamental to order" held by numerous Mississippian-descended tribes in the Southeast. He explains: "Giant water serpents hoisted up the earth from the watery layer below it, and no matter their size or location, they were to be feared and venerated. Their ability to pass between the Lower and Middle Worlds of the universe—by living underground, on the ground, and in trees—made them spiritually powerful and potentially menacing."³⁶ Insofar as serpents possessed the power to unsettle the surface world if humans disturbed them, the snake theory posited a possible anthropogenic origin for the events.

Whether or not they viewed a serpent as the cause, many Cherokee people contended that the quakes responded to human action. Some of these theories tied into deep-seated tensions among Cherokee regarding the degree to which their worlds should be remade in accordance with settler custom. Charles Hicks, a member of the Cherokee elite who had invited the Moravians to establish their mission, followed the missionaries in their biblical assessment of earthquakes as divine chastisement. As the mission diary explained, "The all-powerful God who made the earth and everything on it and to this day has maintained it, also has the power and force to punish it in various ways humans who live in sin, and. . . . He often had used such earthquakes for such a purpose."[37] Others, conversely, held that they condemned Cherokees who, like Hicks, had turned away from Native tradition. Some linked the quakes to settler occupation of the land. According to a group of Cherokees who visited the missionaries in February 1812: "Many Indians believe that white people are responsible for this because they had already taken possession of so much of the Indian land and want ever more. God was angry because of this and he wanted to put an end to it through the earth-quakes."[38] Cherokees who had acceded to settlers' thirst for land were also said to be a target. Big Bear, another Cherokee visitor to the Moravians, narrated a vision experienced by another man in December 1811, after the beginning of the quakes, in which a tall man dressed in foliage gave him pieces of bark to make a broth that would cure his sick children. The tall man said, "I am not able to tell you now if God will soon destroy the earth or not. God is not pleased that the Indians have sold so much land to the white people."[39] The condemnation of Indigenous people's sale of land to whites pointed toward Cherokee elites like Vann, the widow of a wealthy, slaveholding plantation owner who sold land to the Moravians. (Vann was unrepentant; when revivalists, pointing to the earthquakes, called for the disposal of white clothing, household goods, and cattle, Vann purchased and resold those goods in order to demonstrate her disbelief.) The earthquakes were depicted as a corrective to the contamination of Indigenous land and culture by settlers—a kind of self-restoring activity on the part of the land. The tall man, in the vision recounted by Big Bear, is particularly concerned that white people occupying Tugalo, a place sacred to the Cherokee, had desecrated the site. "Tugalo, which is now possessed by white people, is the first place which God created. There in a hill he placed the first fire, for all fire comes from God. Now the white people have built a house on that hill. They should abandon the place; on that hill there should be grass growing, only then will there be peace."[40]

Accounts comprehending the quakes as anticolonial activations of occupied land were tied to an understanding of Indigenous sovereignty as the freedom to make and maintain relations that encompassed the imbrication of humans with land, of life with nonlife—an orientation toward land that was fundamentally incompatible with settler occupation. The earthquakes were positioned as a renewal of origins and a reclamation and re-creation of the land they affected, bringing together the deep past evoked in earth-diver creation stories, the recent history of colonial incursions on the land, and the imminent future. The polychronicity of such prophetic readings demonstrates what Mark Rifkin identifies as prophecy's ability to gather other-than-chronological possibilities. These gatherings, as Rifkin explains, serve to illuminate and intensify the other times pervading the present, opening collective possibilities beyond the settler-national order of things.[41]

Nature in Ruins: Settler Melancholy, Nationalist Messianism

In comprehending the quakes as part of the movement of history, Indigenous interpretations of the quakes designated them as political and cultural resources. They would become resources for settlers as well, although in a very different manner. Settlers in the region also viewed the quakes as a departure from the habitual order. Early reports in newspapers and letters emphasized the chaos they provoked. Focusing on physical and affective description, they eschew the immediate attribution of meaning to the event—an absence of meaning indexed in the withdrawal of language, as writers frequently declared the quakes to be beyond their capacity for speech. A letter about the second major quake reproduced in the *Lexington Reporter* declared: "I cannot give you an accurate description of this moment; the earth seemed convulsed—the houses shook very much—chimneys falling in every direction.—The loud hoarse roaring which attended the earthquake, together with the cries, screams, and yells of the people, seems still ringing in my ears."[42] As the persistence of the roaring suggests, the earthquakes seemed to suspend settler time. Another correspondent observed that in Suffolk, Virginia, "every clock in the place had stopped."[43] An account of the first of the quakes by Eliza Bryan, a white settler who had lived in New Madrid since 1791, depicts a town pitched suddenly and violently out of the ordinary:

> On the 16th day of December, 1811, about 2 o'clock, A.M., we were visited by a violent shock of an earthquake, accompanied by a very awful noise, resembling loud but distant thunder, but more hoarse and vibrating, which was followed in a few minutes by the complete saturation of the atmosphere, with sulphurous vapor, causing total darkness. The screams of the affrighted inhabitants running to and fro, not knowing what to do nor where to go, the cries of the fowls and beasts of every species, the cracking of trees falling, and the roaring of the Mississippi, the current of which was retrograde for a few minutes, owing as it is supposed, to the interruption in its bed, formed a scene truly horrible.[44]

The reversal of the Mississippi River's current, a widely reported detail, embodied the anomaly that the quakes represented for settlers: they went against expected patterns, turning the familiar world into something strange, disorienting, and dangerous.

The tumult eventually gave way to sadness, infusing the withdrawal of the ordinary with a sense of loss taken on not only by the affrighted inhabitants but also by the devastated landscape. James McBride, a merchant, wrote in an April 1812 letter to his aunt that "all nature appeared in ruins, and seemed to mourn in solitude over her melancholy fate." William Leigh Pierce, another merchant, later expanded on this theme: "All nature indeed seemed to sympathize in the commotion which agitated the earth. The sun rarely shot a ray through the heavens. The sky was clouded, and a dreary darkness brooded over the whole face of the creation."[45] Timothy Flint, visiting the area in 1819, described a landscape still in mourning for what had been before: "When I resided there, this district, formerly so level, rich, and beautiful, had the most melancholy of all aspects of decay, the tokens of former cultivation and habitancy, which were now mementos of desolation and desertion."[46] Without a meaningful anchor, settler time threatened to fall into the chasms created by the quakes.

Evangelical Christians were among the first to try to fill the gap, aligning the quakes with the time of the Scriptures. A multidenominational Christian revival movement sprang up in the settlements. The movement soon established a distinctive pattern: converts flocked to churches whenever the tremors intensified, and attendance fell off again as soon as the land became relatively calm. These on-and-off disciples came to be known as "earthquake Christians," their relationship to messianic time shifting in tandem with the ground beneath their feet.[47] Devout Christians depicted the period as the fulfillment of biblical prophecy, a sign that the End Times were at hand. A hymn entitled "A Call to the People of Louisiana," penned several months into the quake series, observed:

> More than six months have past and gone,
> And still the earth keeps shaking;
> The Christians go with bow'd down heads,
> While sinners' hearts are aching.
>
> The great event I cannot tell,
> Nor what the Lord is doing;
> But one thing I am well assur'd,
> The Scriptures are fulfilling.[48]

The hymn divided the settler population along with the chasm-torn ground: the "aching" hearts of the sinners reflect their continued agitation, while the calm submission of the "saved," humbly anticipating the final Judgment, touts the stabilizing power of the messianic. Some evangelists gave this messianism a distinctly local twist. The first report of the quakes in the *Louisiana Gazette and Daily Advertiser*, published in New Orleans, speculated that they might be retribution for the sinful life led in frontier towns:

> The *shake* which the *Natchezians* have felt may be a mysterious visitation from the Author of all nature, on them for their sins—wickedness and the want of good faith have long prevailed in that territory.
> *Sodom and Gomorrha* would have been saved had three righteous persons been found in it—we therefore hope that Natchez has been saved on the same principle.[49]

The *Gazette*'s call for repentance reflected the part played by Christianity in the biopolitics of settlement. In the United States, the first generation of frontier whites was typically depicted as a liminal population: lawless and immoral, in need of conversion and/or replacement by a more "civilized" generation. Christianity thus operated as a means of reforming and regulating white bodies, instilling proper values for imminently national subjects. The quakes, along these lines, became instruments of correction—literally shaking the bodies of errant frontierspeople into submission.

Evangelical Christians were more unified than early nineteenth-century scientists in their understanding of the quakes' cause. The latter proposed a number of theories, including electricity, gas, the collapse of an underground cavern, the gravitational pull of a comet visible over most of North America in fall 1811, and volcanic eruption. Despite their differences, all these theories framed the events as natural disasters, occurring independent of human agency and rendering repentance irrelevant; the only appropriate response to the break in time that the quakes represented for settlers would be repair. This was the part the US federal government would take up. Preoccupied by ongoing conflicts with Indigenous nations and the War of 1812, Congress responded to the earthquakes rather slowly. Eventually, though, it embraced the repair demanded by the natural disaster framework as an occasion to reassert nationalist narratives: American exceptionalism, seen in survivors' ability to persevere through hardship, and American compassion, located in the nation's willingness to assist the earthquake's victims. The General Assembly of the Missouri Territory, in an 1814 appeal to the federal government for aid, vividly depicted the displacement of "our unfortunate fellow citizens, [who] are now wandering about without a home to go to," and affirmed its confidence that "the enlightened humane government of the United States" would provide material aid.[50] The following year, Congress passed the New Madrid Federal Relief Act in response to such appeals. As the act's attempt to reestablish settlers on newly issued tracts of land made clear, the state's concern lay not only with those "unfortunate fellow citizens" but with the future of western settlement, the interruption of which formed part of the national narrative about New Madrid long before the shaking had ceased. A February 1812 letter by Joseph Ficklin of Kentucky declared, "The Indians cannot have suffered much in their tents and bark houses. But the United States will suffer in the sales of their public lands west of the Mississippi for an age. At least the present generation must be buried before the spirit of wandering, in that direction, revives."[51] To prevent such an outcome, the New Madrid Federal Relief Act offered displaced settlers the right to exchange their damaged holdings for equivalent tracts of putatively unclaimed public lands elsewhere in the territory. The act resulted in a land grab heavily marked by cheating and fraud—but one that assured that settlers would continue to claim land in the area. The New Madrid Relief Act's indifference to those not counted as "fellow citizens" matched Ficklin's dismissal of Indigenous suffering. Although the Indigenous population in the affected zone was larger than the settler population, no effort was made to compensate Indigenous tribes, even "allied" ones, for their losses; indeed, the US government did not even try to track those losses or prevent settlers from laying claim, under the terms of the act, to lands occupied by Indigenous people when the quakes began.[52] In the following decades, against the pessimistic predictions of some observers, the settler population in the area continued to increase while the Indigenous population was further displaced.

"Tecumseh's Prophecy" and Settler Catharsis

Despite their divergences, evangelical Christian and US nationalist interpretations of the quakes ultimately worked in tandem as settlement strategies. The messianic impulses of Christians were secularized, folded into the state under the guise of benevolence and continued advancement, even as that state worked to remove Indigenous people from the lands it sought to repair. Meanwhile, the continued appeal of sensational testimonies from those who experienced the earthquakes—testimonies that would circulate well into the nineteenth century and beyond—induced identification with those who had experienced and *lived through* these events. Such accounts demonstrated that such unpredictable, uncontrollable events could be survived, even converted into self-improvement through rededication to Christian faith and/or the secular-nationalist religion of progress.[53]

The US nationalist inclination to self-affirmation in the long aftermath of the earthquakes also took hold of Indigenous earthquake prophecies, turning these, paradoxically, into another testament to settler resilience. White people's awareness of ongoing Indigenous resistance was entwined with their experience of the quakes from the first; indeed, the two were constructed as twinned threats to the settlements. McBride, for instance, reported that he had been able to obtain goods "on very reasonable terms" because "the reports prevailing of the dangers to be encountered from the Indians and the Earthquakes had so much frightened the people that none would venture to encounter them."[54] Pierce's recollection of the first earthquakes, one of the most widely reprinted quake narratives, asserted that Mississippi river boatsmen were on alert against the "Savages, who are said to be at present much exasperated against the whites." Pierce had been aboard a riverboat when the quake hit; in his account, conceptions of Indigenous and geological agency succeeded one another just as rapidly as did the shocks of the earthquake:

> Precisely at two o'clock on Monday morning the 16th instant, we were all alarmed by the violent and convulsive agitation of the boats accompanied by a noise similar to that which would have been produced by running over a sand bar—every man was immediately roused and rushed on deck.—We were first of opinion that the Indians, studious of some mischief, has loosed our cables, and thus situated we were foundering. Upon examination, however, we discovered that we were yet safely and securely moored. The idea of an Earthquake then suggested itself to my mind, and

this idea was confirmed by a second shock, and two others in immediate succession.⁵⁵

By 1820, though, the immediacy of both dangers had begun to fade. Settlers in the region were already depicting regional Indigenous resistance, as well as the earthquakes, as history and had begun to revise and romanticize them both. Since they had successfully turned the quakes to their own national advantage, the prophetic claim that the shaking was meant to displace settlers from the land could be reproduced, in their accounts, without the anxiety that attended earlier reports like the one in the June 1812 letter to the *Louisiana Gazette*.

After 1820, settler-authored accounts of the earthquake prophecy attributed it to the Shawnee military leader Tecumseh, who had been killed in 1813 in a battle with US forces, rather than his brother Tenskwatawa. One of the earliest of these, a transcription of a speech given by Tecumseh on a December 1811 visit to the Osage, appears in the 1823 narrative of John Dunn Hunter, a white man who claimed to have been taken captive and raised among the Osage.⁵⁶ As Donald L. Fixico (Shawnee, Sac and Fox, Muscogee Creek and Seminole) observes, Tecumseh's federation drew on and furthered a complex network of tribal alliances and kinship ties along with the spiritual energy of the revitalization movement.⁵⁷ The earthquakes, in Hunter's account of his oration, are taken up in the service of furthering these alliances. Though many Osage, according to Hunter, worried that the recently begun "violent tremors and oscillations of the earth" signaled an imminent apocalypse, Tecumseh assured them that the quakes would end only the world the settlers were trying to make: "The Great Spirit is angry with our enemies; he speaks in thunder, and the earth swallows up villages, and drinks up the Mississippi. The great waters will cover their lowlands; their corn cannot grow; and the Great Spirit will sweep those who escape to the hills from the earth with his terrible breath."⁵⁸ This speech, as Hunter recounts it, is an interpretation of earthquakes already in action and a prediction of their effects on the settlements. But most post-1820 accounts tell a different story. In these, Tecumseh, on a recruitment visit to the Creeks in the fall of 1811, announces that he himself will cause an earthquake in order to impress them into joining the pan-Indigenous movement. This version recurred often over the course of the nineteenth century, appearing in a few Indigenous oral and written accounts as well as numerous settler-authored histories. Perhaps the earliest report of Tecumseh's visit to the Creeks in the settler press appeared in 1812, when Francis McHenry wrote to the *Georgia Journal* asserting that Tecumseh had predicted both the comet of 1811 and the earthquakes as aids to his campaign against settlers. "The Prophet [Tecumseh], on his embassy to the Creek nation, in the month of August last, pronounced in the public square, that shortly a lamp would appear in the west to aid him in his hostile attack upon the whites, and if they would not be influenced by his persuasion, the earth would, ere long, tremble to its centre."[59] McHenry claimed to have heard this account first from George Stiggins (Natchez Creek), who witnessed the speech, and to have verified it with several other Creeks. He goes on to claim that a teenaged Tecumseh had spent time in Halifax, Nova Scotia, where he learned enough astronomy to enable him to calculate the time of the comet and its supposed seismic influence, which he later used to impress the Creeks. (McHenry subscribed to the belief that the New Madrid quakes had been caused by the pull of the comet upon the earth.)

The story of Tecumseh's astronomical prowess, however, disappeared from subsequent accounts of the speech. Stiggins, who would become the US Indian agent to the Creeks in the 1830s, gave a description of the speech in a history of the Creek Confederacy composed around 1835, though not published until 2003. He cited it to exemplify the irrationality of what he calls the "age of prophecy in the Creek nation," his disparaging assessment of the pan-Indigenous revival's influence on the disputes over governance and land cessions that would ignite the Creek Civil War of 1813–14.[60] Tecumseh's contribution to these debates include the prediction Stiggins dismisses as "coincidence":

> Tecumseh had said to many in private, and to the national council, that he was determined to war with the Americans. He stated the great supernatural powers he possessed. He said if he was to beat the white people they would know it by the following sign: he would ascend to the top of a mountain about four moons from that time and there he would whoop three unbounded loud whoops, slap his hands together three times, and raise his foot and stamp it on the earth three times. By these actions he could make the whole earth tremble, which would be a sign of his success in the undertaking. If such did not happen, they would know that he was to fail in the enterprise.[61]

Stiggins's description, according to Robert Lawrence Gunn, "is [now] regarded as the most authoritative documentation of these events," superior to more widely read settler-authored accounts.[62] The earth's surrogation of the supernatural in this version, he argues, exemplifies the kind of mediated communication that both Tenskwatawa and Tecumseh habitually used to enliven their speech—enacting, in the distribution of their personae through surrogate bodies, "an experience of simultaneity and omnipresence that reinforced [their pan-Indigenous] message of common land, common worship, and collective political action."[63] Although Stiggins professed disbelief in the content of the speech, his close attention to the ritualized engagement with the earth promised by Tecumseh in the speech demonstrates his awareness of the power of this mode of communication. That is, even as Stiggins disdained the possibility that Tecumseh, or anyone else, might possess such supernatural abilities he acknowledged the deep appeal of seeming to speak in tandem with the earth.

The story commonly circulated by settlers across the nineteenth century, however, obscured the spiritual and political dimensions of the speech as reported by Stiggins. Instead, Tecumseh's speech to the Creeks was depicted simply as an assertion of his own great power. This story appears in the US Indian agent's Thomas L. McKenney's three-volume compendium *History of the Indians of North America* (1836–42), where the prophecy is framed by Tecumseh's condemnation of Big Warrior, a Creek leader reluctant to join the pan-tribal resistance: "Your blood is white. You have taken my talk, and my sticks, and the wampum, and the hatchet, but do not mean to fight. I know the reason. You do not believe the Great Spirit has sent me. You shall know. I leave Tuckhabatchee directly—and shall go straight to Detroit. When I arrive there, I will stamp on the ground with my foot, and shake down every house in Tuckhabatchee."[64] Instead of the land's effort to reverse its occupation by settlers, the prophecy, in McKenney's hands, becomes a warrior's boast that he is powerful and divinely favored. McKenney uses the event to dramatize the supposed superstition of the Creeks, representing it as childlike naïveté divorced from the political contexts Stiggins outlines. After Tecumseh's departure, McKenney claims, the Creeks anxiously counted the number of days it would take him to reach Detroit until, on the day of his presumed arrival, "a mighty rumbling was heard . . . the earth began to shake; when, at last, sure enough, every house in Tuckhabatchee was shaken down! The exclamation was in every mouth, 'Tecumthé [sic] has got to Detroit!' The effect was electric. The message he delivered to Big Warrior was believed, and many Indians took their rifles and prepared for the war."[65] McKenney solicits surprise at the occurrence, punctuating its effects with an exclamation point and aligning the reader with the Creeks' awestruck perspective. In the wake of this "electric" moment, however, he debunks the event, asserting that Tecumseh sought merely to frighten the Creeks, "little dreaming, himself, that . . . his threat would be executed with such punctuality and terrible fidelity" as a result of its coincidence with "the famous earthquake of New Madrid."[66] The narrative's double movement with respect to the prophecy's veracity—its appeal to imaginative investment in the thrill of its fulfillment, coupled with its rationalizing dismissal of the reality of supernatural claims—offers a particularly compelling instance of geological fantasy; it flirts with the possibility that humans might actually dominate geological forces but then returns to the more rational ground on which Man stakes his claim. This double movement is echoed in its depiction of Tecumseh himself. Unlike Hunter, McKenney, and Stiggins, who emphasize Tecumseh's rhetorical, political, and, in McKenney's case, scientific acumen and skill at building alliances, McKenney permits him to be read alternately as a savvy, self-promoting politician, cleverly gaging his audience's credulity for his own strategic ends or as a foot-stamping fraud. And while the earthquake accidentally endows him with power, history retracts it, as he is killed just a few months later.

McKenney's version of the earthquake prophecy was reprinted numerous times through the nineteenth century and beyond. Accounts taken (often verbatim) from his text appeared in Benjamin Drake's *Life of Tecumseh and His Brother the Prophet* (1841), James Mooney's *The Ghost-Dance Religion and the Sioux Outbreak of 1890* (1896), Norman Barton Wood's *Lives of Famous Indian Chiefs* (1906), and elsewhere.[67] The story's popularity in these histories has little to do with earlier Indigenous theories about the quakes, which it now almost entirely eclipses. Rather, the primary driver is likely its usefulness in building the legend of Tecumseh as a valiant, but ultimately vanquished, warrior. As Gordon Sayre has shown, white-settler writing about Tecumseh in the decades following his death corresponded to the American mythos around select Indigenous leaders as heroic but tragically doomed.[68] (Tenskwatawa, Sayre notes, was more difficult to enfold into the Western heroic ideal and tended to be demonized in settler narratives.) Tecumseh's heroism in these accounts fueled the anticolonial pride that infused American nationalism in the aftermath of independence from Britain, even as the depiction of his death was a narrative necessity for the colonizing US state. In this sense, Sayre contends, the tragic mythos operated as an impetus to American nationalist catharsis. The earthquake prophecy, in this context, affirmed the romance of Indian intimacy with nature even as it activated "the prejudice that Indians were in thrall to superstitions, omens, and auguries, that they lived in an archaic manner."[69] Even though whites, as Sayre points out, also read natural events as ominous portents, stories like the earthquake prophecy asserted their greater sophistication.

The longevity of the story of Tecumseh's prophecy to the Creeks undoubtedly owes much to the tragic mythos Sayre outlines: it was repeated so often, in part, simply because of Tecumseh's fame. Yet its persistence in multiple contexts also suggests its utility to the geological dimension of national fantasy I earlier outlined: the sense of self-affirmation at having persisted through a cataclysmic event. Or, more precisely, the geological catharsis of imagining oneself surviving an earthquake and the settler-nationalist catharsis activated in the embrace of the conquered Indigenous hero combine, in the story of Tecumseh's earthquake prophecy, to manage anxieties about seismic as well as anticolonial dangers to the nation, suturing geological fantasy to colonial expansion as it celebrates the American ability to triumph over both kinds of danger. Tecumseh's persuasive abilities could be admired from a safe historical distance, removed both from the threat his alliance posed to settlers and from their own complicity in Indigenous displacement; his claim to exercise control over the earth could be enjoyed even as it was disbelieved; and the earthquake itself, along with the pan-Indigenous resistance, could be enfolded into the tale of a young nation that could survive whatever history and geology might throw at it. As a 2006 volume on post-earthquake resilience bragged at the conclusion to its New Madrid chapter—which invoked the prophecy story in its very title, "Tecumseh's Legacy"—"The [earthquake's] impact was minimal at best. Frontiersmen (and -women) are ... made of sterner stuff."[70]

The Geological "Indian"

In the period after the shaking subsided, geology stepped into the gaps left in earlier scientific analyses of the New Madrid earthquakes, seeking to settle the question in more than one sense. Scientists investigating the region posited their superior understanding of earthquakes against backward "superstition," disavowing both Christian and Indigenous readings of the quakes as supernatural events. Yet whereas geologists actively negotiated with Christian origin stories across the nineteenth century, positing biblical analogues for stratigraphy or deferring to the Christian God as *primum mobile* in order to avoid alienating believers, they simply dismissed Indigenous versions of the earth's past. Even as geologists relied in practice on Indigenous guides for vital information about the areas they researched, amusement and/or disdain regarding Indigenous accounts of planetary matters became a rhetorical hallmark of scientific modernity.

Such disdain is evidenced in an 1821 report on the Mississippi Valley region authored by Louis Bringier and published in the *American Journal of Science and Arts*, the leading US scientific journal of the day. Titled "Notices of the Geology, Mineralogy, Topography, Productions, and Aboriginal Inhabitants of the Regions around the Mississippi and Its Confluent Waters," the report formalizes the distinction between rational and superstitious approaches to the earthquake in its two references to the event, one of which is folded into the geological and topographic observations occupying its first half, while the other appears in the second half's ethnographic commentary on "Indian Nations—their Manners, &c."[71] In the first section, Bringier, reporting on an earthquake that occurred in January 1812 while he was traveling near New Madrid, dips briefly into the sensational conventions that characterized many experiential accounts, vividly depicting the "horrible disorder of the trees" and his horse's "panic of terror" as the land around them sank.[72] He quickly pulls back from this mode to the neutral tone suitable to scientific observation, describing the transformed landscape and conjecturing, in a footnote, that the quakes were caused by electricity because their seismic shocks had produced "emotions and sensations, resembling those of a strong galvanic battery."[73] This description forms a striking contrast to the discussion of a Cherokee prophet's account of the earthquake in the ethnographic section of the report. Bringier has earlier dismissed Indigenous prophets' supernatural claims as "absurdities," asserting that "[t]hey are very adroit in playing a number of tricks which, to the Indians, appear to be of a very serious nature."[74] He underscores his properly scientific understanding of these "tricks": their ability to expose themselves to fire without burning, for instance, he ascribes to the protective use of nonflammable substances such as tree acid and silaceous stones. Indigenous prophets, he suggests, improperly utilize natural and geological facts; they are not so much "closer to nature," as the Romantic settler stereotype would have it, as they are distant from modernity and its organization of knowledge about the natural world.

Bringier returns to the subject of prophecy later in the report, as he recounts a speech witnessed in June 1812, delivered by Skaquaw, a Cherokee prophet, at Crowtown on the St. Francis River. Skaquaw narrates a vision experienced the preceding November, shortly before the earthquakes began, in which he was informed that the "Ever-Great spirit" planned to destroy the whites and "save his children alone."[75] He was told that when the ground began to shake, Cherokees living in the region must travel westward to avoid destruction. Remarking on the "singularity of [these] ideas," Bringier reports that three months later, they "abandoned their farms (and some were very good ones too), their cattle, and other property and removed [west]."[76] Bringier fails to provide context either for the Cherokee presence in the region (the result of pressure from the US government to migrate westward, which had accelerated in the years before the earthquakes) or the significant damage caused by the quakes, which drowned much of the Cherokees' land and prompted their move farther west.[77] Instead, he focuses on the seeming irrationality of abandoning good farms, privileging a view of land as intended for domestication and commodity production—a theme he expands on in the following section, where he laments the Cherokees' failure to make good use of their new lands by raising cotton, for which, he insists, the region is especially well suited.

Despite the formal separation between the report's scientific and ethnographic sections, Bringier manages to bring Indigenous people into proximity with geology. Relating a fossil hunt on the banks of the Mississippi near New Madrid, where they found "a great quantity of [mastodon] fossils ... gathered in a small compass," he reasons that prehistoric animals attracted by the water oozing through the then-marshy area had become mired in muck. The explanation resolves an otherwise unsettling discovery, since, he adds, "at first, it seems very strange to see these bones accumulated, like those of some of the extinct Indian tribes in the west."[78] Referencing the Indigenous burial mounds that so fascinated settler scientists, Bringier implies a temporal as well as spatial resemblance between the long-vanished mastodon and the "extinct" tribes to whom the bones belonged, situating them within a geological frame formally distinct from the ethnographic one employed later in the report. The comparison identifies Bringier's participation in what Kyla Schuller calls the "geological machine." Schuller proposes the geological machine as a counterpart to Giorgio Agamben's anthropological machine, an apparatus that differentiates between animalized and fully human populations. The geological machine, in contrast, sorts between populations we might, using Elizabeth Povinelli's framework, designate as "lively" and "inert." The conflation of Indigenous bones and mastodon fossils in Bringier's report exemplifies the machine's outcome in determining that, as Schuller explains, Indigenous tribes "belonged to the earth, not to a people; their vitality belonged to the realm of natural history."[79] Bringier is not wholly ignorant of Indigenous modes of governance; the ethnographic section of his report highlights (with much prejudice) distinctions between tribes—praising the Osage, with whom he may have resided for a time, and deprecating the Cherokee.[80] (This bias is tied into his opinions of colonizing nations: "[I]t is notorious that all the Indian tribes in a state of civilization, within the limits of the United States, are extremely corrupted, whilst those under the Spanish iron rod, are mild, and possess no other vices, except those inseparable from ignorance.")[81] Yet when discussing geology, he gestures vaguely at "Indian" bones too "extinct" to distinguish further. The displacement of Indigenous people from the present tense is accompanied by a quasi-geologic interment within their lands which, shifting from the ethnographic to the scientific register, generalizes them into a species. Indigenous people are thus rendered in the mode of the "fossil other," one of the figures formed around the nineteenth-century scientific revision of Man's overrepresentation as the human.[82] The geological machine takes on a biopolitical function—denying the ongoingness of place-based Indigenous relations to land, it works in tandem with the US state's repositioning and regulation of "Indians" as a racial group.[83]

Another ethnographic/geologic dissolution of Indigeneity's liveness is enacted in the New Madrid writings of Henry Rowe Schoolcraft. Schoolcraft is today best remembered as an ethnographer, the author of *Algic Researches* (1839), the multivolume study of the "mythology, distinctive opinions, and intellectual character" of Indigenous Americans that was used by Henry Wadsworth Longfellow as a source for *The Song of Hiawatha* (1855). Yet Schoolcraft began his career as a geologist. After the glassworks in which he was a partner failed, he published a mineralogical study of Missouri and Arkansas, then the western edge of the United States, titled *A View of the Lead Mines of Missouri*, in 1819. He distributed copies of the report in Washington, DC, in the hope of securing a government appointment. He eventually gained a position as field geologist on Lewis Cass's 1820 expedition to the headwaters of the Mississippi. His connection with Cass secured him an appointment as an Indian agent to Michigan in 1822, after which he married the Ojibwa writer Bamewawagezhikaquay, also known as Jane Johnston, and began publishing ethnologies. But even his geological publications draw upon the stock ethnographic contrast between "Indian superstition" and the scientific modernity he aligned with American industry. In his narrative of Cass's expedition, he describes with amusement the supposed response of some Winnebago observers as he chips off some rock samples: "[T]he moment the Americans get possession of this country, they must come and knock off pieces of the rock and look at them. It is marvelous!"[84] As far as Schoolcraft is concerned, though, the Winnebago are themselves part of that rock; following up with a story about a large lump of copper found in the vicinity, said to have once been a living woman, he sneers: "Such are the imaginative efforts of this race, who look to the eyes of civilization as if they themselves had faces of stone, and hearts of adamant."[85]

The same vision of lithic Indigeneity informs Schoolcraft's mock-epic poem about the New Madrid earthquakes, *Transallegania, or, The Groans of Missouri*, which he appended to some editions of his 1821 geological survey/travelogue *Journal of a Tour into the Interior of Missouri and Arkansaw*.[86] The *Journal* contained just a few sentences on the changes to the lands around New Madrid, making no comment on how these might affect US occupation of these. It did, however, refer the reader to Samuel L. Mitchill's report on the quakes, which, quoted Ficklin's pessimistic prediction that "the present generation must be buried before the spirit of wandering [westward]" would be halted for a generation. Schoolcraft did not include that section of the report in the *Journal*, but *Transallegania*, in essence, transposes it into poetic form. The poem takes on the perspective of the ground as it tries to resist settler "wandering." It opens as the King of the Metals, a fanciful mineralogical sovereign, is woken from his underground slumber by the "tumult" of US expansionism. He travels to the border and looks warily upon "the stream of migration that rolled to the west":

> And all the wide scene—valley, hillock, and glen,
> Resounds with the tumult of business and men:
> They are driving the savage before them amain,
> And people each forest, and culture each plain.

Actual Indigenous people appear in the poem only as passive victims of American expansionism; agency belongs, rather, to the council of metals organized by the King, who foresees the rise of extraction and exploitation of his subjects as capitalism takes root. The council, in this sense, takes the place of the pan-Indigenous resistance movement in its determination to oppose settlement. As the council gathers, the poem makes a shift from epic narrative to scientific didacticism; the metals, in turn, announce their qualities, state where they may be found, and resentfully describe their common uses by humans. Lead, for instance, laments its conversion to wealth in the clutches of industry; Iron alternately bemoans and brags of its utility to humankind. Some of the speeches venture into political commentary. When Paper appears as a representative of Silver, the poem digresses into a disquisition on the evils of paper money. The King of Metals throws Paper out of the cavern, and Silver itself arrives, smirks at the woes humanity has suffered while questing after it, and tauntingly lists silver deposits on the North American continent, confident that these will rest undiscovered as long as the metals protect one another. Eventually, the metals become so numerous and the discussion so heated that pandemonium results and the ground begins to shake:

> And the earth, as if grasped by omnipotent might,
> Quaked dreadful, and shook with the throes of affright;
> Deep northwardly rolled the electrical jar,
> Creating amazement, destruction, and war;
> The rivers they boiled like a pot over coals,
> And mortals fell prostrate, and prayed for their souls:
> Every rock on our borders cracked, quivered, and shrunk
> And Nackitosh tumbled, and New Madrid sunk.[87]

In the cataclysm's aftermath, the King of Metals realizes that settlers are fleeing the west in fear and, consequently, "that the progress of empire was partly allayed."[88] Exultant, he declares that the meeting has accomplished its purpose and sends everyone home.

Appealing to what Schoolcraft elsewhere called a growing "zeal ... [for] geology and mineralogy" among the lay public, the conceit of *Transallegania* diffuses scientific facts throughout the poem.[89] Schoolcraft even managed to promote his own research by indexing where silver and other metals could be found across the continent. His choice of genre, however, indicates a broader agenda, as it situates these scientific facts within a larger conflict between social and geological forces. The poem, which borrows (and misquotes) an epigraph from the celebrated mock-epicist Alexander Pope, mimics Pope's satiric juxtaposition of classical grandeur and modern trivialities. Initially, it seems to deride the ambitions of the young nation, whose westward drive cannot overcome the catastrophic manifestation of natural forces, a move that echoes the conventional use of geology to counter human pride, reminding Man that there are powers greater than itself. Yet the poem's authorship, timing, and placement work against this reading. The close of the poem positions quake-generated chaos and fear as merely a temporary delay in US expansion, a prediction that was, by the year of the poem's publication, already coming true. (Schoolcraft's very career was, indeed, staked on this outcome; his employment as a state geologist, as he well knew, depended on the pursuit of national growth.) What is ultimately satirized, then, is the projected vaingloriousness of the pan-Indigenous movement, transposed onto the poem's animated and contested ground. Though Schoolcraft, in 1820, possessed little to no direct experience of Indigenous people, he might have heard narratives aligning the New Madrid earthquakes with Indigenous resistance, given their frequent appearance in newspapers. He was well aware of Indigenous opposition to the US annexation of the regions he investigated, and though he does not mention him directly, he would doubtless have known of Tecumseh, whose story was already beginning to be romanticized by US writers. And he also would have heard the typically American claim that pan-Indigeneity had failed because of inability of distinct tribes to work together. In this light, the boastful and quarrelsome congress of metals recasts the poem's allegory of Indigenous resistance, insofar as the earthquake results from the chaos that their failure to collaborate creates. *Transallegania* thus suggests, as Schoolcraft maintained across both phases of his career, that Indigenous opposition would, like the earthquake, ultimately pose no obstacle to settlement.

Only a handful of latter-day scholars have taken note of the poem, and none of them have been much impressed with its literary quality. Milton D. Rafferty, editor of a recent reprint edition of Schoolcraft's *Journal of a Tour into the Interior*, describes it as "dreadfully dull," while James Lal Penick notes approvingly that it "sank, like New Madrid, into quiet obscurity."[90] But expecting recognizable literary quality from *Transallegania* misses the point of this particular work.[91] Schoolcraft's intent in writing a mock-epic historico-mineralogical poem was likely not to garner acclaim from the literary establishment but to impress readers with his cleverness and erudition while drawing attention to his geological knowledge. *Transallegania* was penned at a moment when Schoolcraft, seeking a government position as national superintendent of mining (a position which did not exist then), published as much as he could, hoping his writing would gain the attention and respect he needed to land the job. Like the travelogue to which it was appended, the poem was a form of cultural capital intended to demonstrate his worthiness. And as R. H. Stoddard, in an 1855 biographical essay on Schoolcraft published in the *National Magazine*, indicated, this strategy succeeded; although Schoolcraft failed to secure the mining post, John C. Calhoun, then secretary of war, commissioned him to join the Cass expedition after reading his work, and Cass, afterward, helped him obtain the position as Indian agent despite his lack of experience with Indigenous communities.[92]

Anticipating his later ethnographic promotion of the settler fantasy that resistance to civilization would cause Indigenous people to "fade away," Schoolcraft's geological writing, whether fanciful or factual, located them outside the domain of the human, imitating the "clashing of stones" as they acted without intention or orientation—a lack of direction which demanded that they, along with their lands, be overwritten by the progressive time of the nation. As the structure of Bringier's report and the trajectory of Schoolcraft's career similarly indicate, the perceived contiguity of Indigenous people with the geology of their lands, enfolded within a national narrative of conquest and development, was rapidly becoming a matter of settler common sense.[93]

Bringier and Schoolcraft, as geological surveyors, ventured into considerations of the earth's deep past when confronted with fossilized matter; for the most part, though, they engaged the science primarily to open the lands they described to industry, believing, as Schoolcraft asserted in his memoir on the fossil tree, in the primacy of "the national and domestic purposes, to which [the land] is so admirably adapted."[94] The scientific and popular "zeal" for knowledge about the planetary past, however, kept the deep history of the earth in view even when geologists analyzed more recent phenomena. During Charles Lyell's visit to New Madrid, as reported in his geological travelogue *A Second Visit to the United States* (1849), the scientist, while investigating the lingering effects of the earthquake, considered his settler hosts' report that "the Indians, before the year 1811, had a tradition of a great earthquake which had previously devastated this same region."[95] As noted earlier, it was common for scientists working in the Americas to incorporate Indigenous knowledge into their scholarship; for instance, Constantin-François Volney, in his 1804 *View of the Climate and Soil of North America*, adduced as support for his contention that earthquakes did not occur west of the Alleghenies that "the aboriginals of the west have no words in their languages to express earthquakes and volcanos, while equivalent terms are common and familiar in the dialogues of the east."[96] But while Volney and other natural historians employed Indigenous people as guides to the space of the continent, Lyell considered them as conduits to time. He received his hosts' report stratigraphically, noting that "there is so wide an area without sink-holes or, any great inequalities of surface, and without dead trees ... that we cannot suppose any convulsion of equal magnitude to have occurred for many centuries previous to 1811."[97] Correlating Indigenous knowledge with his own empirical observations, Lyell projected the "tradition" beneath the land's surface, aligning it with the geologic past. He knew, of course, that Indigenous people did not actually correspond to prehuman geochronological epochs. Although he reports almost no direct contact with them, he notes, several times, upon arriving at a new site that its Indigenous residents have recently "abandoned" or "deserted" the region, as though they had done so freely, even carelessly.[98] Even the relics he and his fellow explorers dig up are framed in relatively recent terms. Describing the ancient Indigenous burial mounds at Marietta, he reminds his readers that their age could not be compared to that of the land on which they stood.[99] Still, his sense of the pastness of Indigenous culture permitted him, as we saw in chapter 1, to position Indigenous people as analogous to those prehuman epochs—windows into ancient worlds and illustrations of the principle of species extinction, which made geochronology possible. Comparing their removal to the "certain doom of a species less fitted to struggle with some new condition," consigning them to the annals of "poetry and tradition," such as the story of Tecumseh and the earthquake, Lyell, like his North American colleagues, consigned Indigeneity to the realm of the post-animate.

Fantasies of the ethnographic/geological Indian—of Indigeneity rendered as both prescientific and prehistoric—persisted long after the New Madrid earthquakes had receded from US national memory. Indeed, the figure appeared in a 1990 report published by the US Geological Survey (USGS), devoted, as its subtitle declares, to "preparing for the next New Madrid earthquake."[100] The report opens with an overview of the events of 1811–12, featuring a series of vivid eyewitness accounts used to illustrate the potential impact of a (geo-historically likely) seismic repetition. The harm that event might inflict, the report asserts, would be "felt from Denver to New York City, topple chimneys in Chicago, Knoxville, Dallas, and Kansas City, cause architectural damage to tall buildings throughout most of the Central United States, and have devastating physical and societal impacts on the central Mississippi Valley."[101] In the context of the late-twentieth-century scientific report, the image of widespread chimney-toppling is incongruously quaint: given the preponderance of "tall buildings" in the cities named, not to mention other infrastructure systems such as highways, water and sewer systems, and the electrical grid, toppled chimneys are an odd detail on which to focus. They were, however, a widely reported effect of the quake series, and the report, despite its modernity, seems intent on borrowing that event's historical appeal. This explains the cover image: a popular mid-nineteenth-century woodcut depicting people frantically fleeing log cabins that are on the verge of falling into chasms in the earth.[102]

Most telling in this respect, however, is the report's main title: *Tecumseh's Prophecy*—a phrase that presumably encompasses both the last earthquake and the next one. Presented as the stuff of "legend," the story of his nineteenth-century earthquake prophecy (adapted from McKenney's version as reprinted in a twentieth-century history of the events) is recounted on the

Figure 2.1. *The Great Earthquake at New Madrid*, from Henry Howe, *Historical Collections of the Great West* (1854). Source: Wikimedia Commons.

report's inside cover.[103] No contextualizing information is given for the story; its subject is identified only as the "Shawnee Indian chief Tecumseh," who was "travel[ing] south . . . in an attempt to recruit supporters," without clarifying what they might be supporting. Background information on Tecumseh and the broader context for earthquake prophecies is omitted. Though it is anchored by a date (1811), the account, shorn of context, floats at the edge of historical time, endowed with a vague anteriority, as reflected in its position on the inside cover, before the report proper begins; it is employed to endow the pragmatic work of disaster preparedness with an evocative Romantic frame—even as the planning process outlined in the report entirely omits Indigenous knowledge, experience, and participation, past and present.[104] If the report's title, *Tecumseh's Prophecy*, is intended to resonate ominously against its subtitle's reference to the "next New Madrid earthquake," it does so in the double-timed deployment of death that characterizes geology's entwinement with biopower: knowledge of the geological forces posited as Man's limit becomes the means through which he demonstrates his capacity to triumph over limits. Meanwhile, as it frames Indigenous relations to the

Unsettled Ground

land in mythopoetic rather than historical time, *Tecumseh's Prophecy* testifies once again to geology's ability to support settler colonialism's perpetual acquisition of territory.[105]

Nineteenth-century Indigenous citations of the earthquakes, as we have seen, sought to crack open settler time, deploying the polychronicity of prophecy in an effort to sustain and revitalize Indigenous presence. But the earthquake prophecy, in the hands of US historians, became part of settler biopolitics; it joined Christian, national, and geological responses to the quakes as an opportunity for the nation to assert its own worthiness. If the New Madrid series created a rift in time for the settlers who experienced it, it was ultimately used by their descendants to ensure that, as Kyle Powys Whyte (Citizen Potawatomi) puts it, "the future embedded in the landscape is a settler one."[106]

romancing the trace 3
ichnology, affect, matter

ONE SUNDAY IN MARCH 1835, the geologic past put its foot down right in the middle of a quiet town in the Connecticut River Valley, and its reverberations remain with us to this day. On that Sunday, W. W. Draper, a resident of Greenfield, Massachusetts, noticed some curious markings in the paving stones over which he was walking on his way home from church. He showed them to the owner of the house where they were laid, and the owner called in a local scholar, Dr. James Deane, to confirm their antiquity. Deane, who believed the marks to be fossilized animal tracks, sent a copy of them to Edward Hitchcock, then professor of chemistry and natural history at Amherst College and the director of the Massachusetts Geological Survey. Hitchcock went to investigate and a few months later published a groundbreaking paper in the *American Journal of Science and Arts*, in which he declared the marks to be the tracks of three or more long-extinct species of gigantic wading birds, hitherto unknown. Following Hitchcock's paper, the tracks were analyzed by many of the era's most eminent geologists, including Hitchcock's mentor Benjamin Silliman, Charles Lyell, Richard Owen, and Louis Agassiz. They also made their way into literary and popular writing by Henry Wadsworth

Longfellow, Herman Melville, Oliver Wendell Holmes, Thomas Wentworth Higginson, and others.[1]

The popularity of these fossil traces, both within and outside the new field of paleontological inquiry that Hitchcock initially named "ichnolithology" (though William Buckland's term, "ichnology," was the one that stuck), demonstrates that they spoke vividly about the questions and possibilities emerging from the new science that made them legible.[2] Such footprints had, of course, been noted before, both by Indigenous people and by white settlers. To Hitchcock and his contemporaries, however, they resounded in a geological register, evoking the still-new revolutions in scientific thought that have been positioned as modern geology's foundations: James Hutton's recognition of the earth's high antiquity and Georges Cuvier's confirmation of species extinction. In the aftermath of these theories, fossils no longer appeared as mere "sports of nature" or records of species merely displaced from the locations where they were found, two alternate explanations for the phenomena. Rather, they came to embody the vastness of geological time, edged round by the black border of species death. In this sense, the fossil tracks under the feet of Greenfield's residents might threaten to bring the specter of oblivion a little too close for comfort. But the speculative animacy of the tracks helped to ameliorate that threat, turning them from a potential locus of dread into an opportunity for philosophical reflection and imaginative experimentation.

Hitchcock's geological writing coincided with, and took account of, the explosion in the popularity of geological concepts in the United States. A year before Hitchcock began studying the footprints, Samuel Metcalf's April 1834 *Knickerbocker* essay, which declared geology "the fashionable science of the day," affirmed that the fossil record in particular had made this turn of affairs possible; thanks to "the genius of Cuvier," fossils now operated as "a key to unlock the mysteries of discovery—a perpetual light to irradiate the march of future discovery."[3] The fossil record, Metcalf asserted, enabled geology to balance speculation and inductive reasoning so that a general understanding of the "magnificent ... unceasing transposition of matter, by which the surface of the earth is forever renewed," could be broken down, through the clues provided by particular fossils, into specifics—glimpses into different worlds that had arisen and passed away.[4] In this context, the Connecticut Valley tracks captured the public imagination. Some were initially skeptical about Hitchcock's claims, at least until a commission sent by the American Scientific Association in 1841 vindicated them. That same year, Hitchcock released his second *Geological Survey of Massachusetts*, which included an extensive discussion of the tracks. This section made the report so popular that Thoreau, commissioned by Emerson to write on the issue, could not obtain a copy before they sold out. Interest in the question of the earth's antiquity was not the only controversy that developed from Hitchcock's theories concerning the tracks. Also at issue was the question of what type of creatures had made them. Hitchcock maintained throughout his career that they had been made by prehistoric birds, a theory he adopted, initially without credit, from Deane.[5] At first, most prominent geologists who viewed the tracks agreed with Hitchcock on their source, but many soon began to believe that some or all of them had been made by the giant reptilian beasts that would be grouped together in 1842 by Richard Owen as dinosaurs. Hitchcock, however, clung tenaciously to his bird theory, although toward the end of his life, as scientific opinion tilted in favor of saurian origins for the tracks, he proposed that some might have been made by a hitherto unknown four-footed avian species. Because of Hitchcock, it was as bird tracks that the Connecticut Valley marks came into popular consciousness in the US. The familiarity of birds (as opposed to the strangeness of dinosaurs, which would not capture the US imaginary until later in the nineteenth century) meant that these prehistoric figures could establish a certain continuity between the distant geological past and the present. And this continuity meant, in turn, that they could be imagined as vitally active—a circumstance aided by the absence of any fossilized bones or other remnants of the creatures themselves.

Taken together as an event in the historical flow of geological fantasy, the footprints' reverberations clustered around the two genres that have most conspicuously organized that flow. Once geologized, they inevitably spoke of the planet's antiquity. Though the paving stones in which they had first been recognized were human-made objects of relatively recent origin, the footprints turned them into ancient documents. Yet they also testified to the vitality of the material world in a way that complicated, though it did not entirely dissipate, the alienating effect of deep time. As footprints—bird tracks or otherwise—the marks evoked a world of action, indeed of intra-action, indexing the transformative connections between animate beings and presumably inanimate matter. From this perspective, the geological operates not simply as a gateway to a vastness that explodes the human, but as a way for the human to find itself otherwise—to find itself *mattering* in relation to the histories of material agency that geology explores.[6]

In this sense, the footprints connected to the speculative, aesthetic dimension of geological thought, characterized by what Noah Heringman terms "wonder."[7] *Wonder* signifies a mode of invested inquiry that exceeds and redirects the empirical; distinct from awe, *wonder* does not annihilate the subject, but channels it differently, enabling glimpses of life lived otherwise. The material-aesthetic fascination of geological wonder surfaces throughout antebellum US writing on the Connecticut Valley fossil tracks, generating an *ichnopoesis* that articulates itself alongside and within empirical studies of the tracks as well as the literary texts they inspired.[8] The ichnopoetic dimension of the conversation about them kept the marks vibrantly alive, resisting the distancing and deadening implications of the fossil as we saw it evoked in chapter 2. The footprints could still be (and, as we will see, sometimes were) aligned with the trope of Indigenous extinction, rendering them marks of the fossil other. But as animate forms, they also reached past the distance formally separating them from the observing subject, enabling the past they opened to view to mingle with human history, offering alternate perspectives on the present.

This chapter points to a dimension of geological fantasy that has been less prominent in this study until now: the unevenly transformative effect of vibrant material memory, the residue of the "unceasing transposition of matter," even as it operated within the bounds of settler geology. Beginning with a reflection on the interest in fossil traces, the chapter takes up three cases in turn, each of which speaks to a different view of the tracks. The first of these is the enlivening and partly unbalancing investment in something like geological magic that inflects the scientific tone of Hitchcock's earliest writings on the tracks—an article in the *American Journal of Science and Arts* and a didactic poem, published in January and December 1836, respectively. Turning to Henry Wadsworth Longfellow's writing on the fossil tracks, particularly his 1845 lyric poem "To the Driving Cloud," I closely explore the poem's positioning of the tracks alongside the Indigenous "extinction" trope in ways that simultaneously confirm that trope and turn it against itself, denaturalizing the history of Indigenous displacement yet ultimately stranding this fluctuating assessment within the dynamics of moral education so dear to nineteenth-century advocates of geology. The final section of the chapter returns to Hitchcock's writing on fossil traces from 1841 onward, where he engages them in a revision of the fort/da game with geological time that again both replicates and complicates the uses of that game that we have seen thus far, as they unexpectedly coalesce into a material (as opposed to biological) theory of race as constructed in chattel slavery, and then into a model of distributed agency, action suspended between the human and nonhuman/material nature. Ultimately, I argue, the ambivalent operations of the tracks demonstrate both the seductiveness of new materialist takes on geology as a conduit to the possibilities associated with the agency of matter and the limitations it reveals when positioned in relation to all-too-human histories of violence.

Ichnomania

The sort of markings that fascinated Hitchcock and his contemporaries had been interpreted by earlier observers. A Lenni Lenape account held that they were made by an ancient race of monsters who preyed on all other living creatures until they were destroyed by lightning. This account corresponded with Haudenosaunee explanations for the existence of fossilized bones and teeth as well as footprints. In most of these narratives, the fossils are all that remains of a monstrously fierce species that at one point threatened to destroy other animals, humans, or prehuman peoples but which was eventually eradicated, either by those peoples or by earthquakes or lightning. In many of the accounts, one or two especially fierce predators escape the destruction and flee to another region, where, it is suggested, they might still be lying in wait. Adrienne Mayor argues that such stories map earth history as a process of continually rebalancing natural forces, with the surviving predators suggesting that no one species can completely defeat another.[9] The Iroquois believed the prints had been made by the Little People, one of the prehuman races who had destroyed the predatory monsters; seeing the prints as imbued with power, they used them to aid the growth of crops. White settlers, when they came upon the tracks, tended to place them within a biblical time frame and sometimes used them to uphold biblical narratives. Residents of South Hadley, Massachusetts, for instance, found a set of prints in 1802 and identified them as the tracks of Noah's Raven. W. W. Draper believed the Greenfield markings to be 3,000-year-old turkey tracks.

The rapidity with which these markings went geological in the 1830s says a great deal about the appeal of the science in this period. The practical uses of geology had long since been embraced by the young republic; beginning with Lewis and Clark, geological surveys were part of all major western expeditions, and states also began to appoint their own surveyors, starting with the Carolinas in 1823–24 and Massachusetts in 1830 (the latter under Hitchcock's leadership). And as we have seen, once theories of the earth's antiquity began to gain wide circulation (fueled especially by the publication of Charles Lyell's accessibly written *Principles of Geology* in 1830–33), the more speculative aspects of the science began to take root in the popular imagination. In 1836, the year Hitchcock's first report on the fossil tracks was published, an enthusiastic

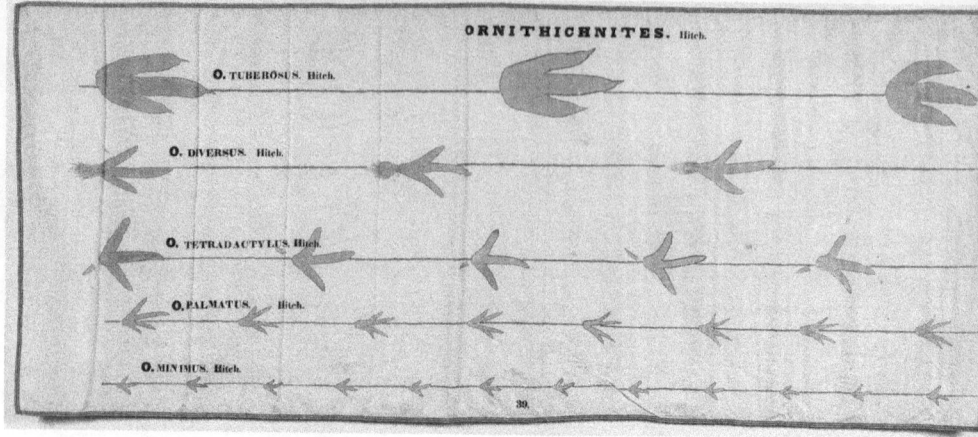

Figure 3.1. Orra White Hitchcock, *Ornithichnites*, ca. 1840. Source: Amherst College/Palatino Press.

twenty-two-page review of the second edition of his *Report on the Geology of Massachusetts* appeared in the *North American Review*. The anonymous reviewer waxed lyrical about the intellectual benefits of geology: "Whoever enters on this study with proper feelings, and pursues it with intelligence and success, can never look back, but is continually urged onward by the discovery of new and wonderful truths, which fill his mind with the most sublime emotions. The world has its history written on its strata: a history so interesting, that the most splendid fictions of the human imagination sink into insignificance when compared with it."[10] The reviewer associates geology with affect: its study requires "proper feelings" and results in the "most sublime emotions." As affective adventure, geology is an inexhaustible source of pleasure, generating a history stranger and more intriguing than fiction. Notably, although the book being reviewed did not mention the footprints, which Hitchcock had not yet studied when he composed it, the review included two pages reporting his findings. Much of that space is spent marveling over his suppositions concerning *O. Giganteus*, Hitchcock's name for the birds he believed to have made the largest of the tracks. Evidently the fossil footprints formed part of the world's "interesting history" for this writer, and the mystery of the lost birds, "stalk[ing] along the shores of a tropical sea, which is supposed to have washed the valley of the Connecticut in olden times," was capable of stirring the feelings.[11]

As we have seen, nineteenth-century interest in geology relied to a large extent on the project of locating the relationship between human and planetary history through the accounts read out of the rocks. That history could offer the stability of self-confirmation through the slow, stately progress that many geological thinkers insisted was the general shape of earth history and that was used to undergird some of the Western world's most familiar self-locating accounts, including white supremacy.[12] Yet its gaps and its differences, its apprehension of the deep past as what Lyell called "the theatre of reiterated change" and "neverending fluctuations," meant that it could also press forward "new and wonderful" visions of life lived otherwise, speculative possibilities for meeting the world on different terms.[13]

We can begin to understand the distinctive appeal of ichnology—literally, the science of traces—in this light. Gayatri Spivak explicates Jacques Derrida's concept of the "trace" as the "mark of the absence of a presence, an always already absent present, of the lack at the origin which is the condition of thought and experience."[14] Yet in the case of fossil tracks (and, as Spivak observes, the French word for trace conveys the sense of *track* or *footprint* more strongly that the English does),[15] we might more accurately refer to the *presence of an absence*: the mark of the here-no-longer that nevertheless remains. This reversal recalls Steven Shaviro's Deleuzian rereading of the positive inflection Derrida gave to the trace in his late work *Specters of Marx*, where the trace reappears as, in Shaviro's terms, a "radical non-negativity, a kind of residual, quasi-material insistence, that disrupts and ruins every movement of negation or negativity."[16] Reborn as the quasi-material specter, that is, the trace haunts the present not with an absence that ruptures presence, but a presence that negates negation.

To some extent, the term *trace fossil*, as it designates the subject of ichnology, might be regarded as redundant. All fossils, in this sense, are traces: lithic ghosts incapable of disappearing, material echoes of past life: forms that, by refusing to vanish into the abyss of time, prevent geological time from becoming merely abyssal. This is true pragmatically as well as philosophically. As we have seen, stratigraphy, the method of mapping the geological past developed in the early nineteenth century by William Smith, relies to a large extent on the correlation of index fossils as well as mineral materials for determining the relative age of strata. As indices, fossils operate as static points for the construction of a progressive time line which surpasses them, suspending them in the immensity of the geologic past. But the repetition in the term *trace fossil* serves to emphasize an intensified form of persistence past extinction located through the prehistoric footprint. As an impression of now-vanished matter, the fossil trace distances the morbidity lithically embodied in other fossils—that is, while the death of the creature that made it is assumed, it is not directly observable, in the form of an ossified body. Moreover, while ordinary fossils offer a record of existence, of being or having-been, fossilized traces, and footprints in particular, appear as a record of action, of doing or having-done—birds "stalking along" prehistoric shores. They seem to open directly onto a dynamic (rather than merely taxonomic) vision of past worlds. Ichnology, as the present-day trace-fossil specialist Anthony J. Martin contends, is "perhaps more than any other part of paleontology... about that exciting intersection between science and flights of fancy."[17] Because it demands the speculative conjuring up of a being from the impression of its presence—rather than working to piece together its remnants—ichnology can offer a fuller, fleshier picture of a creature interacting with a physical environment that was likewise in flux. As it tracks the traces of creatures in motion, then, ichnology points to the possibilities of the geological past as a resource for speculation and sensation rather than a vehicle for annihilation.

"Too Deep for Time and Fate to Wear Away": Hitchcock's Ichnopoetics

Interest in the "fashionable science," in the period in which the tracks were geologized, was by no means reserved for men, but the practice of the science retained a certain masculinist cast. Nineteenth-century geological writing, as Adelene Buckland has shown, often dramatized the quest for scientific knowledge by figuring the geologist as rugged pioneer, bravely ranging over uncharted expanses of space and time to discover (and often to colonize) new worlds.[18] The ichnological writings of Edward Hitchcock, professor of natural history (and later president) at Amherst College, followed suit. Hitchcock depicted himself as a lonely pioneer of ichnology, supported by few and jeered by many until his vindication by the American Scientific Association in 1841. That status, to some extent, has become his legacy, though he did not discover the tracks and though he was accused of adopting Deane's conclusions as his own (which, he admitted, he might have done). His first article—published just months after their discovery—is still recognized today as a masterly work, even though many of its scientific conclusions have been abandoned.[19] Hitchcock returned to the tracks again and again over the course of his career. By 1863, when he authored the memoir *Reminiscences of Amherst College*, he had, he estimated, published "about 550 pages—360 of them quarto—with 116 plates, on the Ichnology of the Connecticut [Valley]" as well as amassed a sizable collection of specimens covering the walls of a room in the sciences building at Amherst.[20]

Hitchcock's extensive 1836 article, "Ornithichnology—Description of the Foot marks of Birds (Ornithichnites) on new Red Sandstone in Massachusetts," published in the *American Journal of Science and Arts* in January 1836, demonstrates how empiricism, the rigorously observational method that nineteenth-century geologists embraced to differentiate themselves from the "fanciful" theories of their predecessors, was an aesthetic form as well as a scientific one. The article sticks, for the most part, to neutral description, provisional taxonomy, and careful hypothesizing. Hitchcock repeatedly proclaims the necessity for wariness in geological study, affirming that "the geologist should be the last of all men to trust to first impressions."[21] Acknowledging that his conclusions run counter to contemporary geological opinion, he more than once invites his colleagues to dispute his conjectures. He permits himself few departures from description, a consistency that renders the exceptions noteworthy. Most significant in this respect is the moment when he diverges from what he calls the "usual" geological perspective on the different pace and style of "early geological changes." Though he accepts this principle in general, in the current case, he declares himself unavoidably "struck with the remarkable resemblance of the state of things, as shown by these ornithichnites, to have existed so many thousands of years ago, and that now passing before our eyes. Our imaginations are carried back by these relics, to that immensely distant period, when the new red sandstone birds were traveling along the shores of the then existing estuaries or lakes, just as is now done by congeneric races."[22] The Connecticut River, as he has earlier explained, looked very different at that time, and the size of many of the fossil tracks suggests that some prehistoric birds were much larger; but the activity of both sets of beings, their interaction with the environment, was, he maintains, roughly similar. His emphasis on that activity in particular, rendered in the past continuous tense accomplishes the temporal bridge, endowing long-extinct creatures with a certain liveness. Completing the work of scientific description, fleshing out the picture gleaned from careful observation and reasoned conjecture, requires a speculative leap; employing the fossil as a conduit to the imagination, Hitchcock collapses the "immense" distance between past and present, emphasizing the continuities between the two worlds. The compellingness of this move is indexed in the paraphrased reproduction of this passage in the *North American Review* essay published later that year.

Although Hitchcock confined his indulgence in such imaginative labors to brief, selected moments in his first scientific publication on the fossil footprints, he allowed himself to expand on these in other genres. In December of that same year, the *Knickerbocker, or New York Monthly Magazine* published a poem about the footprints; it appeared in the pages of the journal without a title, though the issue's table of contents identified it as "Ornithichnites Giganteus, *Redivivus*." The poem was published pseudonymously as "Poetaster," a term designating an inferior dabbler in the poetic arts, which had also, by Hitchcock's time, come to mean one who wrote on mundane subjects. Hitchcock wrote it, though his authorship was never revealed, and both the journal's editors and the prefatorial correspondence from Poetaster, which established Hitchcock's *Journal of American Science* article as the inspiration for the poem, invoked him only in the third person.[23] The *Knickerbocker*'s editors nodded to the earlier article's conclusions without embracing them. Hitchcock-as-Poetaster, though, actively promoted them, affirming that "there was at least probability enough in the theory advanced... [by Hitchcock] to make it lawful to use it in verse."[24] The scientific justification of a "lawful" subject for poetry might seem beside the point to a modern reader versed in the idea of the lyric imagination. It makes sense, though, within the poetic tradition upon which Hitchcock draws, that of scientific-didactic poetry, where the poet serves not only as the conveyor of versified information to the reader but also as an authoritative editor of such information, sorting or selecting among competing theories to present the most accurate facts.[25]

The *Knickerbocker* poem presents three speakers in succession. The first, a solitary geologist examining a set of fossil tracks, muses on the longevity of the prints and the enormous changes the earth had seen since they were made. He enjoins the creature that left them to return, lamenting that modernity has dissipated the magicians who might make that happen. In response, a sorceress appears. Dismissing science's claim to superior enlightenment, she uses her power to cause a huge bird to burst out of the rock in a torrent of water. The bird, identifying itself as the source of the prints, scornfully echoes the sorceress's mocking description of Man, a creature scarcely six feet high, as "creation's lord." Claiming that title for itself, it taxonomizes the amazing creatures of its epoch down from its own ruling position. Once finished, it refuses to remain in the geologist's cold and degenerate world:

> Sure 'tis a place for punishment design'd'
> And not the beauteous, happy spot I lov'd;
> These creatures here seem discontented, sad;

> They hate each other and they hate the world.
> O who would live in such a dismal spot?

The bird sinks back into the rock, and the "vex'd geologist" is left grasping after its form. He laments the loss to science and curses the arts employed by the sorceress,

> Forgetting that the lesson taught his pride
> Was better than new knowledge of lost worlds.

While the geological and paleontological lessons offered in the speech of the geologist and the bird are clear (if now outdated), whatever moral teaching might be overlaid on this scientific substrate—the "lesson taught his pride" said to be missed by the geologist—is less apparent. One possible target of this lesson is the progressivist fantasy that humans live in the best possible version of earth as it has evolved over the eons. If the bird's speech is taken at face value, the poem reads as a rebuke to the geologist's supposedly ideal world; the bird describes it in quasi-apocalyptic terms, calling it "well nigh worn out" and predicting that its occupants are "soon/in nature's icy grave to sink for aye." Poetaster, in a footnote, acknowledges the bird's view as a potentially rational conjecture in light of the evident cooling of the globe: "If it be admitted that the climate, vegetation, and animals of [the Connecticut] valley really were tropical, when this bird lived, who will say that its present condition might not seem, even to a rational being, in similar circumstances, to be one of deterioration and approaching ruin?"[26] Jordan D. Marché II reads this reference as a remnant of diluvialist views of the pristine prehistoric past, positioned as a contrast to the broken world in which we now live.[27] This is the kind of earth history presented in biblically based geological writing such as Thomas Burnet's 1681 *Telluris Theoria Sacra*, though the idea of a cooling earth was also embraced by the more secular Comte de Buffon. The consideration of the earth's deep past would, from this perspective, operate to counter human "pride," rendering the sandstone footprints a planetary manifestation of the Puritan death's head—a lithic *memento mori*. (The decline of the planet, on this view, offers an earlier version of the geological chastisement often said to be the effect of deep time.)

Yet Hitchcock, as Marché acknowledges, was more inclined to the progressivist view of earth history established by Charles Lyell. In this light, it is also possible that the "lesson" taught to the geologist might not target his assumed anthropocentrism after all. Rather, it may be aimed at the geologist *as* geologist, and the hastiness that, Hitchcock believed, characterized the thinking of some of his scientific contemporaries. Hitchcock's geology was more modern than Burnet's by far; he embraced both the post-Huttonian geological timescale and Cuvier's proofs of species extinction, though along with Cuvier, he refused theories of evolution. The geological past appeared, in his view, as a series of perfectly integrated ecosystems. In his *Elementary Geology* textbook, first published in 1840, he depicted this history in a paleontological chart based on the then-common trope of the "tree of life." That the diagram looks more like a bush than a tree reflects Hitchcock's conviction that all plant and animal classes had been present since the beginning of life, though they had become more sophisticated and more diverse over time—hence the spreading of the branches. The positing of birds as the makers of the Connecticut Valley tracks was crucial to this picture. As noted in another footnote to the *Knickerbocker* poem, the bird tracks displaced the saurian fossils which had, up until the discovery of the former, been thought to be the "most perfect animals" this far down in the rock record. Although the lack of evidence of birds in the fossil record had led many geologists to infer that they did not exist then, the discovery of their footmarks, Hitchcock had argued in the January 1836 *Journal of American Science* article, might therefore "prove . . . an instructive lesson to the geologist," leading him to "enquire, whether he has not been too hasty in inferring the non-existence of the more perfect animals or plants, in the earlier times of our globe." This claim was disputed in a later issue of the journal, in an article authored by its editor-in-chief, Silliman, though printed anonymously. (Marché suggests that Hitchcock may have published his poem to strike back at his mentor.) If the "lesson" taught to the geologist in the poem is the same as the one Hitchcock posited in the earlier article, which Poetaster identifies as his guide, we might understand the poem as layering similar moral-methodological instruction onto its scientific didacticism, with the intention of correcting an overreliance on empiricism and a corresponding lack of principled speculation that might hold open a place for the yet-to-be-discovered.

Both these readings, though, assess the poem as a conversation between masculine figures, the geologist and the lordly bird, overlooking the fleeting but crucial appearance of the sorceress who responds to the geologist's wish by making the bird appear. Hers is a strange interlude, set apart metrically from the matching styles of the geologist and the giant bird; they speak in the pentameters favored in Anglophone scientific-didactic poetry, while her brief speech, in rhymed tetrameter couplets, evokes Shakespearean invocations of the supernatural, such as the witches' song in *Macbeth*. Yet even as her arts accomplish what the empirically bound geologist cannot, the sorceress

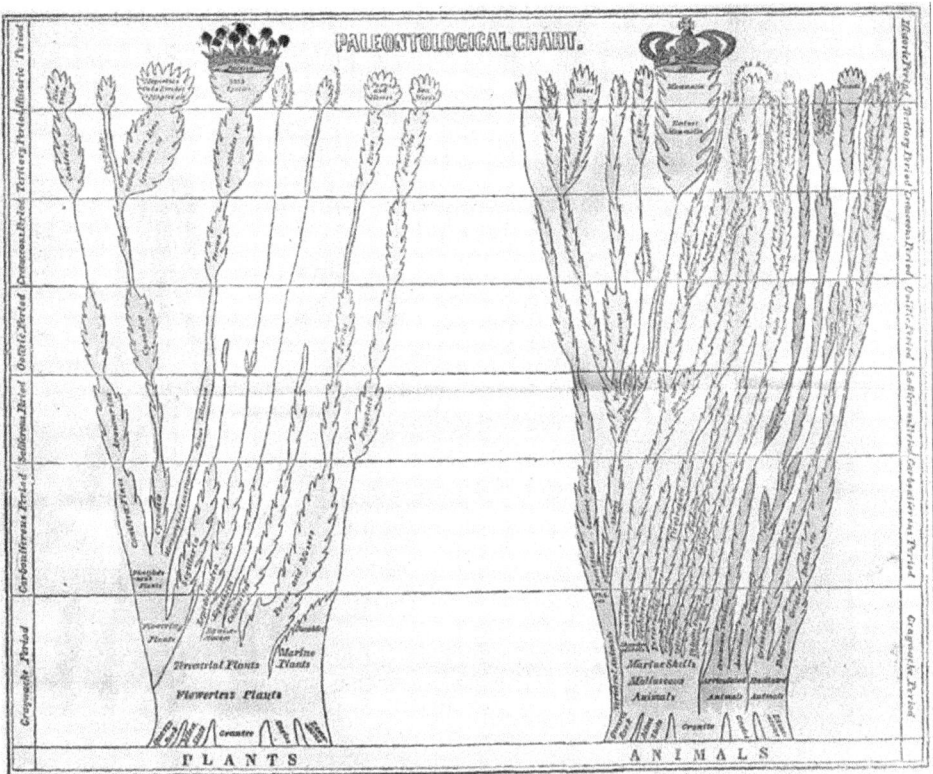

Figure 3.2. Foldout paleontological chart from Edward Hitchcock's *Elementary Geology* (1840). Source: Wikimedia Commons.

herself has been conjured, inadvertently, by the geologist's own wish, which alludes to a biblical figure commonly identified as the Witch of Endor, whom the geologist identifies as having "broke[n] the prophet's slumbers."[28] The story, from the first book of Samuel, runs thusly: King Saul, anxious about an impending battle with the Philistine army, tells his servants to bring him to a medium. Visiting her in disguise, he enjoins her to summon the spirit of the prophet Samuel. The spirit appears, cranky about having been disturbed. He chastises Saul for disobedience to the Lord and prophesies his downfall, which takes place as promised the following day. Much commentary on this incident holds that its point is not Samuel's prophecy per se (indeed, his appearance is said by some to be a trick, since the dead, in orthodox Christian theology, are not believed to return, with one significant exception), but Saul's lack of faith (a later verse from 1 Chronicles affirms that Saul's death was a punishment for various acts of "unfaithfulness," including turning to a medium rather than the Lord), along with his hypocrisy, since as the witch herself points out, he had banished sorcerers from the realm. The poem may likewise condemn the geologist for falsity to science, since he claims, at the outset, that such enchantments are banished from the modern "age of light." Summoning the sorceress, in this sense, is both hypocrisy and scientific impiety.

Reading the Witch of Endor allusion in a strictly biblical frame is complicated, though, by the sorceress's Romanticism: her metric alterity, her scorn (cut from the published version) at the scientific arrogance of naming what remains inaccessible, and, most importantly, the visual and poetic revisions of the Witch by Romantic writers and painters (Henry Fuseli, William Blake, George Byron) that the poem would also bring to mind for Hitchcock and his contemporaries. In Romantic visions, witches defiantly maintain their place in a present that would banish them but cannot, precisely because they occupy a site less supernatural than psychic: the site of interiority, the turbulent and half-occluded domain of the emotions that surround our desire for and fear of the past. In this context, then, the sorceress would be linked less strictly to religious or secular-scientific heresy than to the omnipresent yet potentially heretical energy that drives scientific inquiry—the wondering intensity of the geologist's deep desire to know the geological past. Hitchcock's appeal to the imagination, in both article and poem, to supply missing details about the birds, to flesh out the picture of the geological past, is a consequence of wonder. Wonder operates as the vitalizing force that enables the imagination to access prehistory; it is necessary to kindle the drive to scientific discovery.[29] At the same time, Heringman reminds us, wonder was viewed as something that needed to be carefully controlled, and it was repeatedly disavowed by scientific writers. What we can, in line with the sorceress, understand as the enchantment of the geologic past points toward embodied, potentially feminized, knowledges that surpass taxonomy, challenging the masculinized domain of scientific discovery. If wonder was given license, there was no telling what might quicken through the rocks.

"That Have Left Us Only Their Footprints": Longfellow's Lyric Ichnology

Much of the knowledge about Indigenous people possessed by American Romantic poet Henry Wadsworth Longfellow had come to him by way of a former geologist: Henry Rowe Schoolcraft, author of *Algic Researches*, a compendium of sources on the Ojibwe, which Longfellow, as I noted in chapter 2, used as a resource for the composition of his 1855 epic poem *Hiawatha*. But this was not the first time Longfellow had composed the figures he called "Indians" in the shadow of the geologic. A lesser-known work, his 1845 poem "To the Driving Cloud," seems to have been inspired in part by the enthusiasm surrounding the Connecticut Valley tracks in the years following their rendition as geological artefacts. The poem compares the footsteps of an Omaha chief identified as Driving Cloud to the bird tracks. It isn't clear what, if anything, Longfellow knew about the Omaha, whose imminent displacement focalizes the poem, and who were, at the time of its publication, struggling to hold onto their traditional lands west of the Missouri River, a struggle they would lose a decade later.[30] Yet his own lifelong interest in geology meant that he almost certainly knew something about the Connecticut Valley footprints. The first stanza of "To the Driving Cloud" positions those fossil traces as an antecedent for an Omaha chief's passage through the streets of an unnamed city:

> Gloomy and dark art thou, O chief of the mighty Omahas;
> Gloomy and dark as the driving cloud, whose name thou hast taken!
> Wrapt in thy scarlet blanket, I see thee stalk through the city's
> Narrow and populous streets, as once by the margin of rivers
> Stalked those birds unknown, that have left us only their footprints.
> What, in a few short years, will remain of thy race but the footprints?

The Omaha chief is initially aligned with the "gloomy and dark" trace of a different natural object, the "driving cloud, whose name thou hast taken." But the comparison shifts from meteorological to geological as the poem references the fossil traces of those "birds unknown." The traces mark an absence from the present—a mysterious extinct species—that both parallels and prefigures a future absent presence, Driving Cloud and the Omaha for whom he stands in, now present to white settlers *as* an imminent absence. In bringing the footprints into association with the Omaha, Longfellow drew upon the familiar trope of Indigenous extinction; indeed, "To the Driving Cloud" reads, to a significant degree, like a somber transcription of Andrew Jackson's 1830 *Annual Message to Congress* into unrhymed hexameters. Jackson there declares:

> To follow to the tomb the last of his race and to tread on the graves of extinct nations excite melancholy reflections. But true philanthropy reconciles the mind to these vicissitudes as it does to the extinction of

one generation to make room for another.... Nor is there any thing in this, which, upon a comprehensive review of the general interests of the human race, is to be regretted. Philanthropy could not wish to see this continent restored to the condition in which it was found by our forefathers. What good man would prefer a country covered with forests and ranged by a few thousand savages to our extensive republic, studded with cities, towns, and prosperous farms, embellished with all the improvements which art can devise or industry execute, occupied by more than 12,000,000 happy people, and filled with all the blessings of liberty, civilization, and religion?[31]

Jackson's use of the extinction trope in the *Annual Message* characteristically obscures the cause of this extinction, depicting it as a natural event, an inevitable succession. Following the progressive logic of natural theology, the new lifeworld encompassed by "our extensive republic" is seen as an "improvement" over the last one. The "melancholy reflections" inspired by the act of "tread[ing] on the graves of extinct nations"—a striking interment of Indigenous people as protofossils, buried within lands being annexed—are, apparently, fleeting philosophical interludes, replaced by the "happiness" settlement enables.

But while Jackson's deployment of the Indigenous extinction trope masks the violence of removal in the guise of a natural process, Longfellow's invocation of the fossil footmarks and other geological markers is more ambivalent. Even as it prefigures the Omaha chief's "disappearance" from the historical stage, the materiality of Longfellow's geological metaphor presses forward another kind of presence. Lloyd Willis has written of Longfellow's consistent representation of the natural world as "an explicitly terrestrial and material, grounded and tactile phenomenon."[32] Longfellow's nature insists on its own *there*-ness, physically impressing itself on both poet and poem.[33] The incorporation of a geological perspective on the natural world in "To the Driving Cloud" extends this impressibility across time as well as space. The geological dynamics of the poem might, in this light, be said to resist the preemptive equation of Indigenous culture with death and disappearance, insofar as the fossil footprints that (literally) ground the extinction metaphor introduce what we have seen as the temporal permeability of the trace fossil—its evocation of the presence of an absence, its ability to press forward from the past rather than merely carry the present observer backward in time. Materializing what Naomi Greyser has called "sympathetic grounds," the earth's ability to convey affect across space and, in this case, time, the Omaha chief's footsteps do not merely convey an imminent absence; they continue to press his claims against the encroaching settlements, insisting on his ongoing present-tense presence as he moves through a city already populated, implicitly, with European migrants.[34]

The ambivalence of the extinction metaphor and the politicization of geological material resurface later in the poem, as the speaker muses on the dangers facing the Omaha chief:

> Far more fatal to thee and thy race than the tread of Behemoth,
> Lo! the big thunder-canoe, that steadily breasts the Missouri's
> Merciless current! and yonder, afar on the prairies, the camp-fires
> Gleam through the night; and the cloud of dust in the gray of the daybreak
> Marks not the buffalo's track, nor the Mandan's dexterous horse-race;
> It is a caravan, whitening the desert where dwell the Camanches!
> Ha! how the breath of these Saxons and Celts, like the blast of the east-wind,
> Drifts evermore to the west the scanty smokes of thy wigwams!

The "Behemoth" allusion references a settler transposition of Indigenous accounts of mastodon extinction. White settlers, moving westward, are said to pose a greater threat to Indigenous people than did the figure of the Behemoth, a monster "who, unharmed, on his tusks once caught the bolts of the thunder,/ and now lurks in his lair to destroy the race of the red man." The figure's most proximate reference, for Longfellow, would likely have been Cornelius Mathews's popular 1839 novella *Behemoth: A Legend of the Mound-Builders*, whose author's notes draw extensively on contemporary geological writing about the mastodon based on studies of fossil remains. The plot concerns a battle between humans and a single, monstrous mastodon who has survived the extinction of his species. Mathews indirectly acknowledges Indigenous sources for this tale; he admits to having adopted the titular figure from Delaware and Upper Cree stories about conflicts between earlier humans and megafauna, known to him from transcriptions by Ross Cox and Thomas Jefferson.[35] Yet Mathews's novel was written to support the then-popular settler myth of a prehistoric European-descended race that had preceded Indigenous peoples as residents of North America and which, believers insisted, had built the Indigenous burial mounds found across the continent; these supposed early Euro/Americans, not Indigenous people, serve as the tale's protagonists.[36]

Longfellow retains the name given the mastodon by Mathews, though he restores the story to the Indigenous context. Yet even as the poem cites the legend, it asserts that the mastodon's prehistoric threat is nothing compared to the present historical impasse; the real danger is "the breath of these Saxons and Celts, like the blast of the east-wind." The extinction metaphor is carried forward, in the poem, by the vehicles—the steamboat and the caravan—transporting those clamoring Europeans westward. In place of the geological climate change understood by nineteenth-century scientists as the primary cause of species extinction, Longfellow's poem identifies social and cultural climate change—strikingly conveyed in the "whitening" of the desert sands—as the cause of an undeniably anthropogenic extinction, underscoring the inseparability of natural and social history. Whereas most instances of the "vanishing Indian" trope place responsibility for remembering Indigenous presence with white settlers—as in Jackson's "melancholy reflections"—Longfellow's poem assigns this responsibility instead to the objective testimony of the rocks. (It may, in this sense, be regarded as an early example of Anthropocene poetry.)[37]

Yet the poem, on the whole, tends toward resigned lamentation rather than protest—or rather, it situates lamentation as its (largely inert) mode of protest. After marking the chief's presence, the speaker reverses perspective, pressing the starving masses of Europe against the Omahas' right to the land based on a numeric calculus of asserted need rather than the fact of long-term presence and relation. Indeed, the symbolic weight of Indigenous presence decreases as the Europeans disperse themselves over their lands; by the end of the poem, the figure that conveys Indigeneity has been displaced from ground to air—the smoke of the wigwam, blown westward by European breath—echoing centuries of theft of Indigenous land. As signaled by its repeated interjections ("O"/"Ah!"/"Hark"/"Ha!"), the poem apostrophizes its subject, displacing him from the historical present even as he is retained in earthly memory. Longfellow's poetics, in this sense, accomplishes what a dynamic reading of the footprints resist. As Willis observes, Longfellow's eventual disillusionment at American encroachments on nature led him often to represent both nature and, crucially, the Indigenous cultures with which he habitually aligned it, as "glorious ruin[s]."[38] Read in the mode of the ruin, the Driving Cloud's footsteps become fossilized once again, indexing not animate but post-animate nature. The fossil, like the ruin, is rarely complete and no longer functional; it operates as the memory of vitality rather than the thing itself, positioned as material for contemplation rather than action.

Even as they press the claims of the Omaha chief, the fossilized footprints ultimately work the same way.

The self-enclosure of the ruin is mirrored by the social practices that guided the reception of Longfellow's poetry—what we might identify, with Virginia Jackson, as *lyric reading*. The historical process that Jackson identifies as the lyricization of poetry constitutes "the shift from many verse cultures articulated through various social relations ... to an idea of poetry devoted to the transcendence of those relations."[39] Jackson, citing a poem that may be an earlier example of Longfellow's ichnophilia—his 1838 blockbuster "A Psalm of Life"—sees Longfellow as a pivotal figure in this transition. Though the poem's connection to the Connecticut Valley footprints is by no means as firm as it appears in "To the Driving Cloud," at least one critic has interpreted the poem's best-known line—"footprints on the sands of time"—as a direct allusion to prehistoric footprints preserved in sandstone, since otherwise the image would lack any duration.[40] The footprints, like the fossil tracks, convey an image of action remembered; yet Jackson argues that the notoriously nonspecific exhortation in "A Psalm of Life" ("Act! Act! in the living present") converts the didactic instruction of the traditional psalm, its elaboration of specified rules for living, into a vaguely instructive observation regarding the spontaneous overflow of feeling into generic action—transmitted, through the "footprints," heart to heart. As Jackson notes, "Longfellow's 'Psalm' was made for all possible purposes, because it could be adapted to 'any fate' at will."[41] The footprints can go anywhere—and for that reason, they lead nowhere. Lyricization challenges the potentially dynamic effect we might want to ascribe to traces of material presence and/or nonhuman agency in literary writing, insofar as lyric reading tends toward the reabsorption of nature, however material or geological, into affirmative but inactive circuits.[42]

Lyric reading, as Jackson assesses it, organizes the way the impress of history, geological and social, on "To the Driving Cloud" is received. While the poem denaturalizes Andrew Jackson's account of Indigenous extinction, underscoring its settler-driven causes, that exposure is ultimately contained within the process of lyric reading as a mode of reading for the *feel* of poetry. The poem's exposure of the anthropogenic agency behind Indigenous extinction, that is, confers a kind of agency on its reader that is finally no more specific than that of "A Psalm of Life," where "action" and "feeling" spiral through time in a self-confirming loop. Deciphering the testimony of the rocks, both the Massachusetts sandstone and the whitening desert sands of the Great Plains, the superimposed footprints in "To the Driving Cloud" relocate that testimony within a self-referential temporal fold where what is gained from the moral education of reading the rock record is finally not a blueprint for action, but a lesson in the desirability of moral education.[43]

Distributed Geology and Material Memory

The forms of moral education the fossil footprints provided for white settlers were multiple. Though one "moral" reading of the footprints views them as a geological *memento mori*—remember you must die—another assessment, which Edward Hitchcock began developing in the 1840s, moved in a different direction: also remember, you *may not*. This caveat is not quite as triumphalist as it might at first sound; the capacity to survive across eons is not only a testament to the success of humans but also potential testimony to their perpetual fallibility. This shift in emphasis results from changes in the framework in which Hitchcock read the footprints, moving away from the "tree of life," the organic metaphor he earlier employed as a means of grappling with the past presented in the footprints, and toward the mechanistic model indexed in Charles Babbage's *Ninth Bridgewater Treatise* (1837–38). Hitchcock's incorporation of this mechanical model made room for an increased attention to the mobility, malleability, and vitality of inorganic as well as organic material.

Babbage, a controversial Cambridge mathematician and inventor now recognized as an early pioneer of the computer, composed his own unauthorized addition to the eight official *Treatises on the Power, Wisdom and Goodness of God* exploring the contributions of different sciences to natural theology commissioned by the Earl of Bridgewater. Annoyed because his Cambridge colleague and rival William Whewell had remarked in his *Treatise* that there had been no positive moral contribution made by mathematics, Babbage sought to illustrate the possibility of using math to discern the unity and beauty of the Divine Plan, in part through tracing the cosmic implications of the principle of action and reaction. Matter, he asserted, was permanently affected by motion, which effectively never ceases: once sent into the air, the energy that carries a given sound remains even after the sound itself has ceased to be heard. The principle applies to liquids and solids as well, so that "the solid substance of the globe itself, whether we regard the minutest movement of the soft clay which receives its impression from the foot of animals, or the concussion arising from the fall of mountains rent by earthquakes, equally communicates and retains, through all its countless atoms, their apportioned shares of the motions so impressed."[44]

The deep memory of the earth, Babbage notes, is too subtle to be perceived by ordinary human senses but might be tracked mathematically: were there a being who enjoyed perfect command of mathematics, he observed, it would be able to follow and potentially to predict the course of all motion—though even this being, "however far exalted above our race," would come nowhere near the intelligence of the Deity. The legibility of the past and the predictability of the future in this model have led commentators such as Alan Liu to view Babbage's computational theology as a largely deterministic one, with the fate of the universe effectively scripted in advance. But it may actually be more flexible, more open to chaos and contingency. As Tina Young Choi argues, "Babbage's account focuses on change, on the shifting paths, extinctions, and redirections that result from 'altered physical circumstances,' all of which a superior providential plan, like a superior computational one, can accommodate."[45] Divinity, that is, signals not a rigid refusal of flux and contingency but a supremely advanced ability to cope with it.

Hitchcock first linked Babbage's speculation on matter's memory to the footprints in his 1844 "Report on Ichnolithology, or Fossil Footmarks," published in Silliman's journal. The report punctuated a lengthy review of data gathered thus far with a nod toward some of the "valuable morals" that the field provided. First among these was the proposal that ichnology "shows us that the most trivial movement of ours may make an impression on the globe that shall be brought out ten thousand years hence with unimpaired freshness—that shall in fact be immortal." Hitchcock goes on to posit that the fossil tracks are "almost a realization of the ingenious thought of Prof. Babbage, founded on the principle of action and reaction, that oft-cited declaration that 'the air is one vast library, on whose pages is written all that man has ever said, or woman whispered; while the waters and the more solid materials of the globe bear equally enduring testimony of the acts we have committed.'"[46] The promise of immortality, the time-defying evocation of freshness: Hitchcock's geologic framing of this oft-cited passage from Babbage in the 1844 report approaches Longfellow's "footprints on the sands of time," establishing ichnology as a site for the transcendence of time, perhaps the ultimate location of human mastery. Babbage's thinking is positioned by Hitchcock as a guarantee of the permanence of human action—so much so that Hitchcock feels the need to balance this affirmation by pointing "human ambition" to "a lesson of an opposite character" reflection in the official Bridgewater Treatise composed by William Buckland.[47] Buckland there points to the triviality of the kind of motions that bring about the objects of ichnological study, conspicuously opposing the geologizing of the unexceptional everyday action—walking in mud—to the dramatic events that Man thinks will bring historical significance, like going to war. "The proudest monuments of human art will moulder down and disappear," Hitchcock adds, "but while there are eyes to behold them, the sandstone of the Connecticut valley will never cease to remind the observer of the gigantic races that passed over it."[48] Though Hitchcock here underscores the insignificance of human history, his reference to observing eyes makes room for geologists to posit a kind of compensatory fantasy in their ventures across deep time. Geology alone, Hitchcock asserts, holds the key to the "almost immeasurable past": "And is it strange that the geologist should manifest a deep and even enthusiastic interest, when he discovers and attempts to describe these archives of new, unknown, and peculiar animals that peopled the world untold ages before man became its possessor? . . . The solid strata reveal to him the history of those ages, so near the birth of time, with all the distinctness of yesterday; and he finds the laws by which Jehovah governed the universe then, engraved, like those given at Sinai, upon tablets of stone."[49] Nineteenth-century geology's inclination to "moral education" finds its way into Hitchcock's 1844 report, identifying geologists as, in essence, prophets rivaling Moses as they reveal the will of the divine carved into the rock record.

The report sets up Buckland's reflections as an "opposing" corrective to the potential excesses of hubris opened by the suggestion of human immortality. But Babbage's system also implicitly posits its own built-in check: the kind of impression one makes cannot be known or tracked in advance; nor can it be controlled or erased. Babbage suggests toward the end of his chapter that the fact that the earth will record *all* actions, good, evil, and in-between, ought to give us pause about the impact of our deeds. This dimension of his thinking becomes clearer in Hitchcock's later return to the Babbage principle in his 1858 volume *Ichnology of New England*. There, his concluding reflections, which he identifies as "curious speculations," expand the claims from the 1844 report to underscore the operation of the will alongside the taking of action: "the slightest action of ours, *even the most unnoticed decisions of our wills*, may make an impression on the globe, which will endure, and may be read, as long as the earth exists."[50] Babbage is not directly quoted in this version, though he is referenced in a footnote. Instead, Hitchcock walks through the making of fossil footprints meticulously in order to illustrate his claim. Pointing to some of the plates of fossil tracks reproduced in the volume, he describes in extensive detail how they reflect not just the presence of prehistoric birds and insects but also the specific muscular actions they took to make particular impressions legible to the trained geological eye across vast spans of time. Instances in which the tracks veer from a straight path, he declares, show that

> this change in the animal's course must have required the use, and the increased or diminished action, of certain muscles in its legs. We have, then, in these curved tracks, certain evidence of the peculiar action of the Adductor, or Gastrocnemian muscle, or all of them, together, in the leg of a small bird; nay, of a small insect; perhaps ten, perhaps fifty, perhaps a hundred thousand years ago! Still further, that muscular movement implies a previous action of the animal's will, and that implies, as we now know, an electric current inward along the sensor nerve, and outward along the motor nerve. With the register before us of the decision of an insect's will, made fifty thousand years ago, and the corresponding movement in the muscles of its legs, who will dare to say that any action of ours, or any operation of the human mind, will certainly be so lost that it may not reappear in all its freshness ten thousand ages hence![51]

Hitchcock's minute description of how a footprint happens maps the motion of the body in almost exhaustive detail. Even as he locates the movement itself in a specific set of muscles, though, he shifts focus to mark its origin in "the decision of an animal's will." This extension of the durable "moral" implications of fossil impressions from the afterlife to the inner life reflects his developing conviction that thought counted as a kind of action and, hence, could also have lasting material effects. Thought, in this light, possesses geological as well as moral significance.

This detailed description of the connections between thought or will (animal or human), the "electrical" structure of the nervous system, and the muscles of the body as they made contact with the then-plastic sandstone, alongside his previous account of the subsequent climatological and geological forces, the perimineralization, sedimentation, and erosion that led to the chance event of an impression's stony preservation, sketches a version of distributed agency across deep time. Even as Hitchcock distinguishes between human or animal vitality or mental activity, the physical body, and the material world; that is, his description underscores the necessary connections between thought, energy, flesh, mud, minerals, sediment, wind, and water, underscoring this preservation as a collaborative or compositional process as well as a matter of chance or speculation. The lithic materialization of such traces of action, unlike the certainty of Babbage's system, is only a possibility, a matter of chance, dependent on a number of factors beyond one's own agency. The preservation of such traces is as much outside one's control as the erasure thereof. Yet for Hitchcock, just as for Babbage, this possibility provides a kind of moral oversight on action, since anyone's false moves may be preserved and read until the end of the earth.

The potential preservation of human action across earthly time (the word *immortality* is notably absent in Hitchcock's 1858 revision) also implies the unforeseeable moral, geological, and environmental consequences of any move we might make—even, potentially, of any given mindset. In this sense, Hitchcock's "curious speculations" anticipate similar reflections on the environmental implications of distributed agency as it has been taken up in recent years by new materialist ecocritics, who address "the world's phenomena [as] segments of a conversation between human and manifold nonhuman beings," as Serenella Iovino and Serpil Oppermann explain.[52] In new materialist thought, distributed agency has both analytic and ethical implications based on the recognition that we can't entirely know the effects of our own actions. To affirm the potential durability of human action is also, paradoxically, to recognize a certain limit to human agency or at least the necessity of conscious collaboration with other material entities, as that action is thrown into a deep future that humans can neither predict nor control.[53] The diminishment of autonomous human agency amounts for new materialists—as for Hitchcock—to an intensification of human *responsibility*: the human inability to fully predict or control the behavior of the nonhuman world, they assert, might lead us to generate deeper ethical reflection on the potential implications of any given action or relation.

The "moral lesson" Babbage's thinking provoked for Hitchcock, sketched in the scientific papers, was brought out most emphatically in his 1851 series of lectures, *The Religion of Geology and Its Connected Sciences*. There, in a chapter titled "The Telegraphic System of the Universe," he again cites Babbage's illustration of "the principle of reaction" in reference to the fossil tracks as he declares, "Not a footprint of man or beast is marked upon [earth's] surface, that does not permanently change the whole globe"; though we are unable to see most of these, he insists, "in a higher sphere there may be inlets of perception acute enough to trace [them]."[54] Hitchcock expands on this claim by quoting in full a paragraph added to the second edition of Babbage's *Treatise*, which contends that the planet itself will remember the inhumanity of the slave trade:

> We cannot regard the glowing language of Babbage an exaggeration, when he says, "The soul of the negro, whose fettered body, surviving the living

charnel-house of his infected prison, was thrown into the sea to lighten the ship, that his Christian master might escape the limited justice at length assigned by civilized man to crimes whose profit had long gilded their atrocity, will need, at the last great day of human accounts, no living witness of his earthly agony: when man and all his race shall have disappeared from the face of our planet, ask every particle of air still floating over the unpeopled earth, and it will record the cruel mandate of the tyrant. Interrogate every wave which breaks unimpeded on ten thousand desolate shores, and it will give evidence of the last gurgle of the waters which closed over the head of his dying victim. Confront the murderer with every corporeal atom of his immolated slave, and in its still quivering movements he will read the prophet's denunciation of the prophet king."[55]

The "glowing language" that Hitchcock quotes extensively here is not followed up with respect to its subject matter. Indeed, on the whole, *The Religion of Geology* is not centrally concerned with the Atlantic slave trade or the slave system in general.[56] (Nor, for that matter, was Babbage's book: the passage in question was added to the second edition of his *Treatise* in 1838, after Babbage read of slave ships dumping their human cargo overboard.) Though it is not analyzed at any length, the slave system appears, in both texts, as the historical apotheosis of the circuits of evil with which the authors are concerned, while the image of a recording earth is posited as a rebuke to and redress for a legal system that fails to arrest these practices.

Hitchcock's lifelong descriptive and speculative engagement with fossil tracks does not resolve into anything like a clear cosmology, much less a plan of political action responding to slavery or other social problems. Yet in the context of something like a "religion of geology," his adaptation of Babbage's reflections on the slave trade instantiates a different framing of the matter of race than the one geology was usually employed to shore up in this period. In evolutionary thought, *race* constitutes a kind of species-belonging, a form of biological life marked by a set of hereditary traits moving forward across time. In this sense, it is subject both to extinction and to arrest under the sign of fixity—two modes of racial stratification which drew upon the geological imagination. Yet while the becoming-biological of race situated geology as a key part of modern biopower, Hitchcock's citation of Babbage instead endowed the science with a lively mechanicity that diverges from the biopolitical; it proposes a vision of the historicity of race not as a kind of autonomous life or heritable biological matter, but as a material relation, manifested in a series of abusive transactions whose vibrant affective residue is archived by the inorganic material of the earth.⁵⁷ Hitchcock's geologizing of the passage from the *Ninth Bridgewater Treatise* opens a view of race not as narrowly biological but as broadly ecological, determined, in this instance, by the brutality of the slave system in its dehumanizing construction and disposal of Africans as "waste material." In this speculative, re-godded guise, ichnology again serves to illuminate the persistence of a presence that denaturalized the violent histories involved in the construction of Man.⁵⁸

Reminiscing, in the October 1891 *Atlantic Monthly*, on his correspondence with Emily Dickinson, Thomas Wentworth Higginson remarked that her "handwriting [was] so peculiar that it seemed as if the writer might have taken her first lessons by studying the famous fossil bird-tracks in the [Amherst College] museum," which Hitchcock had founded.⁵⁹ As Virginia Jackson notes, Higginson manages, by means of Hitchcock's by-then-outdated theory, to make a connection between Dickinson and the figure of the bird, which stood in, through the nineteenth century, for lyric poetry.⁶⁰ Aligning Hitchcock's collection of fossil tracks with the feminized figure of the songbird-poet, Higginson also implicitly registers the lyrical self-containment that had come to characterize moral readings of the rock record. By the time Higginson wrote, the tracks were generally understood to have been made by several species of dinosaur. The new framework departed from the continuity between past worlds and our own implicit in Hitchcock's avian-origin theory, replacing it with an emphasis on radical alterity that masked the late nineteenth-century fascination with the fierce, imperial potential of the Mesozoic lifeworlds evoked by the dinosaur.⁶¹ (Though the British paleontologist Thomas Henry Huxley speculated on a possible evolutionary link between birds and dinosaurs as early as the 1860s, the connection did not become widely accepted in the field until the late twentieth century.) The new investment in dinosaurs thus took up the mode of geological fantasy exhibited in Andrew Jackson's address, positioning geology as a means of naturalizing and depoliticizing colonial conquest. Against this developing saurian obsession, the deliberate anachronism of the "bird-tracks" reference appears as both feminizing and quaintly antiquarian, folded tidily away from the fiercer geology of the present—a version of femininity that critics past and present have frequently (and wrongly) imposed on Dickinson.

For Hitchcock and his contemporaries, though, the Connecticut Valley fossil tracks were vital and somewhat messy objects, despite scientists' best attempts to clean them up and set them in order. The footprints both tamped down existing geochronologies, along with the racial hierarchies that had become entwined with them, and kicked up prehistoric dust: bringing the distant past alluringly close, blurring the edges of scientific knowledge with the seductiveness of wonder, suggesting a co-agential model that intensified human responsibility to the world, and pressing against—though not unsettling—those hierarchies. The multiplicity of these inferences speaks to the way vibrant geologies—geologies that emphasize the mobility of matter as well as its active memory—can cut athwart the alternating uses of deep time as a limit to the human and scaffolding Man. Hitchcock's writing on the footprints suggests an ethics inspired by the inhuman that might be extended toward intrahuman accountability. But as he makes only glancing contact with the human contexts this mode of ethics might speak to, it remains without a politics to guide it. Longfellow gestures toward a form of land memory that might contest settler presence thereon. The geologic lyricism of his poem, however, converts that possibility into a self-confirming lament; drained of their dynamism, in the end the Driving Cloud's footprints might as well be displayed on the walls of the Amherst museum.

Positioned at the "exciting intersection between science and flights of fancy," fossil tracks point toward another perspective on the material world: a more speculative engagement with matter and time that, in the case of the Connecticut Valley tracks, opened onto radical revisions of agency, new mediums of remembrance, even alternate takes on the historicity of race. As evidence of creatures long extinct, they contributed to the geologic mapping of the earthly past; but as traces, as *specters* of those creatures, they *insisted*, per Shaviro's framing, on something more, a "quasi-material" presence that encounters time otherwise. The more vibrant geology they inspire generates compelling glimmers of worlds otherwise, future as well as past. It remains to be seen, though, how these might connect with our own.

matters of spirit 4

vibrant materiality and white femme geophilia

WHAT IS THE SPIRIT OF STONE? Giorgione Willoughby, the narrator of "The Amber Gods" (1860), a short story by Harriet Prescott Spofford, a white, New England–based writer, is determined to find out. Though the profoundly narcissistic Giorgione, called Yone by her family, is interested in how precious stones look on her, she takes even more pleasure in speculating about how they feel. Rhapsodizing over a set of aquamarine jewels given by her father to her cousin Louise, Yone brushes over their surface properties and gets right to the heart of the matter: the oceanic reverie that she locates at the center of the gemstone—a "dream of vast seas, a glory of unimagined oceans."[1] The stone possesses a music that she can feel but can't quite find. As she envisions the elegant crystallization of the gem—"each speck of it floating into file with a musical grace, and carrying its sound with it"—she concedes that such strange sounds might not sound like music to human ears; but that, it turns out, is part of the attraction, the "charm of gems": "You feel that they are fashioned through dissimilar processes than yourself,—that there's a mystery about them, mastering which would be like mastering a new life, like having the freedom of other stars."[2]

Yone's interest in the material qualities of gemstones is not unusual in itself; the ability to talk about the "fashionable science" would have been de rigueur at the Willoughby mansion in the mid-nineteenth century. Her decidedly sensual investment in that composition, though, goes beyond those expectations. She seems to have taken William Buckland's insistence that geological education should bring its devotees into "immediate contact with events of immeasurably distant periods" all too literally.[3] For Buckland, such contact would catalyze an interest in the science that would ultimately confer morally beneficial effects—effects that made geology a subject suitable for the education of young ladies. In Elizabeth Stoddard's 1862 novel *The Morgesons*, for instance, Cassy Morgan, the novel's adolescent protagonist, is told to study geology when she arrives at a new school. "It is important," Miss Black, her teacher, affirms, "for it will lead your mind from nature to nature's God."[4] Cassy finds the subject boring, complaining that "it never inspired me with any interest for land or sea"; eventually, she throws her book at the head of a classmate, earning a punishment from the teacher.[5] Geology holds more interest for Spofford's Yone—the mere mention of fossils sends her into rhapsodies—but it likewise has no effect on her moral constitution. Indeed, geologically inflected flirting plays a part in her brazen seduction of Louise's longtime paramour, the painter Vaughn Rose. Though their marriage turns out unhappy and childless, geology permits her to situate herself in queerer genealogies: "In some former state," she muses, "I must have been a fly embalmed in amber."[6]

Such genealogies fell athwart the gender- and repro-normative frame that nineteenth-century childhood educators assigned to the study of geology. As we saw in chapter 1, the science was celebrated for its ability to steer boys and young men away from idle entertainments and toward more robust and potentially profitable activities. Its importance "to females," according to Almira Hart Lincoln Phelps, a writer of popular science textbooks, was likewise informed by gender norms: it "enlarge[d] their sphere of thought, rendering them more interesting as companions to men of science, and better capable of instructing the young."[7] Granville Penn's *Conversations on Geology* (1828) modeled this capacity by couching its lessons in the form of a mother, Mrs. R., setting a course of geological study for her two children, Christina and Edward.[8] Though Mrs. R. entices her children to the subject by describing geology as a "romantic science," she insists on approaching it through facts and systems, dismissing speculative theories of earth out of hand. These, she tells her children, are based in imagination rather than observation, the work of unscientific men; and though it is "not a little amusing, to follow them in their fancies and their waking dreams," they should be regarded as poetry rather than science.[9] The learned ability to distinguish poetry from science, like the careful curtailing of wonder discussed in chapter 3, formed no small portion of the moral education geology was intended to impart, and in Penn's *Conversations*, this was a lesson best begun at mother's knee. Routed through women, geology could help to secure and improve the future, but only if it was properly controlled, purged of fancy and caprice.

This sort of control was central to the workings of biopower. According to nineteenth-century theories of impressibility, mothers were capable of transmitting more than verbal instruction to their children. An understanding of minds and bodies as impressible, highly susceptible to external influences that shaped both health and character, dominated nineteenth-century physiology. Impressibility theorists were particularly concerned with women's bodies, which were held to be capable of physically transmitting such influences to their children during pregnancy as well as morally influencing them during childhood. As Kyla Schuller observes, the anxieties clustered around impressibility created a demand for "sensorial discipline," allying science and sentimentality, that was keyed to race.[10] The belief in racial improvement through positive impressions was not limited to whiteness; as we will see in chapter 5, the African American writer and physician James McCune Smith embraced the Black body's openness to geologic impressibility as a counter to racial determinism. Yet what Schuller calls the "racial common sense" developed by white scientists and sentimentalists maintained a belief in the superior sensitivity, and hence the greater vulnerability, of white bodies, particularly those of white women, which demanded both stimulation and discipline to ensure that the properly raced future would arrive as planned.[11] Imaginative flights of fancy and wayward sensations placed that future in peril as they threatened to pervert lines of descent. Even geological instruction required regulation, lest the attempt to fathom the nature of rock wander too far astray. Yet given the breadth of the subject—the vastness of its timescale, the magnitude of the planet on which it focused—there was certainly room to wander. Even the most disciplined of scientists, as we saw in chapter 3, permitted themselves an indulgence in imagination from time to time—indulgences that could overly excite the impressible. The young Emily Dickinson seems to have been one such case. Dickinson studied geology at Amherst Academy, where Edward Hitchcock's *Elementary Geology* was the textbook. In an 1845 letter to her friend Abiah Root, she lauded its expansiveness, along with her three other subjects, Mental Philosophy, Botany, and Latin: "How large they sound, don't they?"[12] Dickinson, of course, would go on to write some of the queerest poetry in the nineteenth century, much of which reveals the impress of a wild geological imagination—precisely the kind of thing Mrs. R., concerned as she was about the need to distinguish science from poetry, sought to avoid.[13]

The disciplinary impulse that regulated geologic instruction resisted the enticements of what Jeffrey Jerome Cohen names geophilia: "matter's queer, inconstant and promiscuous desire to affiliate with other forms of matter, regardless of organic composition or resemblance to human vitality."[14] Formal study of the rock record, which insisted on an orderly logic of geohistorical progression, sought to counter the potential unruliness catalyzed by geophilia.[15] This insistence, as we have seen, owed more to natural theology than to the material evidence contained in that record. In this sense, the road that Stoddard's Miss Black marked out from geology to God was actually a circular path, beginning and ending with religious discipline even as the science insisted on its secularity. Yone's attempts to find the music in stones testifies to a geophilic and decidedly un-Christian investment in the spirit of matter that defied such efforts to keep geology on the straight and narrow—an investment that anticipates contemporary new materialist thought. Something like the spirit of matter—the quality that animates it—emerges in new materialist discussions of the *matter-energy* shared by geologic and human bodies alike. Attention to matter-energy permits humans to comprehend themselves in geologic terms—to understand, in Manuel de Landa's phrasing, what they "have in common with rocks and mountains and other nonliving historical structures."[16] The pull of matter-energy thus enacts a kind of mattering of the human, an awareness of oneself outside the bounds of species and the hierarchies associated with Man. Though there is nothing inherently spiritual about the concept of matter-energy, its alignment with being-in-common—the capacity to overcome boundaries and generate something like unity—renders it amenable to spiritualization. Indeed, Jane Bennett frames it in explicitly nonsecular terms: her *Vibrant Matter*, something of a new materialist Bible, closes with an adaptation of the Nicene Creed: "I believe in one matter-energy, the maker of things seen and unseen."[17] As the motor of geophilic desire, matter-energy moves across forms, inorganic and organic, bringing substances into relation, coaxing affinities from differing materialities.

But the geologic mattering of the human body can be radically estranging; regardless of what humans might have in common with rock, "dissimilar processes" of composition and organization remain. For those invested in the coherence of the self, the sanctity of the soul, and/or the progressive temporality associated with Man, the process of mattering indexes the vulnerability of those forms. In this sense, it recollects the discontinuity marking the modern understanding of life as Foucault explains it in *The Order of Things*: "the living being wrap[ped]... in its own existence."[18] If the material body is understood to constitute the existence in which the living being is wrapped, the *mattering* of human beings, even as it opens onto "new life," may also activate the deathly limits with which life is understood to be perpetually surrounded. It is not surprising, then, that racial difference is so often proximate to nineteenth-century invocations of geological humanity insofar as race, as Foucault would come to argue, was central to modern biopower as a set of strategies for managing and maximizing life while designating certain populations as deathly threats to its continuity. The excessive carnality attributed to these populations aligned them with the supposed stasis of the material world against the optimized and future-directed life assigned to those designated as fully human.

This chapter addresses forms of geophilic fantasy constructed in some nineteenth-century white women's experiments with geological existence—embodied experiments that take place outside the bounds of Christianity and exceed the decorum of proper white femininity. It consists of two case studies, the first of which focuses on two feminists associated with the Spiritualist movement, Elizabeth M. Foote Denton and Annie Denton Cridge, the wife and sister, respectively, of the geologist William Denton, discussed in this book's introduction. The trio collaborated in an extended project of unorthodox research in both geology and archaeology that was enabled by the psychometric abilities—the capacity to "read" the energetic residues of an object's experience—claimed by the women. The second case returns to Spofford's Giorgione Willoughby, dwelling on her sensual fascination with amber, which she views as an imaginative and potentially material conduit to past geological epochs. Yone's intimacy with the amber that makes up a necklace of carved beads depicting pantheistic gods facilitates the construction of a new understanding of sex, departing from nineteenth-century sexual typologies. In both cases, though, geologically impelled dissolution stops at the border of race: whiteness is maintained even as gender and sexuality are transformed. In this sense, they suggest that the figure of "woman," which is, Schuller argues, an effect of racial thought, may remain so even when she moves, geologically, toward the inhuman.[19] The chapter thus continues the consideration of the question posed in chapter 3: whether the vibrations of the geologic inhuman can participate in the undoing of intrahuman relations of exploitation.

Visceral Geology: *The Soul of Things*

The belief in physical connections between geological matter and human bodies is nothing new. In Greek and Babylonian mythology, humans are created out of clay; the Book of Genesis declares that they were made from "the dust of the ground." When the geological timescale enters the picture, though, things become a little more complex. Human bodies and deep time don't seem to connect well. As the paleontologist Steven Jay Gould declared, "an abstract, intellectual understanding of deep time comes easily enough—I know how many zeroes to place after the 10 when I mean billions. Getting it into the gut is quite another matter."[20] When the two do manage to connect, deep time doesn't always sit well in the body, even for those who, like Gould, locate their intellectual and professional lives within it. John Playfair's emphasis on the giddying effect of the "abyss of time" is complemented by Charles Darwin's confession of "deep but ill-defined sensations" upon observing the "boundless" plains of Patagonia, which "bear the stamp of having lasted, as they are now, for ages, and there appears no limit to their duration through future time."[21] Engaging with the depths of the earth in the depths of the flesh—getting deep time into the gut—is felt as disorienting precisely because, as I have shown, the planet's antiquity, since the inception of the concept, has been posited as something external to Man, a kind of exoskeleton that helps to secure his status as a modern, scientifically aware subject. What we might call visceral geology, embodied contact with geologic concepts or their material/mineral instantiations, effectively folded Man in upon himself, a structural collapse that opens the body to experiencing itself not as form nor even as flesh, but as matter. Gilles Deleuze and Felix Guattari describe this state as "the unformed, unorganized, nonstratified or destratified body and all its flows."[22] Darwin's "deep but ill-defined sensations" constitute one likely response; Yone's "having the freedom of other stars" is another.

Both of these responses appear in *The Soul of Things*, the three-volume report, published between 1865 and 1874, of the psychometric research collaboration between Elizabeth and William Denton and Annie Denton Cridge, also joined, in the second and third volumes, by Elizabeth and William's son Sherman. (The first volume was published under William and Elizabeth's dual authorship, though the second and third were credited to him alone.) William Denton accomplished much of his geological research by conventional means. He is best remembered for having verified the antiquity of what would turn out to be hundreds of fossilized remnants of Miocene-era life at Rancho La Brea, now known as the La Brea Tar Pits, in southern California; when he died in 1883, he was serving as lead geologist on a protocolonial exploration of New Guinea sponsored by an Australian newspaper.[23] At the same time, along with Elizabeth and Annie, he was active in Spiritualist circles and a firm believer in psychometry, a capacity Elizabeth and Annie both claimed, though William did not. The trio were also actively involved in feminist and progressive causes. Annie published a Spiritualist and reformist newspaper, *The Vanguard*, along with her husband Alfred Cridge; Elizabeth and William met when they worked at the Cincinnati-based phonetic newspaper, *The Type of the Times*.[24]

The synthesis of science, Left Utopianism, and Spiritualism that marks William Denton's career as a geologist was more than a century old by the time the trio's work began. Geology helped to shape the Modern Spiritualist movement from its outset; Emanuel Swedenborg, the eighteenth-century Swedish philosopher who inspired much Anglo-American Spiritualist thought, began his career as a geologist, and that knowledge filtered down through the mid-nineteenth-century writing of the "Poughkeepsie seer" Andrew Jackson Davis. Davis was widely recognized as the father of Modern Spiritualism, a diffuse movement devoted to communication with the departed, which believed that spirits returned not only to console their loved ones but to educate and elevate society at large. For Davis, the history of the earth served to illustrate that "matter contains within itself an eternal Law of progressive activity" corresponding to the development of the human spirit. The "useful" discoveries of geology held a distinctive place in the scientific unfolding of this spiritual truth, as the science made possible the development of knowledge about the material world to which humanity's spiritual progression would correspond: it "contributed to promote liberal views and speculations, and ha[s] greatly dispersed the darkness that has so long concealed the origin and primitive history of our earth."[25]

Like Davis, William Denton was invested in geology's capacity to "disperse the darkness," not least as a lever for displacing the oppressive weight of Christian tradition. He believed, as we saw in this book's introduction, in geology's capacity to reveal "progress [as] the law of our globe" and oriented his lectures on geology, published as *Our Planet, Its Past and Future*, toward this end.[26] The book's affirmation that the planet was developed "for man" transposes natural theology into a Spiritualist register, eschewing the Christian god; instead, the material universe was depicted as self-regulating—not the result of intelligent design, that is, but of an intelligence intrinsic to matter as such.[27] *Our Planet* rode geology all the way to a future utopia in which the planet and humanity would evolve in tandem toward perfected states, the former eventually ridding itself of volcanoes and earthquakes and substantially increasing the size of its landmasses, while the latter would abandon war, slavery, and bigotry, instead focusing its energy on projects like developing new methods of agriculture to feed a greatly increased population.

Although *Our Planet* contained only a brief hint of his Spiritualist convictions, William's belief that geology illuminated a brighter future led him to align the science with the quest beyond the visible world. Psychometry is formally distinct from Spiritualism as such insofar as it does not address the spirits of the dead; rather, it is based on a belief that physical residues of past experience, thought, and sensation accrued on objects over time, congealed by means of "radiant force," an energy said to suffuse and connect all matter. Mediums sensitive to these residues could "read" them and report their content. William first encountered psychometry in *Buchanan's Journal of Man*, which reported on Joseph Buchanan's experiments with "impressible persons" who claimed that they could detect the register of human character upon objects touched by the original subject.[28] Buchanan imagined psychology, aided by psychometry, walking "hand in hand" with geology as the two sciences unfolded the history of the earth and its human inhabitants. William Denton went further, asserting that psychometry could also support geological research, filling in the aporia in earth history created by gaps in the fossil record.[29] Indeed, the geological timescale meant that rocks were better conveyers of their own history than objects in the human world could be, as they had more time to absorb impressions. "Radiant force" thus comprised a form of matter-energy that transcended time, enabling the "rock record" to be read as sensuous object.

As was the case for Spiritualist mediumship, the receptivity associated with psychometric reading was considered a feminine capacity, the result of "woman's superior sensitiveness" on both mental and physical levels.[30] This sensitivity was modeled on the affective receptivity, or "sympathy," ascribed to the impressible sentimental subject. Typically white and educated, the sentimental subject was deeply attuned to the emotional transmissions of others and hence to the deeper moral truths that emotions conveyed.[31] Psychometers and spirit-mediums, often called "sensitives" within the Spiritualist movement, simply intensified this capacity by virtue of an amplified physical predisposition to affective and sensory porosity, described by Buchanan as the possession of "mental cultivation and refinement, acute sensibility, delicacy of constitution, a nervo-sanguineous temperament, and a general predominance of the moral and intellectual organs."[32] Not all "sensitives" were women, though many of the men who practiced mediumship were said to have a feminine constitution. Yet white women's bodies were believed to be most sensitive, inclined to what Buchanan termed the "sympathetic perception of character"; when balanced by the "cultivation and refinement" that Buchanan also stressed, they were also said to be more capable of a properly selective porosity.³³ The valuation of feminine sensibility as a regulatory and reparative force points to a gendered division in the figures overrepresented as the human, to recall Wynter's phrase. Apart from (and alongside) the bounded figure of Man, a porous and prototypically white feminized figure emerged, in sentimental culture, as the model for and archivist of a "humanizing" emotional sensitivity, bearing primary responsibility for affective labor.³⁴

The porosity of mediums, like that of other impressible subjects, was a risky matter. Psychometers were therefore encouraged to regulate their impressibility rather than be overtaken by transmissions from another realm. Most of the readings of matter recorded in *The Soul of Things* are affectively moderated and orderly. Each case study hews to the empirical method followed by geologists: first closely descriptive, then cautiously correlative. When Elizabeth is handed a piece of anthracite coal, for instance, she describes in detail a warm, boggy forest typical of the Carboniferous period, from which most of the planet's coal originates. William then interprets and contextualizes this report, declaring that "such examinations have given me a more vivid and, at the same time, what seems to be a more correct idea of the Carboniferous era."³⁵ Even as psychometry was said to accelerate scientific understanding of the "rock record," the moral implications of psychometric geology exceeded those of ordinary versions of the science. Psychometry's moral value lay not only in its expansion of knowledge but also in its surveillant capacities. As the psychometers learned more about the physical world through traces left on impressible matter, they also reminded other humans that they, too, were leaving impressions behind that would testify to their conduct and character. The possibility that these might later be read augmented Hitchcock's warning about the lasting impressions one's action might leave. "The very rocks drink in the character of the people of the country in which they exist," William warned, "and give this out again ... to the sensitive psychometer."³⁶ Psychometric geology's ability to access these records revealed a planetary panopticism that demanded continuous human self-regulation and consequent improvement.

But just as an ostensibly "improving" education in geology could go astray when the lure of matter's energy became too strong, psychometric contact with geological matter could come closer than was deemed advisable. Psychometric reading, the Dentons explain, is a full-body experience, involving "sensing" as well as "seeing." Sensing enabled the psychometer to penetrate the depths of a scene. When reading in this mode, her body mingled with the object and its sensations, a mingling which could escalate to the point William describes as the "complete identification... of the psychometer with the thing psychometrized, or the animal with whose influence it is imbued."[37] This is the point at which psychometric geology becomes visceral. In a section dubbed "The Autobiography of a Boulder," for instance, Elizabeth narrates, in first person, the sensations of a rock, beginning with its surfacing: "Mercy! What a whirl things are in.... This is the strangest feeling I ever had... I am sent up whirling in a torrent of water, mud and rocks; not sent out, but it is puff, puff, whirl, whirl, all of us flying round together."[38] The account progresses through the boulder's eventual glacier-borne drift across the globe, during which Elizabeth remarks on the disorienting, uneven slowness of the movement and, shivering, draws her seat up to the stove. The rock finally comes to rest on the side of a mountain—at which point, Elizabeth is physically too exhausted to continue and breaks off contact.

In volume 2, William lauds the way the multisensory capacity of psychometry maintains the liveliness of past worlds: "The cheek felt the hot breath of the volcano as easily as the ear heard its sullen roar; while the tongue tasted the sweet fruit or the luscious juice, and enjoyed their flavor almost as much as if the psychometer had been present in proper person."[39] Sensory data remains scientifically valuable; William uses the boulder's autobiography, for instance, to explicate the geological history of Wisconsin, where the rock specimen is from. Yet the excitement of embodied contact with the geological past—the hot breath of the volcano on the cheek, the lusciousness of the juice on the tongue—outstrips its utility. *The Soul of Things*' clarity of moral purpose wavers as the psychometers' readings vary in intensity and closeness. Shifting into the embodied experience of an object muddles the orderly work of stratigraphic correlation, instead emphasizing the waywardness of sensation in an interconnected material world where matter connects, geophilically, to matter as well as to mind. As the boulder, Elizabeth, after becoming frozen into a vast sheet of ice, reports, "my connection with the ice seems to give me a connection with all the country round, so that now I can see for many miles."[40] Object exchanges can also bridge time and space, as evidenced in the conflicted testimony given by Elizabeth in response to a meteorite fragment; initially, she reports, "I am a very large—a monstrous beast.... My proportions are huge," before reverting to the expected experience of being "a great rock... flying, going, going."[41] William deduces that the mixed report is the result of specimen miscegenation: the piece of meteorite Elizabeth held had previously been wrapped up in a bag along with a fossilized mastodon tooth and "had apparently imbibed considerable of its influence."[42]

The ability of objects to "influence" one another complicates the understanding of the material world put forth in the introduction to *The Soul of Things*. There, each object is seen to possess its own sensory history, inscribed by radiant force and sedimented in linear time. Objects, that is, are understood as individuals, like the human spirits cherished and perpetuated in Spiritualism's hyper-individualist theology, while each object's radiant force builds upon itself like geological strata. But objects that "influence" one another are more difficult to put in place; their conglomerated layers of sensation tell a different story. The messiness, or queer meshiness, of the cases in which the discrete identity of objects slides into the sensory networking of matter develops a picture of the material world as weirdly and unpredictably imbricated. Elizabeth's intimacy with the boulder narrates the uncomfortable experience of the human subject as it becomes viscerally aware of this intermeshing. Her contact with the boulder's sense-memory is both exhaustive (condensing millions of years into the experience of an hour or so) and exhausting; being-boulder, moving swiftly across deep time, wears her out.

William's description of sensory psychometry as "complete *identification* with the object" does not quite match the psychometers' narratives; the accounts they produce from such experiences outline something closer to an affective and sensory mingling or embodied geo-affective duality. Elizabeth speaks, mostly, as the rock, living its sensations and movements, even as she retains a degree of physical control as a human, managing to pull her chair closer to the fire to counter her sense of glacial cold. She affirms her conscious presence throughout the encounter, translating lithic sensation into human language and correlating its perceptions with her own experience; of the miles-wide glacier, she observes, "How insignificant a tree or a house would be in its pathway!"[43] Nevertheless, it remains difficult to know precisely where the rock ends and Elizabeth begins—whether, for instance, the "strange feeling of passiveness" she describes is the rock's, or her own.[44] The disorientation and estrangement that marks this account recurs in numerous other cases of sensory reading. After contact with a fossil mastodon tooth, Elizabeth reports with satisfaction on the sweet succulence of the Pleistocene plant she is eating; yet when asked if the taste is savory in human terms, she makes a face and pronounces it "sickish" and unpleasant. The feelings resulting from these moments of sensory estrangement fail to dissipate immediately after contact with the object is broken off. Traveling with an ice-age glacier leaves Elizabeth tired out and shivering; her response to the flowing lava enlivened by contact with a volcanic fragment is so strong that, as William remarks, "the feeling of terror, produced by the sight, did not entirely pass off for an hour."[45]

Annie is likewise "terribly" affected, after contact with another fragment of meteorite, by the sensation of traveling headlong toward a moon, and breaks off contact in a panic prior to impact.[46] Such visceral geological experiences make the psychometers conscious of sensations that cannot be easily reaggregated into what it means to be a subject, a person, or even alive. *The Soul of Things*, to be clear, does not suggest that object-channeling makes the body into the objects channeled: Elizabeth, as the boulder, is not actually turning to stone. Yet in channeling the rock's experience, she is confronted with the experience of being rocklike, of being radically other than human. Within its deep-temporal history, nothing familiar offers itself as a point of orientation. As the geological object, in its radical difference, asserts itself psychometrically, the medium's body is forced on some level to become aware of what it has in common with it—to recognize itself as strange, or estranged, matter. The object's "queer, inconstant and promiscuous desire to affiliate with other forms of matter" exceeds the mind's ability to regulate the body's materiality.

In marked contrast to the generally positive inflection that the interconnectedness of matter is given in contemporary new materialist thought, though, overclose encounters with the nonhuman in *The Soul of Things* are, in the end, more disturbing than wonderful. When geological objects come too close, when what Timothy Morton affirmatively calls the "mesh of strange strangeness" feels too estranging, the psychometers expend considerable energy trying to get back to the world as they know it: a harmonious and progressive universe led by reasoning creatures with the capacity for unceasing self-improvement.[47] They seek the position of the distanced, objective observer to restore their status as thinking, rather than merely sensing, beings; even when immersed in nonhuman sensation, they struggle to interpret, not simply to describe, these experiences—speculating, for instance, that the fragments causing otherworldly sensations "must be meteoric." That process activates the biopolitics of cultivation and refinement as well, as they attune themselves to the kind of racial "common sense" that situates whiteness at the forefront of civilization. In volume 1 of *The Soul of Things*, Elizabeth is given a fragment of ancient pottery found on Starved Rock in Illinois, so named, William reports, because of "a legend which states that the remnant of an Indian tribe was starved to death upon it, being surrounded by their enemies."[48] She proceeds to channel a human consciousness which seems, at first, likely to be that of a member of that legendary tribe who, she reports, is hiding from a group of "shout[ing] and whoop[ing]" Indians. After they move away, she remarks: "I have come to the conclusion that they were not after me [the person whose experience she is channeling]. I seem to have too much calm, steady thought for an Indian."[49] William speculates that the unknown consciousness must have been that of a pioneering white "explorer," distancing it from the possibility of Indigeneity and implicitly allying it to the psychometric investigators as versions of the geologic conquerors we saw in chapter 1.[50] Elizabeth's casual demotion of Indigenous people to subrational status recalls the toggle between the anthropological and geological machines that we saw in chapter 2 of this book. "Indians" are at once animalized, making noise that does not qualify as language, and, like the rocks and fossils she channels, deemed capable of sensation but not sensibility.[51]

If psychometric geology, as I have been suggesting, bears some resemblance to new materialist philosophy, it is especially visible in Jane Bennett's intriguing consideration of hoarding. Bennett comprehends those who hoard objects as possessing a similar extraordinary sensitivity; they are, she proposes, "good at reception: [their] perceptual filter is unusually porous."[52] As a result, they are especially responsive to geo-affect, the vibrancy of vibrant matter, which she terms "inorganic sympathy."[53] The transmaterial agency accessed in inorganic sympathy pulls the subject away from itself; hence, Bennett proposes, it might operate as an impetus to the ethical project of learning to feel other than human, or at least to understand the "non-human components that are always at work inside" human social practices.[54] Despite their ostensibly progressive feminist and Spiritualist politics, however, this is not a project that Cridge and the Dentons embrace. For them, the spirit of matter must be arranged for the benefit of (certain) humans; accordingly, they retreat into a bounded whiteness characterized by rationality, sensibility, and cultivation, interposing Indigenous bodies between themselves and the "indeterminacy" of the inorganic world.[55] This retreat creates a disruption in the flow of matter-energy, a kind of deadening of the subject's response to the object. The impulse to hierarchize, to order the mesh of geophilic waywardness, expressed in the Christian insistence on the mental progression from "nature to nature's God" ends up shaping the Dentons' Spiritualist geology as well, although their destination is not divinity, but the perfectibility of Man's overrepresentation.[56]

All the World's History: "The Amber Gods"

"The Amber Gods," published when the then-unmarried Harriet Prescott was just twenty-four years old, proposes a picture of what the history of sexuality might look like were it not organized around the biological imperative intended to further the "progress of the race." The most familiar nineteenth-century figures of sexual deviancy—the onanist, the spinster, the hysteric, and, by century's end, the homosexual—are all dissidents from the developmental trajectory that upheld that reproductive imperative, governing the child's growth into a responsible, procreative adult.[57] In contrast, Spofford's Giorgione Willoughby might be said to follow a geological imperative. Yone is in many ways a typical "bad girl," unabashedly sensual, casually amoral ("I'm not good, of course; I wouldn't give a fig to be good," she declares in the story's first part), and profoundly self-centered, situated in highly conventional opposition to her dutiful, virtuous cousin Louise, whose happiness she thwarts by seducing Vaughn Rose.[58] Yet Yone's passionate investment in amber, and in the geological past it recollects, gives an unconventional turn to her waywardness, triggering a tangle of relations between animate and inanimate objects that gesture toward another kind of deviation: not only is Yone indifferent to the hallowed figure of the child, that most cherished object of the reproductive future, she even wanders away from the form of the human altogether. This inhuman turn partly discomposes the clichéd love triangle around which the tale is ostensibly organized. And though most readings of the story view it as chastising Yone for her immorality—she dies at the end of the tale, implicitly of hereditary syphilis, and is transformed into a specter in the story's last paragraph—it is more equivocal with respect to her investment in matter.

If "The Amber Gods" can be said to possess a "morbid, unhealthful tone," as one reviewer complained, it could not be blamed on the romance between Louise and Vaughn Rose, childhood sweethearts reunited after Rose's return from a European sojourn. As if underscoring their wholesomeness, they enact a springtime ritual in which Rose brings Louise a yearly shower of mayflower blossoms because, he says, their sweet, pale blooms remind him of her. The ritual connects the pair's attachment, through an imaginative dilation upon the mayflower, symbol of a gently rejuvenative nature, to the foundation of the nation; they envision the blooms as "fair little Puritans" greeting the "winter-worn mariners of Plymouth" and helping to renew their spirits as they herald the return of spring.[59] But the force of Yone's investment in amber generates a wilder and more eventful comprehension of the natural world than do mayflowers, which she considers "useless things."[60] The stone in question enters the story in the guise of an intricately carved necklace depicting a series of gods and goddesses, which Yone's father brings home along with the aqua-marina. Though she admires the clear blue stone, Yone greatly prefers the amber; the former captivates with its intimations of a mysterious elsewhere—the "glory of unimagined oceans"—amber, as a fossilized substance, carries with it an else*when*. When Rose wonders at her investment in amber, she turns the question around on him:

> "Just tell me, sir, what is amber?"
> "Fossil gum."
> "Can you say those words and not like it? Don't it bring to you a magnificent picture of the pristine world,—great seas and other skies,—a world of accentuated crises, that sloughed off age after age, and rose fresher from each plunge?"[61]

Amber opens onto an epoch of wild exuberance, a differently paced, less predictable, more sensual, and more capacious time, which charges the present with its allure.

Yone's understanding of the prehistoric past as a time of "accentuated crises" reflects the belief that geological events in the deep past were more intense than those at present—a theory that originated with Georges Cuvier, who, as we saw in chapter 1, correlated geological and cross-cultural textual evidence to support his theory of a global catastrophe, probably a flood.[62] Cuvier's belief in the flood was not a matter of biblical literalism, as has sometimes been claimed, but this line of thought, belatedly dubbed catastrophism, could and did make room for biblical correspondences with geological history for some of its adherents.[63] Yone's catastrophism is also infused with sacred time, though not in the Christian sense. Sacred time, set apart from the ordinary, designates the time of origin—the "pristine," or prehuman, world—which recurs in religious rites and festivals, something like the iteratively self-renewing world of her amber-induced vision.[64] Indeed, it could be said that the geological is Yone's religion, though different, again, from the Christian implications of the science narrated in Hitchcock's *Religion of Geology*; instead of scientific teachings, the sense of the spiritual here is derived from the eventfulness of geological matter. Planetary renewal, here, is something far different from the springtime rejuvenation of Louise and Rose's mayflower ritual; a world that "slough[s] off age after age" and rises "fresher from each plunge" comes closer to Georges Bataille's unsentimental conceptualization of nature as a "squandering of living energy and an orgy of annihilation." Nature's squandering signals an eroticism defined against the reproductive drive; nature is not bound to that drive, but rather comprises "a movement which always exceeds the bounds, that can never be anything but partially reduced to order."[65]

Amber itself is direct evidence, for Yone, of the wild geologic past's resistance to order. Departing from the stable, generational propagation of sameness, amber's genesis is associated with moments of transformative passion animated by an inspired materiality that evokes the supernatural. What she calls the "witchery of amber" is "that it *has* no cause,—that all the world grew to produce it, maybe,—died and gave no other sign,—that its tree, which must have been beautiful, dropped all its fruits,—and how bursting with juice must they have been—".[66] This account of amber positions it as the very emblem of nature's "squandering," as the stone takes the place of the reproductive process that the fruits should have catalyzed. As the lingering trace of primordial jouissance, amber survives through the ages as the lithic preservation of a supremely annihilating pleasure, a case in which, as Nigel Clark and Kathryn Yusoff put it, "survival ... is but a fortuitous side effect of exploring and elaborating upon the play of the earth itself."[67] The deliberate perversion of amber's origin story in the fruit-dropping account suggests Yone's intentional embrace of this form of pleasure above conventional modes of reproduction. Rose interrupts to remind her the trees that generated amber were not fruit-bearing but "coniferous," according to the contemporary scientific consensus. Yone is aware of this; indeed, just a few sentences earlier in her narrative, she has identified amber as a product of resin, "fine solidified sunshine" "ooz[ing]" from the pores of trees.[68] Her deliberate substitution, in the conversation with Rose, of fallen "fruits ... bursting with juice" seems to be designed to underscore the waywardness at amber's origin, its turning aside from the expected order. Even when she acknowledges the official geological version of amber's genesis, she narrates it in sensual terms: "I like amber ... because I know how it was made, drinking the primeval weather, resinously beading each grain of its rare wood, and dripping with a plash to filter through and around the fallen cones below."[69] The account of amber as a dripping, plashing prehistoric substance again depicts it as departing from its proper place to pursue its own gratification. Amber signals another mode of production for Yone: accidental and unforeseen, and valuable precisely for that reason.

Vaughan Rose senses the threat to the modern order lurking beneath this kind of geophilic waywardness. In response, he declares himself disgusted by amber, calling it an "unnatural" thing with "no existent cause."[70] Rose finds amber hateful because "when we hold it in our hands, we hold also that furious epoch where rioted all monsters and poisons—where death fecundated and life destroyed,—where superabundance demanded such existences, no souls, but fiercest animal fire."[71] Rose's illustration of this "furious epoch" corresponds in substance to Yone's depiction of a "world of accentuated crises"; the two imagine the planetary past roughly along the same lines, but for Rose such worlds are horrifying rather than exhilarating. Amber, in Rose's view, brings the present into direct contact with an undirected, undifferentiated existence, obliterating the individual and the capacity for spiritual elevation in its insistence on the merely carnal. This, perhaps, is why he conjectures that the elaborately carved gods and goddesses on Yone's string of amber beads represent "all those very Gnostic deities that assisted at Creation."[72] In the Gnostic account, the creator-deities generated a world bound entirely to material existence, without avenues for transcendence. Yone enthusiastically aligns herself with the world of the amber gods, a version of her pristine world. When Rose admits that amber suits her, she responds, "you mean that it harmonizes with me because I am a symbol of its period. If there had been women, then, they would have been like me,—a great creature without a soul, a—".[73] Rose cuts Yone off before she can finish this heretical thought, but her synthesis of geology and Gnosticism avows both the "voluptuous" substance of amber and the ferocity of "animal fire"—two inhuman incarnations alongside which this "great creature" feels at home.[74]

Yone locates the ecstatic inhumanity of planetary forces in other spaces and other species as well. She lauds the "fierce heat and panting winds" of the tropics, which she credits with having rebirthed her during a visit to a Caribbean island taken for the sake of her ailing mother's health. Yone recalls, "all that tropical luxuriance snatched me to itself at once, recognized me for kith and kin; and mamma died, and I lived."[75] In its tropical manifestation, nature, instead of propping up the family form, possesses the power to kill the mother and substitute itself as an alternate lineage. As with Yone's conviction that in a "former state, [she] must have been a fly embalmed in amber," she is enfolded, here, in a queer planetary genealogy intensifying her susceptibility to inhuman energies—heat, wind, sunlight, rain. Impressibility manifests otherwise here: affected by planetary forces, Yone does not improve or degenerate in ways that might be transmitted to her offspring, but turns away from biological reproduction altogether. The purpose of planetary forces, on this view, seems to be the production of pleasure, and the "accentuated" time of the geologic past manifests this principle vividly.

Such paeans to inhuman pleasure periodically interrupt Yone's account, given on the morning of her wedding to Rose, of her victory in the heterosexual love triangle, accomplished in part by her strategic loan of the amber necklace to Louise after learning of Rose's antipathy. In the midst of the romance, these repeated digressions from the human bring about what Gilles Deleuze and Felix Guattari would term a molecular sexuality, moving "beyond the anthropomorphic representation that society imposes on th[e] subject."[76] The molecular names a level on which "sexuality" breaks free not simply of the obligation to biological reproduction but also of the perpetual reproduction of a field marked out by the distinction between idealized and deviant typologies, such as the familiar set of perverse figures we saw at the outset of this section. The geologic eros of Spofford's tale suggests a practice of pleasure that thwarts the regulation of "impressible" white feminine bodies by the shadow of the reproductive future. Yone's strange, inhuman intimacies, so far astray of both law and norm, move otherwise: establishing erotic pathways between light and flesh, finding fulfillment in a plash of dripping resin. Along with new forms of pleasure, they are inventing new worlds—or, rather, reviving old ones. "What if in some piece of amber an accidental seed were sealed; we found, and planted, and brought back the lost aeons?" Yone wonders.[77] This fantasy of return resists the progressive model of planetary history and its depiction of the geological past as the necessary (but lesser) precursor to a more highly developed and superior mode of existence. The possibility that the age of accentuated crises remains suspended within the present, available for reactualization, undermines the conviction that human civilization constitutes the apex of geohistorical development, proposing that it might, instead, be simply another incident in the long and lively history of the planet.[78] Yone's geologic eros allies itself with this liveliness, embracing prehistory's potential to activate the undoing of Man.

But the tale complicates this geophilic vision by underscoring the narrowness of its focus. Yone's preoccupation with geological time and inhuman worlds is pointedly juxtaposed to an indifference bordering on inhumanity to an unnamed Asian girl enslaved by her great-grandparents, from whom her family stole the amber necklace. Her account of the girl—which she recounts in order to explain her possession of the beads—is riddled with gaps: the girl's name, her ethnicity and place of origin (Yone refers to her both as "Asian" and "islander" and describes her skin color variously as "brown" and "black"), and even her language (composed, Yone insists, of "short screeches and shouts") all remain unidentified. She enters into Willoughby family lore when Yone's slave-trading American great-grandfather brings her, along with the carved amber beads that she carries everywhere, home from a voyage without explanation. His wife tries to train the girl as a servant, but she refuses to adapt, wreaking havoc on their costly possessions and even trying to set the house afire. After Yone's great-grandmother, fed up with the girl, commands her husband to send her back, she becomes the sole survivor of a shipwreck, which Yone's family imagines her causing through a spell cast by her amber beads, and she somehow ends up in Europe. Many years later, Yone's father, on a visit to Italy, encounters her in service as lady's maid to the daughter of a wealthy Fiesolan family. He ends up marrying the daughter despite the now-elderly Asian woman's fierce opposition. After her death some years later, the family sends the beads to Yone's father in defiance of the woman's wishes.

Yone's unsentimental attachment to the inhuman seems to have desensitized her both to the girl's story and to colonization and slavery in general. Her sensational depiction of the unnamed girl underscores the developing nineteenth-century designation of Asians in America as irredeemably alien. Iyko Day documents the "destructive, unrepresentable abstraction attributed to Asian bodies" in the United States; assigned the racialized, immutable qualities of "inscrutability, perpetual foreignness, transnational mobility, and flexibility," they are ultimately deemed wholly excludable, in contrast to the African-descended enslaved, whose alienness is violently enfolded into the economy.[79] Yone's identification of the Asian girl as a "slave," albeit one who is ultimately cast out of the nation, touches on both forms. Enslaved African-descended people are susceptible to retention, in her view, though not of inclusion into the category of the human. She approaches the Atlantic slave trade, on which her family's wealth is founded, as neither an ethical nor an economic/political problem but an aesthetic question, declaring, in a rhapsody on the luxuriance of Caribbean foliage, "What a blessing it is that the blacks have been imported there,—their swarthiness is in such consonance!"[80] (Rose counters this comment with a compressed critique of New World history, saying simply, "No—the native race was in better consonance."[81])

Ignorant of or unconcerned with histories of Indigenous displacement and African captivity, Yone overlooks their local manifestation in the Asian girl's enslavement, which contains within it hints of the sexual trauma that structures those histories. The gaps in the girl's story raise a number of questions: why the great-grandfather brought her home in the first place and why, in contrast to her fierce resistance to domestication while living with the Willoughby family, she remains with the Italian family for decades.[82] Yone conjectures vaguely that an "ague" the girl contracted during her journey shook the "effervescence" out of her.[83] Behind this account, though, the fusion of colonial and sexual violence offers pregnancy as another possible explanation, the result of sexual abuse by Yone's great-grandfather and the reason for his wife's sudden ejection of the girl from her house. Her devotion, as an older woman, to the young Italian girl—she even gives the girl the amber necklace, her most cherished possession, though she takes them back upon her marriage to Yone's father—also suggests a possible blood tie between them, the consequence of the Fiesolan family's adoption of a child fathered by the elder Willoughby. (This possibility introduces the specter of incest into the story, which would account for the woman's furious, yet futile opposition to the marriage to Yone's father.) In this case, Yone would, without realizing it, be the Asian girl's granddaughter.[84] Yone insists on her own whiteness, although an ethnically inflected one, as she affirms herself "streak[ed]" with "little weak Italian traits." But that insistence may shield an unconscious awareness of her own problematic family history. (She remarks, in response to her father's insistence on marrying her mother over the Asian woman's objections, "The Willoughbys are a cruel race."[85]) Even as Yone seeks out a new mode of liveliness in geologic existence, she holds on to the biopolitically maximized and privileged form of life to which she has been assigned.

The family's posthumous theft of the Asian woman's necklace, in this light, echoes and underscores the earlier theft of the body that is, as Hortense Spillers has argued, the constitutive condition of enslavement.[86] The shadow history of slavery and sexual violation that presses through the gaps in Yone's account of her family's acquisition of the amber beads introduces another form of time into the narrative, though it is one that cannot be easily reconciled with the sensual persistence of the deep past associated with amber. As chapter 3 suggested, fossils can be considered geologic revenants, suffusing the human world with what Yone regards as a generative untimeliness; their presence-ing of the past resembles what Steven Shaviro identifies as the quasi-material insistence of Jacques Derrida's figure of the specter. But the persistent presence of historical violence associated with the Asian girl's story recalls another aspect of the Derridean specter: its demand for justice. Derrida identifies the specter as the "Thing" that "looks at us and sees us not see it even when it is there," its unceasing gaze demanding recognition and a reconceptualization of justice as ongoing.[87] As a "Thing," a figure beyond the human, the specter may track the kind of dehumanization recounted in this story, slavery as thingification. The Willoughby family describes the girl in just this way; as they reflect on the shipwreck, "they framed many a wild picture of the Thing enchanting all her spirits from their beads about her." These wild pictures convey the recognition, however reluctant, of the injustice of the girl's captivity, as they imagine that enchantment sinking the ship, drowning the great-grandfather and her other "capturers."[88]

As adjunct to the Asian-girl-as-specter, distinct from their geologic function, the amber beads evoke another kind of history, one that is untimely, belated, a time "out of joint." The specter, Derrida observes, is what "secretly unhinges" the living present, recollecting its responsibility to those who are not there, those whose deaths are counted as part of the cost of modernity, sacrificed to maintain the life of Man.[89] Two nonlinear temporalities—one indexing geologic plenitude, the other historical trauma—manifest in and around the amber necklace. Yet the coincidence of these temporalities does not in itself resolve their divergence. The lack of reconciliation becomes clear in the celebrated ending of Spofford's tale, when Yone herself becomes a ghost. The second, much briefer, section of the story, set ten years after the first, takes place at Yone's deathbed, where she lies dying of an unnamed disease, likely hereditary syphilis (looking up at portraits of her ancestors, she reflects that she has inherited "all their little splendor ... their sins and follies; what slept in them wakes in me"). Her marriage to Rose has not been a happy one, and she remembers an overheard exchange between him and Louise which suggests that they will reunite after her death. Strangely, despite her illness, she suddenly rises from the bed, declaring, "Out, out into the gale! Back to my elements!" and passes down the stairs. Only when she sees the discrepancy between the chime of the hall clock and the position of its hands does she realize her condition, revealed in the story's celebrated final line: "I must have died at ten minutes past one."[90] The gap in time points us back to the aforementioned gap between geological and human-historical temporalities; as if to underscore their lack of reconciliation, the string of amber beads, which Yone, on her deathbed, had been clutching, breaks just before she dies, and the beads tumble onto the floor.

"The Amber Gods" closes on a fracture in time—a rupture that leaves open the question of how the broken corporeality of historical trauma can be justly brought together with the pleasurable intensities and transformative suspensions that mark Yone's geologic erotics. In evoking the former, Spofford's tale does not simply disavow the latter, despite Yone's own culpability within that history: the fantasy of geologic plenitude is too generative—too productive of pleasures apart from kinship, modes of production other than childbearing—to jettison. The "new life" Yone associates with crystallization, the "accentuated crises" that the time of amber opens to view—these mark out forms of eros that depart from the biopolitical deployment of sexuality. But within a present built upon chattel slavery and colonization, that departure risks becoming another instance of geology's claim to political innocence. Spofford's tale poses, and yet leaves open, the question of whether geology can bring about new worlds in which pleasure is not only reinvented but also redistributed.

The Soul of Things and "The Amber Gods" alike bear out Almira Phelps's conviction that geology would render the young ladies who studied it "more interesting"—though not quite in the way she meant. Their exuberant experiments with geologic ways of knowing and visceral travel across deep time propose a radically expanded timescale for the decidedly queer practices that Elizabeth Freeman names "sense-methods." Sense-methods, for Freeman, are ways of living time otherwise: "tap[ping] into other rhythms, other ways of feeling like [one belongs] to a history, and/or other modes of arranging past, present, and future, that will foster new forms of being and belonging."[91] The utopic future that the Dentons harnessed psychometric research to bring about, the lush "lost eons" that Yone imagined taking root in the present, constitute some of these other arrangements. Geophilia, on this view, appears as a sense-method that involves the channeling of geologic matter through the body to make room in time for these new forms.

The expansive effects of the geologic turn away from the human seem, however, to be balanced by a corresponding contraction when these subjects turn back to intrahuman relationships: a retreat to whiteness and the raced hierarchies that uphold it. The Dentons' experiments naturalize and obscure this retreat, leaning on scientific authority to distance a raced otherness they associate with the nonhuman world; Spofford's tale, ending on a temporal fracture, makes it visible, though in doing so it leaves the question of "belonging" up in the air. In this sense, I propose, it can also point us toward a comparable suspension in contemporary new materialist thought, which also might be understood as a kind of sense-method in search of intimacy beyond the human. Chapter 3 asked whether something like a geologic theory of distributed agency might generate the more capacious ethics that new materialists seek; but the answer was equivocal at best. The white feminine experiments explored in this chapter end in much the same place. Bennett observes, in her essay on hoarding, that new materialism—a field dominated, in its early years, by white feminists—might be understood as an experiment in taking material agency, the "'call' from things," seriously, in the hope of catching a "glimpse, through a window that opens, of lively bodies unparsed into subjects and objects."[92] Yet as she goes on to acknowledge, "this window has a rickety sash liable to slam shut without warning."[93] That sash, I contend, is its insufficient comprehension of the "human" whose status it hopes to trouble. Without a stronger understanding of how racial hierarchy has historically stratified the matter, geologic and otherwise, to which it seeks to respond, its vision will remain partial, underattuned to intrahuman injustice and unable to access the new genres of the human and modes of belonging that might emerge in the interstices of Man's overrepresentation.

the natural history of freedom 5

blackness, geomorphology, worldmaking

EVEN IN LIGHT OF THE FOSSIL'S FREQUENT PRESENCE in antebellum American writing, the one that appears in the introduction to Frederick Douglass's *My Bondage and My Freedom* (1855) comes as something of a surprise. The introduction's author, James McCune Smith, a New York–based physician, activist, and writer who often composed pieces for Douglass's newspaper, found in the fossil a universal right to freedom. McCune Smith depicted Douglass, in his youth, "peering and poking about among the layers of right and wrong, of tyrant and thrall, and the wonderfulness of that hopeless tide of things which brought power to one race, and unrequited toil to another, until, finally, he stumbled upon his 'first-found Ammonite,' hidden away down in the depths of his own nature, and which revealed to him the fact that liberty and right, for all men, were anterior to slavery and wrong."[1] The reference to the ammonite, the fossilized remnant of a form of marine mollusk that went extinct 66 million years ago, points back toward McCune Smith's comparison, earlier in the same paragraph, between *My Bondage and My Freedom* and the autobiography of Hugh Miller, a Scottish geologist, who, McCune Smith claimed, resembled Douglass in his curiosity about the moral nature of the world.[2] In his autobiography, *My Schools and Schoolmasters*, Miller describes coming upon an example of the prehistoric mollusk on a walk by the ocean. The fossil's beauty and its connection to the "ancient world," Miller declares, launched his lifelong investigation of geology.³ McCune Smith's adaptation of this scene to Douglass's life implicitly figures long-sedimented social hierarchies as the layered rocks of Miller's seaside as it transposes material nature, where Miller finds his fossil, into the interior of Douglass's being. Drawing on geology's ability to furnish the voice of nature with a deep, epochal undertone, McCune Smith aligns the concept of natural rights, upon which this understanding of universal freedom was founded, with planetary time. Rooted in the "ancient world," the universal right to freedom not only preceded the historical imposition of slavery; it preceded human history itself.

Douglass's recognition of a right to liberty founded in external nature, a kernel of which was hidden within his own, kindles a process of personal growth that McCune Smith also figures as natural. Moving from Douglass's childhood through his liberation from captivity and into the present, where he has "raised himself by his own efforts to the highest position in society," McCune Smith explains this outcome through a theory of organic progression:

> Naturalists tell us that a full grown man is a resultant or representative of all animated nature on this globe; beginning with the early embryo state, then representing the lowest forms of organic life, and passing through every subordinate grade or type, until he reaches the last and highest—manhood. In like manner, and to the fullest extent, has Frederick Douglass passed through every gradation of rank comprised in our national make-up, and bears upon his person and upon his soul every thing that is American. And he has not only full sympathy with every thing American; his proclivity or bent, to active toil and visible progress, are in the strictly national direction, delighting to outstrip "all creation."⁴

Britt Rusert characterizes this passage as describing the "queer human-animal-vegetable alliances" rather than discrete biological species that structured McCune Smith's understanding of evolution. These alliances, she contends, challenge the anthropocentric norm that underlies both contemporary ethnographic thought and biographical narratives like Douglass's (organized, as she notes, around the "slave-becomes-man archetype").⁵ Outstripping all creation, Douglass demonstrates the limitlessness of Black progress, which surpasses not only the extant form of the nation but also that of the human itself. Even as McCune Smith's category-confounding reflection on Douglass's triumphant adulthood unsettles the human, his earlier inclusion of the ammonite in the story of Douglass's youth also enfolds the mineral within this queer alliance. Embedding Douglass's expansive growth in a geological time frame, McCune Smith keeps it vibrantly alive through the ages in a more-than-human world.

Freedom's ammonite, in McCune Smith's introduction, reorients the claim to racial innocence that structures the geology of Man. As we have seen, geology was seen to maintain a kind of political innocence by virtue of its concern with prehistoric lifeworlds and inanimate matter even as geological fantasy shored up the geographic and racial hierarchies associated with Man's overrepresentation as the human. McCune Smith's association of that matter and those lifeworlds with a universal and natural desire for liberty engages geology's putative distance from politics differently as it reduces the institution of slavery from "God-given" status to the purview of the merely human, which, unlike the immensely broader and older natural world, is capable of error. The fossil's innocence of race, that is, illuminates the guilty uses of that category in the service of overrepresented Man. In McCune Smith's hands, geology lent itself to what Rusert identifies as "fugitive science": the unleashing of scientific knowledges against their state-approved uses, toward resistance and freedom. Insofar as geology offered a deep-temporal corrective both to narrowly biological, hereditarian arguments about racial capacity and to the sedimented chronologies associated with the Western world's institutionalization of chattel slavery, the science's postulated preracial concerns could be put to novel antiracist uses. What we might, following Rusert, call *fugitive geology* opens a speculative window into other material processes, other times, other worlds, suggesting the subterranean possibilities and alternative practices of freedom that lay within our own.

Despite its alignment with the construction and maintenance of the figure of Man, geology did not only ossify nineteenth-century US racial hierarchies; rather, its revelation of what Samuel Metcalf called the "magnificent... unceasing transposition of matter, by which the surface of the earth is forever renewed" could also catalyze racial renewal.[6] In the hands of antebellum African American writers, geology was, paradoxically, livelier than biology—livelier, at least, than white supremacist biological thought, with its self-serving insistence on racial fixity. African American geological thought and geo-affective fantasy embraced the vitality of matter in motion to create new forms and futures for Black life. In the hands of the writers considered in this chapter, geological fantasy became a means of re-emplotting Black intimacies with the earth. The science's affiliation with self-improvement and uplift, along with its much-vaunted ability to "tell... directly of the thoughts and creative acts of God," could offer a foundation for models of Black manhood based on heroism, hard work, and faith.[7] At the same time, geology's focus on the mobility and agency of the inorganic world over time also suggested new forms that pushed beyond these models of manhood, expanding extant genres of the human—although the strategic avoidance of biology in these discussions limited their capacity to address the reproductive violence and consequent gender de-formation inflicted by the slave system.

I consider, in this chapter, how affective and speculative engagements with geology by African American writers functioned in proximity to questions of enslavement and Black freedom in the antebellum period. Following recent work on African American science by Rusert and Gordon Fraser, among others, I identify geology as a source of alternate Black worldviews, ways of understanding the earth as a space capable of gathering not just deep histories of freedom but also reenergized presents and alternate futures. An overview of articles about geology appearing in African American journals from the 1840s through the 1860s, documenting the Black press's participation in the national conversation about geology as well as some of the sources for African American geological fantasy, highlights their attention to the power of volcanoes and the processes of geologic worldmaking. These articles resonate suggestively against the familiar antislavery trope of the slumbering volcano, which, in the hands of Black abolitionists Douglass and J. Sella Martin, operated both as a symbol of Black heroic leadership and the source of alternate geologies and ecologies suggesting new genres of the human. Counterpointing the volcano trope, the chapter turns to an exploration of the ways geology shaped the writing of McCune Smith, considering both his environmental theories of race and his geologic figuration of Black energy over the longue durée. The vitality of Black thought and the immensity and intricacy of earthly forces comes together, in these writings, to (re)make the world.

What a Volcano Can Do

In 2009, exploratory drilling in the Krafla volcanic caldera in Iceland struck magma, making contact, for the first time in human history, with this subterranean substance. Nigel Clark, Alexandra Gormally, and Hugh Tuffen argue that this event might point us toward a speculative, geologically inflected revision of time, one that understands events as generating time rather than simply existing within its flow. "That we experience eventful time as *erupting*,

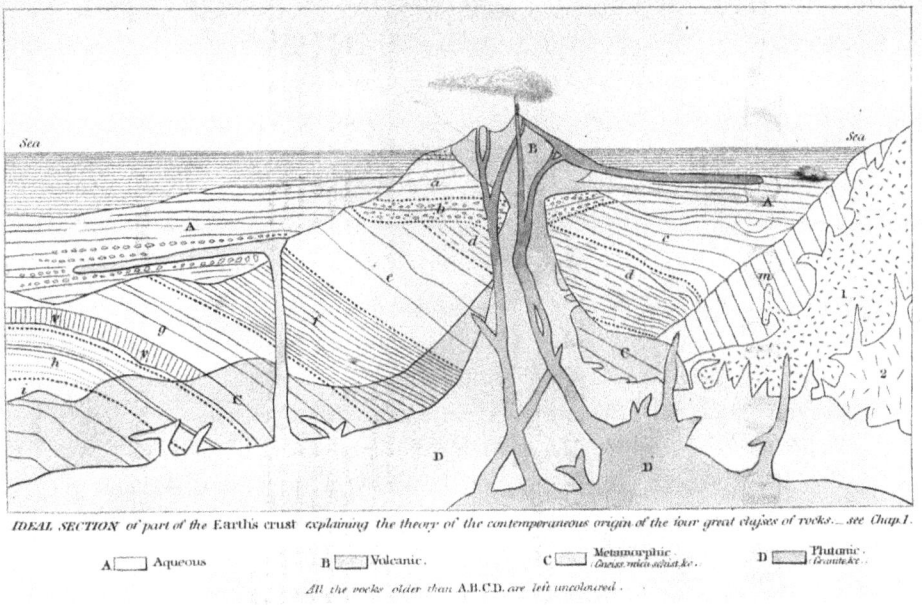

Figure 5.1. Frontispiece from Charles Lyell, *Principles of Geology* (2nd US ed., 1857). Source: Wikimedia Commons.

irrupting, interrupting suggests memories of those ruptures that our planet delivers now and again," they observe.[8] But geological fantasy has not, historically, required physical encounters with magma to engage in this sort of reshaping of time; descriptions of volcanism on their own sufficed to generate an understanding of time as irruptive. In the decades before the Civil War, popular interest in geological theories about the earth's interior grew. At the same time, antislavery sentiments mounted toward what many believed would be an inevitable eruption. The figure of the volcano would bring together these two developments, geologizing revolutionary feeling.

As theories of eruption evolved toward an assessment of volcanoes as release valves for pressures generated by the earth's interior, the geosocial imaginary channeled these to figure the conditions of revolution. Mary Ashburn Miller, tracking the evolving uses of volcanic metaphor in France during the revolutionary period, outlines a turn from repression to rebellion—from the volcano as figure for concealed dangers, employed to amplify calls for "vigilance and surveillance," to its embodiment of "revolutionary force, power, and passion," fires that burned for purification rather than destruction.[9] The volcano took a similar turn in US antislavery writing. Increasingly common after 1830, the metaphor was, as William Gleason notes, a strikingly malleable one.[10] In some contexts, volcanic eruption signified the immorality of the slave system, representing it as "cataclysmic disruption of the natural order," in Maggie Montesinos Sale's evocative phrasing.[11] In 1830, Abraham Lincoln referenced the "great volcano at Washington, belching forth the lava of political corruption."[12] William Lloyd Garrison inveighed against slavery as "a volcano of lust and impurity . . . throwing out its lava-tide of desolation and death, rolling over the land, blasting and blighting every green thing therein."[13] And in June 1861, when US troops were already massing in the capital, Frederick Douglass told a Rochester audience that "[Slavery] is not a Vesuvius which, belching forth its fire and lava at intervals, causes ruin [only] in a limited territory; but slavery is felt to be a moral volcano, a burning lake, a hell on the earth, the smoke and stench of whose torments ascend upward forever."[14] Yet the trope more often invoked a different relationship to the natural world, drawing on geological accounts that comprehended eruption not as an unnatural event but a necessary planetary mechanism required for the periodic relief of subterranean pressure.[15] In this light, it operated, as Gleason observes, to show that "in the face of white incalcitrance, violent insurrection is not only inevitable but also natural."[16] Antislavery rhetoricians drew on the geological, rather than moral, understanding of volcanoes to present slavery itself as an unnatural institution and to suggest that that institution, because of its repression of the natural rights of African Americans, would eventually blow up in the slaveholders' faces.

US-based writers adopted the volcano trope from its use in the late eighteenth century in reference to Haiti, both before and after the 1799 revolution. McCune Smith's "Lecture on the Haytien Revolutions" (1841) includes an oft-cited observation attributed to the Comte de Mirabeau, an early French revolutionary leader, concerning Haitian slaveholders' lack of concern over insurrectionary movements discovered in the summer of 1791: "The colonists slept upon a Vesuvius, nor were awakened by the first jets of its eruption."[17] US antislavery activists also seized upon the trope to describe the discontent among the enslaved elsewhere. In 1837, a *Colored American* article, "Letters from the West Indies," linked the dormant volcanos of Montserrat to the unrest fomented there by the "apprenticeship" system, which replaced slavery in the British colonies: "Traces of volcanoes, I am informed, are yet found in various places. These have ceased to burn for very many years, but the elements of another, a different kind, but not less fearful, still exist in its midst, and threaten to pour desolation through its whole social and political system. The apprenticeship is adopted here, and is heaping up materials and kindling a flame that will, I fear, break forth on that community in conflagration and ruin."[18] For US antislavery writers, the figure of the dormant volcano, as it concealed the "elements" within, lent itself to vivid depictions of the explosive passions of the enslaved. The anonymous author of "Letters from the West Indies" went on to detail the anger spreading throughout the island's Black population: "[A] bad spirit is excited by the vexatious treatment which they receive, the petty but severe aggressions which are made on their privileges and rights,—the last acts of the tyrant whose power is soon to be wrested from him. They are exceedingly restless and irritable."[19] The outside of the volcano concealed these passions from view, but anyone who understood its mechanisms knew that they would eventually manifest in a sudden eruption. Similarly, a report on the debates over slavery in the Virginia House of Delegates published in the *Liberator* in May 1832 noted that prior to these debates, "The inhabitants of our sister states of the South seemed to have long slumbered on the brink of a volcano, unconscious of the dangers to which they were daily and hourly exposed."[20] By the mid-1830s, Gleason points out, the figure of volcanic revolt had become so common that "at least one southern respondent felt moved to rebut the repeated insinuation: "It is not true that the South sleeps on a volcano—that we are fearful of murder and pillage."[21]

In antebellum Black and antislavery newspapers, the antislavery volcano trope circulated alongside popular reporting on geological research, including theories speculating about the earth's core and its link to volcanic eruptiveness. The number of articles about geology reflected the widespread national interest in the topic as well as the African American press's commitment to racial uplift. Geology, as a subject that improved the mind, the body, and the spirit, was ideally suited to this task; as the 1841 reprint of an article by Josiah Holbrook in the *Colored American* declared, its study would "diffuse knowledge over the globe ... increase wealth ... improve morals ... [and] promote religion," among other things.[22] Hence the appearance of geological theories about volcanoes in the Black press served a number of purposes; it was not simply a scientific screen for revolutionary desire. At the same time, the copresence of scientific and antislavery representations of volcanic activity points to the emergence of what Fraser identifies as an "emancipatory cosmology," a way of conceiving relationships between political matters and the matter of the world.[23] Even as geological fantasy sought to close the gap between "human" self-conception and the immense force and age of the earth, fugitive geology worked to correct the distorted conception of the human that permitted slavery to continue.

In February 1849, the *North Star*, a newspaper edited by Frederick Douglass, discussed a passage from Benjamin Silliman's writing under the title "Terrific Theory." In the passage, Silliman, observing during the drilling of deep wells that the temperature of the earth increases steadily the farther down one goes, conjectures that "the whole interior portion of the earth, or, at least, a great part of it, is an ocean of melted rock, agitated by violent winds."[24] In support of the theory's possibility, the article's author points out that Silliman, in good uniformitarian fashion, is "reasoning from causes known to exist." These causes turn out to be volcanic eruptions. The molten-interior theory, according to Silliman, "is ... rendered highly probable by the phenomena of *volcanoes*. The facts connected with their eruption have been ascertained and placed beyond a doubt. How, then, are they to be accounted for?" Rejecting the argument that internal combustion was responsible for volcanic eruption ("All the coal in the world could not afford fuel enough for a single capital exhibition of Vesuvius"), Silliman asserts that "we must look higher than this; and I have but little doubt that the whole rests on the action of electric and galvanic principles, which are constantly in operation in the earth."[25] The idea of the earth's molten core did not originate with Silliman, of course; yet his sublime depiction of volcanic eruptions as touched off by storms on a fiery interior sea endowed that theory with particular interest. A similarly vivid reflection on the potential link between volcanoes and the igneous interior of the planet appeared in an article anonymously reprinted in *Frederick Douglass' Paper* in August 1855, which bore the provocative title "Is the Center of the Earth a Mass of Fire?"[26] Opening with a paragraph explicating the "generally credited hypothesis" named in its title—that "the interior of the earth is now a fluid mass of fiery matter"—the article defended this theory against a recent essay in the *Scientific American* positing alternative explanations for such phenomena as mineral hot springs and the higher temperature of mines relative to the surface, which testified to some underground source of heat. Although the author characterized the arguments put forth in the *Scientific American* as "very plausible," the article nevertheless sided with the "internal fire" position, which was supported by a "vast majority in the scientific world." Though the new arguments might explain thermal springs and mines, the author asserted, it failed to explain away those "mighty stores by which rivers of fire are poured from the bowels of the earth."

Alongside the editorial expectation that African American readers would be interested in keeping abreast of contemporary scientific conversations, such provocative headlines and lively descriptions also indicate the attractiveness of the molten-core theory within the context of the African American print public sphere. "Terrific" as they might be, such theories also rendered the earth as a lively object, heated, like the warm-blooded creatures that walked its surface, from within; this liveliness, in turn, suggested a parallel force within those creatures that might emerge to refashion their worlds. The focus on interior heat was coupled with an investment in the external effects of volcanoes that hinted at parallels between those events and the imminent eruption facing the United States. On April 13, 1861—the day after the first shots were fired in what would become the Civil War—the *Christian Recorder*, an African American newspaper based in Philadelphia, printed a review of significant eruptions throughout recorded history under the title "The Force of Volcanos." The article combined startling facts (such as the volcano's ability to disgorge matter far in excess of its own mass) with observations emphasizing the volcano's power:

> Cotopaxi, in 1738, threw its fiery rocks three thousand feet above its crater, while in 1744 the blazing mass, struggling for an outlet, roared so that its awful voice was heard a distance of more than six hundred miles.... The stream thrown out by Etna, in 1810, was in motion at the rate of a yard per day, for nine months after the eruption; and it is on record that the same mountain, after a terrible eruption, was not thoroughly cooled and consolidated ten years after the event.... Vesuvius has thrown its ashes as far as Constantinople, Syria, and Egypt; it hurled stones, eight pounds in weight, to Pompeii, a distance of six miles, while similar masses were tossed up two thousand feet above its summit ... Sumbawa, in 1815, during the most terrible eruption on record, sent ashes as far as Java, a distance of three hundred miles of surface, and out of a population of twelve thousand souls, only twenty-six escaped.[27]

The timely appeal of this catalog of destruction, evidenced by the number and persistence of its reprints, was suggested by the paper's decision to reprint the same article on November 2, 1861—by which time the war was well underway—under the title "What a Volcano Can Do."[28]

The *Christian Recorder*'s attention to volcanos was not limited to documenting their immediate destructiveness. It also published pieces whose deep-temporal perspective enabled their generativity to come into view. In October 1868, three years after the close of the war, the journal printed a selection from a recent article in the *New York Times* under the title "The Use of Earthquakes." The lengthier original had appeared a few weeks earlier under a more equivocal title ("EARTHQUAKES: Their Volcanic Origin and Their Function in Nature. The Earth in a Continual State of Perturbation. Possible Methods of Rendering Earthquakes Harmless") and opened in a catastrophic register, highlighting the "afflictive picture of horror and utter wrack" drawn by reports of a recent South American earthquake.[29] The *Christian Recorder*'s selection, however, skipped over this event, drawing attention instead to "the important part [earthquakes] play in preventing all earth from being washed away into the ocean." The omission of the "afflictive picture" bypassed the solicitation of sympathy for the earthquake's human victims, foregrounding, instead, the nonhuman perspective offered by geological time. The selection portrayed the rise and fall of continents as a battle between stone and water—"the sea... constantly at work warring against the land"—which required a geologic time frame for its course to manifest: "This process is slow, but it goes on forever, and the result is, that in time (that is, in the secular time in which geology works) the structure of continents is entirely worn away, and new ones are formed out of the ruins of the former ones." Both earthquakes and volcanoes, the extract emphasized, prevented the sea from winning the war outright. Operating on the side of land even as they wreaked havoc upon it, they "place[d] themselves in opposition to this destructive [oceanic] tendency, so that we may regard the igneous agents as in constant antagonism to the aqueous agents—the latter laboring incessantly to obliterate the land, while the former are equally active in restoring it."[30] At a moment when the "horror and wrack" of the war still loomed large in the public memory, the editorial decision to privilege "use" optimistically directed attention to the long-range effect of these events: the restoration and renewal of the nation and the revitalizing of Black worlds following emancipation.

The restoration of the land, in the article, could ultimately be traced back to the earth's fiery interiority, which caused both volcanoes and earthquakes and which illuminated the activeness of the planet: "Beneath the crust of the earth there is a sea of liquid fire, on which the continents and the land underneath the ocean are floating. This central fire is not only incandescent matter, but it is matter in a state of energetic elasticity, continually reacting upon the structure of the earth, and making itself felt more or less palpably."[31] An abiding presence, the lively matter inside the earth is understood as perceptible even though it was visible from the surface only rarely. Hence, those cases in which that matter could be seen—catastrophic seismic events—needed to be comprehended from a geologic perspective, in their land-restoring capacity, to be fully appreciated. As an outlet for the interior incandescence of the planet, seismic events channeled the earth's energy to reconstruct the world.

Volcanos, as these illustrations made clear, could inspire as well as condemn, construct and restore as well as destroy. On the level of the human, they appeared as harbingers of death; but from the much larger, longer-term perspective embodied by the planet, they were lively and creative expressions of the inner fire that sustained it. These inferences, as we will see, also came to characterize citations of the volcano trope by Douglass and Martin in which the temporality of the present manifested otherwise in view of the need for long-term transformation of national life. Both men found, in the time of eruption, an eventful reorientation, guided by the "inner fire" of Black life, that might enable other worlds to come into view.

Frederick Douglass's Fire

The abolitionist activist, author, and newspaper editor Frederick Douglass had a particular flare for using geological metaphor to activate the time of the "ever-living now"—a sacred temporality that opened the present to unforeseen possibilities.[32] Seismic activity resounds through his writings and speeches: in the speech now known as "What to the Slave Is the Fourth of July?," he declares that the hypocritical nation needs "the storm, the whirlwind, and the earthquake" to enliven it; in "The Revolution of 1848," he describes the battle against slavery as a globe-shaking contest; and in "What of the Night?," he asserts that European revolutions are "proclaim[ing], in the ears of slave-holders around the world, with all the terrible energy of an earthquake, the downfall of slavery."[33] His use of the volcano trope was even more suggestive. In Douglass's writing, the antislavery volcano took on a number of implications: it was intended to alarm the slaveholding class but also to affirm African American masculinity and to imagine and activate modes of Black connectedness.

A surface reading of the volcano trope would see it as directed toward southern whites, as an attempt to persuade them to abandon a system that would eventuate in violent revolt. On this view, it is directed toward a hypothetical future, one that may yet be averted. But in some renditions the time of the volcano's eruption approaches that of the earthquake: it is already shaking things up. The *Liberator* printed, in June 1832, a letter from a "New York philanthropist" that asserted, "The oppressed may sing and laugh and 'appear to take comfort,' but their mirth is that of the maniac or the desperate—in whose breast the flames of vengeance are already kindled, ready to burst onto the secure, and guilty, like those of the volcano on Pompeii and

Herculaneum."³⁴ Like the oblivious colonists in McCune Smith's citation of Mirabeau, the slaveholders here seem unlikely to awaken in time to avoid the already kindled flames—they are imminent ciphers, like the cavities of incinerated victims left in the lithified ashes of Vesuvius.³⁵ The letter is less concerned with them than with the fire itself: the affective *now* of the enslaved.

Even this concern, though, is ultimately oriented toward white readers. The New York correspondent's emphasis on the "maniac[al]" and "desperate" emotions of the enslaved, concealed behind a seemingly happy façade, employs another device common within antislavery writing—activating what Saidiya Hartman terms the "spectacular nature of black suffering" within (and beyond) the genre.³⁶ Such reflections provide occasions for white witnesses to emphasize their own grasp of human nature: as Hartman observes, in these scenes "the elasticity of blackness enables its deployment as a vehicle for exploring the human condition."³⁷ The possibility of Black agency, though, is undermined in the very gesture of affirming Black humanity, as the possession of reason that leads to this type of observation on human nature is not extended to the enslaved whose action is anticipated; they are depicted as beyond reason, maniacal, and desperate, descriptors presumably intended to heighten the imminence of antislavery violence but that enact a kind of violence on the enslaved, depicting them as automatons at the mercy of their explosive feelings rather than subjects who might plan and enact deliberate campaigns of opposition. The spectacle of suffering that might erupt in rebellion is also witnessed, as Hartman notes, from a distance. Distance enables readers to experience the thrill of violence without risking their own integrity, all the while producing Blackness as affective mechanicity so that the "circumscribed recognition of black humanity itself becomes an exercise of violence."³⁸

Frederick Douglass, Hartman points out, also comments on such affective contrasts, noting the suffering imperfectly hiding behind singing in plantation life and linking it, similarly, to a volcanic assessment of human nature. Slaveowners built in occasions for amusement among the enslaved, he asserted, as "safety-valves to carry off the explosive elements inseparable from the human mind when reduced to the condition of slavery."³⁹ Alongside this analysis of the geophysics of oppression, Hartman identifies a "longing for a culture of resistance," one that Douglass used the volcano metaphor to express. Avoiding the spectacular approach of the New York correspondent, though, Douglass approached the fire within as something more sensed than seen.⁴⁰ This is evidenced in his speech to the Anti-Colonization Society meeting in New York on April 23, 1849, which contains what is probably the best-known deployment of the trope. Usually reproduced under the title "Slavery, the Slumbering Volcano," the speech marks Douglass's first public affirmation of the desirability of slave rebellions; it was also, and not incidentally, the first time he delivered a speech before a large assembly (over one thousand) of African American men.[41] Douglass deliberately directs the volcano trope toward a dual audience; he addresses himself consciously and forcefully to a Black audience while also pointing out that the speech would be reported and recirculated well beyond that room, reaching white readers, including Southerners, as well. His assertion that "the slaveholders are sleeping on slumbering volcanoes, if they did but know it" is thus intended, in part, for the audience outside; he declares his intention to "alarm the slaveholders... to show them that there is really danger in persisting in the crime of continuing Slavery in this land."[42] But this affirmation is also directed at those who would rebel, as he continues:

> and I want every colored man in the South to remain there and cry in the ears of the oppressors, "Liberty for all or chains for all." I want them to stay there with the understanding that the day may come—I do not say it will come, I do not say that I would hasten it, I do not say that I would advocate the result or aim to accomplish or bring it about,—but I say it may come.... Those who have trampled upon us for the last two hundred years... may expect that their turn will come some day.[43]

The same duality of perspective marks his poem "The Tyrants' Jubilee!" written in response to the 1856 discovery and suppression of numerous rebellion plots in slaveholding states and published in *Frederick Douglass' Paper* in January of the following year. "The Tyrants' Jubilee!" testifies to Douglass's increasing skepticism about the likelihood of preventing armed conflict.[44] Its primary speaker is an unnamed southern slaveholder who initially celebrates the obliteration of the insurrectionary movement but who gradually comes to realize that it has only been deferred. The end of the poem reflects this realization as it contrasts the oblivious warmth of the plantation's domestic hearth to the volcanic conflagration that may yet consume it:

> Our sacred firesides, beaming with affection
> Might be sunk in a flash, through fierce insurrection,
> In one single night that fiend of desolation,
> Might spread his black wings in every direction.
> The fire thus kindled, may be kindled again;
> The flames are extinguished, but the embers remain;

The Natural History of Freedom 149

> One terrible blast may produce the ignition,
> Which shall wrap the whole South in wild conflagration.
> The pathway of tyrants lies over volcanoes;
> The very air they breathe is heavy with sorrows;
> Agonizing heart-throbs convulse them while sleeping,
> And the wind whispers Death as over them sweeping.[45]

Unlike the 1849 speech, in which the slumbering slaveholders are unaware of their situation, in "The Tyrants' Jubilee!" the speaker recognizes his continued peril. Yet whether any change will result from that recognition remains unclear. Although the speaker concedes that "Nature, with her million tongues," speaks on behalf of the enslaved, he declares no intent to free them, instead avowing the need for "eternal vigilance" against the rekindling of the flames.[46]

The antislavery volcano trope, seemingly situated as a warning to the slaveholding class, ultimately constitutes a planetary judgment of that class. In the end, the poem's perspective aligns with the volcanos rather than the tyrants. As the speaker retreats from the possibility of corrective action, the poem retreats from his perspective: the passionate first-person embrace of *our* firesides gives way to an objective third-person depiction of *their* sorrowful convulsions. The point at which the poem definitively abandons the slaveholder's voice, shifting to a third-person depiction of their imminent situation, is the moment of the volcanoes' appearance against "tyrants" in the fourth-to-last line. From that point on, the situation of the whites—asleep once again—is instead described in one of nature's "million tongues": the sulfurous volcanic air, heavy with sorrow, whispering Death. Yet the planetary perspective has been present all along, finally consolidating, in the volcano trope, the incandescent imagery that recurs throughout the poem, as it gestures to previous rebellions led by "sable forms illumined with great Liberty's fire."[47] As with the New York correspondent's nod to "flames ... ready to burst," the eruptive agency of the enslaved is pointedly contrasted to the obstinate inaction of the slumbering slaveholders; the poem is ultimately less concerned with awakening them than it is with illuminating and celebrating the flames' ongoing ability to burn.

Douglass's antislavery volcanos counter Mary Ashburn Miller's contention that naturalistic tropes of revolution ultimately risk "complacency." Miller argues that while natural metaphors possess obvious appeal, they ultimately "leav[e] individual agency, responsibility, and will as mute bystanders to the march of Nature."[48] To say this, however, requires a view of humanity as defined through "individual agency, responsibility, and will," existing apart from

Nature and able to separate itself from nature's progression through Man's time. This kind of separation captures the position of the static slaveholders in "The Tyrant's Jubilee!": they not only stand outside nature but have turned against it, ignoring its cries on behalf of the enslaved. The rebellious captives, however, are *not* separated from nature; aligned with geological forces, they are open to its immanence—and therefore to their own.

The natural fire celebrated in "The Tyrant's Jubilee!" bears a complex relationship to the concept of natural rights. The latter conventionally affirms a mode of humanness that takes shape around the notion of self-possession based on a natural desire for freedom and verified by the drive to self-definition and self-defense. But insofar as self-possession is denied to the enslaved by definition, they will have a different relation to this genre of the human. They are not denied humanity entirely; rather, as Zakiyyah Iman Jackson explains, it "function[ed] as a plastic limit case" for what was "proper to man."[49] That positioning, Jackson aptly observes, renders the labor of the enslaved "an essential enabling condition of the modern grammar of the Subject, a peculiar grammar of kind or logic of species . . . that approaches and articulates the planetary scale."[50] This enabling labor manifests not only geopolitically (as Jackson, following Denise Ferreira da Silva, observes)[51] but also geologically: as we saw in the case of the *Liberator*'s New York correspondent, the antislavery volcano trope could operate as evidence of (human) nature without attributing full human agency to the enslaved. But Douglass's rendition of the trope operates differently. In "The Tyrant's Jubilee," the predicted volcanic liberation of the enslaved neither reduces to a version of nature that stands in for human social and civic action nor speculates on human nature as a self-elevating exercise; rather, it overcomes slavery's disruption of a flow between the natural and the social, releasing a more-than-human energy that may be channeled rather than a mechanics that defaults to a given operation. In this sense, the geologic instantiation of "natural" desires and drives in the figure of the volcano does not negate the self-defining agency of the enslaved, but enables it to manifest in and as potentiality; the observation of the volcano's latent force constitutes a recognition of the power to act. The volcano, that is, does not even need to erupt—the affirmation that it is capable of doing so is a form of self-realization in itself. On this view, the trope not only allegorizes but *enacts* a selfhood forged through the enlivening recognition of one's own potential.

As a performative figure, the volcano disrupts the time of slavery, which Douglass elsewhere describes as a "perpetual chronic insurrection"—an insurrection against time itself, arresting its flows as it piles outrage upon outrage.[52]

The desire to resist the sedimentation of this arrest of time explains why Douglass's writing, as Jeffrey Insko comments, is strewn with "seismic events" for which Douglass "can hardly wait." Insko identifies this anticipatory sensibility, which charges the present by "drawing otherwise distant or remote futures nearer to hand," as the keynote of Douglass's sense of the historical.[53] Geology, in these events, does not diminish human history but enlivens it; the earthquake and the volcano enact the drawing-near of the "otherwise distant" by concentrating the immensity of geological time to an explosive moment. Indeed, the performativity of the volcano trope—its ability to create the kind of self-possession that the anticipated rebellion will confirm—folds anticipation in on itself: the volcano-affirmed self is already the self it aspires to be by virtue of that aspiration. Alongside the volcano's imminent eruptiveness, then, the deployment of the trope signifies an irruptive immanence: the presence of a time that manifests as more than the present can formally recognize. In line with Clark et al.'s insistence on the volcano's ability to revise time, the traditionally timeless time of the free citizen's inception—that is, the originary time of nature in which natural rights are founded—returns, in the volcano trope, as a *force* of nature, the disruptive act of setting history aright.

Irruptive immanence permitted the volcano to be invoked with a satisfaction derived from both the achievement of empowered selfhood and the realization of nature's intentions rather than with fear or awe. That satisfaction manifested audibly in the rumblings of pleasure and pride that greeted Douglass's speech in New York City. As Douglass turned his focus from the predicament of the slaveholders sleeping on volcanoes to the empowering possibility of rebellion being fomented within, he was frequently interrupted by outbursts of applause that actualized the irruptiveness of the trope.[54] Douglass affirmed the pleasure to be found in eruption. Nodding to the fact that colonization supporters and slaveholders would likely read reports of the speech, he proclaimed that as a Black man and a fugitive he would "greet with joy the glad news" of an insurrection. As he continued, "It is not impossible that some other black men may have occasion at some time or other, to put this theory into practice," his prediction was punctuated, after the words *black men*, by a voice crying out "we are all so here."[55] The eruptive response indicates Douglass's ability to channel volcanic affect toward Black masculine self-definition, the ratification of a selfhood understood as naturally affirmed but socially denied, which the response folds into the present: we *are* all so here.

Maggie Montesinos Sale has documented the association of volcanism with heroic Black revolutionary leadership, which was well established by the 1849 delivery of this speech. It appeared, for instance, in a description of Joseph Cinqué, leader of the Amistad rebellion, published in the *Colored American* in 1839: "His eye is deep, heavy—the cloudy iris extending up behind the brow almost inexpressive, and yet looking as if volcanoes of action might be asleep behind it."[56] Douglass reproduced it in the story of Madison Washington, who led an 1841 revolt aboard the slave ship *Creole*, and who became the subject of Douglass's only novel, *The Heroic Slave* (1853). Washington—whom Douglass describes, in the 1849 speech, as "an illustration of the spirit that is in the black man"—returned to Virginia after escaping to Canada, intent on rescuing his wife, who remained there in bondage. He was captured and imprisoned below decks on a New Orleans–bound ship but succeeded in unchaining himself and other captives. In Douglass's narration of the event, they lay in wait until the following day, when Washington looked out onto the ocean, felt its winds, and leapt through the hatch, leading a successful charge against the ship's crew. Douglass's retelling of the story, Sale contends, "recasts the legacy of the Revolution from an oppositional perspective, arguing that the national community needs to be reconceptualized in order not only to include, but to serve, African American men, enslaved and free."[57]

Sale defends the orientation of volcanic antislavery action toward the production of the exemplary individual—the shape commonly taken by the ideal of American revolutionary manhood—as an attempt to prioritize political legibility. The emphasis on action also attempts, as I have suggested, to overcome the loss of agency inherent in the spectacularizing of Black suffering. Yet despite Douglass's deft negotiation of these frames, he cannot entirely avoid what Jackson identifies as the "near-inescapable paradoxes of liberal humanist recognition" that "return us to racialized, gendered master narratives of identity and feeling."[58] The propulsive force with which the volcano endowed Black masculinity, for instance, ultimately rendered that ideal vulnerable to what Hartman describes as the postemancipation insistence that "the individual prepared to meet the challenges of freedom and ready to make a man of himself was deemed capable of throwing off the vestiges of slavery by his own efforts."[59] The strategic attractiveness of what Sale recognizes as a "new politics of masculine solidarity," founded on the heroically self-possessed and fully agential form of the exemplary individual, is thus undermined by that form's continued dependence on ideals constituted through the ongoing subjection of Blackness.[60]

At the same time, Douglass's deployment of antislavery volcanism may suggest to us another inflection, one that regards the volcano not solely as a producer of self-possessed individuals who erupt from its cone, much as

Madison Washington leapt onto the deck of the *Creole*, but also as a site that intimates a subterranean coming-together, charged with the affects implicated in the *becoming* of becoming a movement. In addition to kindling the proleptic coming-to-oneself of the heroic individual, that is, the volcano also gestures to the unglimpsed force of what remains underground, the "incandescent matter" of the earth's interior. From this perspective, it recollects what Hartman identifies as the "usually subterranean" practices enabling captives to maintain a connection to freedom's possibilities beyond recognized political forms. Hartman argues that the desire to discover resistance in the speech and practice of the enslaved, as it leads auditors to privilege those recognized forms, perpetuates the assumptions about agency and individuality they carry. (Sale's defense of revolutionary masculinity is a self-aware case in point.) In contrast, Hartman highlights practices such as "stealing away," the surreptitious meeting-up of enslaved people for ordinary purposes (praise meetings, dances, connecting with lovers or friends), as they generated modes of connection that moved against the terms of dispossession without being formally oppositional.[61] Such practices, she asserts, occurred "in the absence of the rights of man or the assurances of the self-possessed individual," developing another set of possibilities "outside the 'political proper.'"[62] These relations and possibilities, I suggest, may also attend African Americans' coming together for recognized political actions; for even those modes of meeting up that fell under legibly oppositional rubrics—whether planning insurrection or considering possibilities for Black social and political organization, such as objecting to colonization—generated a connectedness that provided sustenance in excess of their official purposes. The "*we . . . here*" framing the audience member's affirmation of Douglass's reference to Black manhood suggests this kind of connectedness—a sense of *being* together in Black space that overflowed even the satisfaction of being *men* together in that space. The New York City Anti-Colonization meeting could not have been described as "subterranean"; it was widely reported, sanctioned by the rights of freedom of speech and of assembly. Yet it too would have been inflected by the awareness and, for some audience members and for Douglass, the personal memory of prohibitions on the movement and meeting-up of the enslaved. And even as Douglass orchestrates an identification between the Black men in that room and those among the enslaved who might someday rebel, the affective energy that fueled those associations also recollected the sociality that made possible "the articulation of insurgent claims that make need the medium of politics."[63] Those claims are, like magma, subterranean by nature; once they reach the "surface" of liberal political discourse, they necessarily change form, just as magma becomes lava, hardening into various kinds of rock when it pushes through the earth's crust.

The New York audience's satisfaction in Douglass's affirmation of their presence as a gathering of Black men, in this sense, points at once toward and beyond the legibility of civic form to modes of social connection that exceed it—charged, more-than-political modes of being (and of being-together) that flow like dense, superheated magma beneath the surface of what we have come to know as political speech but that nevertheless exert pressure on its articulation and reception. On this view, the volcano operates not simply as an imminently eruptive trope, nor even, necessarily, as an irruptively immanent one insofar as such forms of being (together) may *persist* rather than inevitably *erupt*. It functions, rather, as a medium, a means of communicating with the earth's depths from its surface and a way of comprehending their coexistence whether or not they are seen to come together in time.

J. Sella Martin's Irruptive Atmospheres

The aforementioned citations of the antislavery volcano understand it as a mechanism connecting the surface of the earth to the layers below: as a geologic pressure-valve and/or an apparatus for seeing underground. A different analysis guides the Reverend J. Sella Martin's adaptation of the volcano trope in a speech commemorating John Brown. To Douglass's focus on the fire underground, Martin added fire from the skies. In his rendition, volcanic eruption is one aspect of a larger environmental/social event, part of a natural circuit of freedom encompassing the sky as well as the earth.

John Sella Martin, a Boston-based antislavery lecturer, Baptist minister, and poet who had escaped slavery at the age of twenty-four, had recently returned from a speaking tour of the Northeast discussing Nat Turner's rebellion when Brown was executed on December 2, 1859, by the state of Virginia.[64] The date was designated a day of mourning by antislavery activists nationwide, and a mass meeting was held in Tremont Temple, where Martin was then preaching. In the speech he delivered that day, which was reprinted in full in the antislavery newspaper the *Liberator*, Martin denied that the October raid on the armory at Harpers Ferry had been a failure because it did not result in a mass rebellion of the enslaved as Brown had hoped. Instead, he insisted that the inspiring model of Brown's campaign, and the outrage generated by his execution, would catalyze the coming eruption:

> It is thought by the slaves—and it is a beautiful conceit, though coming from slaves—that the meteors from the heavens are sparks that escape from the storehouse of the lightnings to strike upon the craters of volcanoes, and that is the cause of their eruptions. From the firmament of Providence to-day, a meteor has fallen. It has fallen upon the volcano of America's sympathies, and though for a while, it may seem to sleep, yet its igneous power shall communicate itself to the slumbering might of the volcano, and it shall burst forth in one general conflagration of revolution that shall bring about universal freedom.[65]

Martin's depiction of this theory of volcanic causation as a "beautiful conceit" implicitly acknowledges that it would not be widely recognized as scientific. Some Euro/American geologists had, in the past, assigned eruption to an external electrical stimulus, but by the middle of the nineteenth century that theory had been displaced by the understanding of volcanos as thermodynamic phenomena. But Martin's citation draws upon a different cosmology altogether: one in which the link between atmospheric and subterranean events signals the interconnectedness of the physical world, traversed by an energy that animated and bound it. This vision of the supercharged atmosphere's enlivening effect on the earth resists the geological fragmentation of the planet's surface ecology, anticipating, instead, the attention to "integrated systems of interacting components" that would come to characterize earth system science.[66] In the world the conceit depicts, atmosphero-volcanic events are not aberrations but alterations in the natural order, at once extraordinary and part of its comprehensive flow.

The "beautiful conceit" Martin uses to illustrate Brown's revolutionary effect—the figure of the meteor-sparked volcano as part of an interconnected and electrified ecology—may be understood in terms of the counterecologies Christina Sharpe describes in *In the Wake: On Blackness and Being*. Counterecologies emerge as Black responses to what Sharpe terms the antiblack "weather" of the Americas. Weather, here, signals not a swiftly changing condition but an enduring and all-permeating atmosphere: the longue durée of the New World in which "antiblackness is pervasive *as* climate."[67] The trope of the weather conveys not just the pervasiveness but the materiality of antiblackness, the way it shapes lives physically as well as socially. Yet while the weather cannot be escaped, it can be countered, Sharpe writes: "The weather trans*forms Black being. But the shipped, the held, and those in the wake [of enslavement] also produce out of the weather their own ecologies."[68] Martin's environmental volcanism seeks a permanent change in the weather. The electric counterecology he adapts from the enslaved is a transformation about to happen—the lightnings stored up in the heavens animating, through Brown's meteoric act, the sympathies awaiting within the volcano, meeting to ignite the "general conflagration of revolution" that will alter the conditions of African American life.[69]

Martin's deployment of the volcano, which was delivered in front of a mixed-race audience in Boston, differs from Douglass's use of the trope to channel Black affect. For Martin, the volcano contains not only the feelings of rebellious captives soon to take revolutionary action but also generalized national "sympathies" that will erupt responsively in actions less clearly mapped out. Martin's lack of specificity about the "general conflagration" might be taken, in this context, to soothe anxieties about violent rebellion, especially among the white members of the audience, many of whom deplored Brown's methods even as they honored his martyrdom. Yet Martin professed no such anxieties. Although he described himself, like Douglass, as a "peace man," he dismissed the "quibbling" and "querulousness" over the propriety of endorsing Brown's violent methods and declared himself fully prepared to approve them. To say this, he insisted, was not necessarily to speak the language of rage, insofar as celebrations of the US revolution endorsed the same methods, "the only difference being, that in our battles, in America, [these] means have been used for white men and that John Brown used his means for black men." Indeed, beyond endorsing Brown's willingness to use violence, Martin criticized Brown for not being willing *enough*. Brown's unwillingness to shed blood "was one of the faults of his plan" because the enslaved were unconvinced of his sincerity without bloodshed: "They have got sense enough to know that until there is a perfect demonstration that the white man is their friend—a demonstration bathed in blood—it were foolishness to cooperate with them. They have learned this much from the treachery of white men at the North, and the cruelty of the white men at the South, that they cannot trust the white man, even when he comes to deliver them." Brown's inability to see beyond the limitations of whiteness—his failure to understand that professions of solidarity alone would not suffice to persuade the enslaved that he was entirely their ally—explains the reluctance of the enslaved to join his campaign, Martin avers. This critique, coming in the wake of Martin's lecture tour on "Nat Turner and the destiny of the Negro race in America," underscored not only the necessity of violent revolution (as biographer R. J. M. Blackett put it, Martin believed that "the sword, once unsheathed, should not be replaced until the job was completed") but also the essential need for that revolution to be guided by Black perspectives and dedicated to Black futures.[70]

Martin's emphasis on African American perspectives, and specifically the perspective of the enslaved, anticipates his positioning of the antislavery volcano trope, at the close of the speech, within the larger framework of the "beautiful conceit" derived from cosmology of the enslaved. Yet as Astrida Neimanis argues with respect to Sharpe's invocation of the weather, the electrified antislavery ecology is not only metaphorical. Sharpe's term, Neimanis observes, "implicates matters discursive, structural, material, and environmental."[71] In fact, one materialization of this ecology, in the effects of an actual volcanic eruption, may have played a role in Nat Turner's 1831 rebellion. As Fraser reports, Turner's 1825 vision of a strangely darkened sun, which touched off his belief that he was intended to lead a revolt against slavery, coincided with the eruption of a volcano in the Aleutian islands that had changed the color of the skies across the North American continent.[72] Although Martin's implication of the weather—the storehouse of lightnings, the electrification of antislavery activism, launching Brown-as-meteor to ignite "American sympathies"—is clearly metaphorical, his suggestion that Brown's mistake must be corrected, that the revolutionary electrification of the national climate must be guided by Black knowledge collected over centuries of captivity and white treachery, also points toward an affective and material transformation of Black life. The arrival of "universal freedom" would change the air itself, permitting the liberated captives to breathe freely.

James McCune Smith's Geologies of Blackness

Like Martin, James McCune Smith envisioned a liberated Blackness energizing the nation. His geologic thinking inclined, however, to the accretive instead of the eruptive, a vision of African American worldmaking unfolding across deep time. Like Martin, McCune Smith comprehended geology as part of a larger planetary system. His environmental/geological theory of race underscores the centrality of planetary factors—the vitalizing material influence of land, ocean, and climate on human bodies—in the development of race and culture, countering the racial paralysis asserted by biologically minded white supremacist thinkers. His thinking transformed the electrified ecology outlined in Martin's lecture into an account of the Black body's enfolding of planetary matter that would, in the long run, expand the possibilities of Blackness. Katherine McKittrick has shown how African Americans resisted the constraints of the plantation through "black geographies," which marked out the "terrain of political struggle."[73] In McCune Smith's thinking, Black geologies also animated this terrain, enlivening it through the enfolding of planetary force and extending it across planetary time.

McCune Smith was a polymath: the first African American to receive a regular medical degree (from the University of Glasgow), he was also a well-known writer who contributed regularly to *Frederick Douglass' Paper* and other publications, an abolition and racial-uplift activist, a statistician, and an ethnologist; toward the end of his life, he was offered a chair in anthropology at Wilberforce College, though he was unable to take it up for health reasons.[74] His long-standing interest in geology accompanied and wove its way through these other pursuits. Geology, in McCune Smith's writing, became a means of both envisioning Black progress and establishing racial malleability. Carla Peterson asserts that "well before critical race theorists, he grasped that race is not a fixed phenomenon but an evolving social and historical construct."[75] Geology helped him to materialize these ideas.

McCune Smith was well aware that geological writing had become a platform for debating the status of Blackness in America. An 1854 sketch titled "The Schoolmaster," part of the "Heads of the Colored People" series he wrote for *Frederick Douglass' Paper*, takes up that debate as it inflected the writing of the British geologists Charles Lyell and David Ansted. The latter had recently published a geological travelogue, *Science, Scenery and Art, Being Extracts from the Note-book of a Geologist and Mining Engineer*, which asserted that the free Black population of the United States was degraded and diminishing. When emancipated, he claimed, "the coloured race disappears, not by absorption into the white, but by a process of absolute extinction"; he insisted that free Blacks should join the colonization movement rather than remain in "a country not suited to [their] physical constitution, and, as far as one can learn from the statistical facts, destined to be the grave of [their] race."[76] In McCune Smith's sketch, his schoolmaster-narrator runs across the text in a bookstore; drawn to it by Ansted's reputation as a geologist, he is distressed by "finding parts of at least ten or fifteen pages devoted to the most cruel abuse and misrepresentation of the free colored people of our free States!"[77] The schoolmaster goes on to refute Ansted's antiblackness by countering his flawed and partial statistics, but not before setting his work up unfavorably against Lyell's: "I will not be so uncharitable as to say that the Professor was paid to come over and write up a rebutting testimony to the hard (because calm and quiet) blows dealt against slavery by his brother geologist, Sir Charles Lyell; but the thing has that look."[78] In his popular geological travelogues *Travels in North America* and *A Second Visit to the United States*, Lyell's moral stand against the slave system was extended by his beliefs about racial plasticity, which he supported with reference to successes among the free Black population.[79] The suspicion that Ansted's claims were meant to undermine Lyell's leads the Schoolmaster to depict Ansted as a profiteering fraud, "bent on traveling and disposed to turn a penny thereby."[80] Ansted's propensity to cash in on his geological knowledge (also exhibited in the speed with which *The Gold-Seeker's Manual* was published) is thus tied to his insistence on racial hierarchy: both, the Schoolmaster suggests, are about money rather than science.

These characteristics would qualify Ansted, in McCune Smith's view, as the remnant of another geological epoch. In a lively debate with William J. Wilson, writing as "Ethiop," published three years earlier, McCune Smith, who wrote as "Communipaw," derided the pursuit of wealth and influence (which, Wilson contended, would be the decisive factor in Black liberation), asserting that "such ichthyosauri and plegiosauri as wealth and caste only half lunged" would soon become extinct, to be succeeded by a "freer, hopefuller, happier time."[81] As Derrick Spires observes of this passage, McCune Smith "merges the scientific, the spiritual, and the political as he outlines an evolutionary millennialism that applies evolutionary theory to human development and enshrines 'Liberty' as humanity's ultimate end."[82] His analogy between the "ichthyosauri and plegiosauri [plesiosauri]," marine creatures from the Early Jurassic era, and the current obsession with "wealth and caste," which renders the present as the deep past, points toward a future in which "the spirit of God will pass over the great deep and the mountains and the dry lands and the atmosphere," generating "holier and happier beings . . . higher laws and higher organizations."[83]

Not only the spirit of God would be responsible for that elevation; in McCune Smith's geological/environmental thinking, "the great deep and the mountains and the dry lands and the atmosphere" would contribute materially to the coming of this brighter day. He outlined this thinking in two critiques of scientific racism published in the *Anglo-African Magazine*, a new monthly that he coedited, in 1859 (though likely composed in the previous decade). The first of these, "Civilization: Its Dependence on Physical Circumstances," which appeared in the first number of the journal, laid out a general theory of human physical development with respect to climate and location, while the second, "On the Fourteenth Query of Thomas Jefferson's Notes on Virginia," published a few months later, pointed back to the first article's understanding of "natural progress" as a critique of Jefferson's belief in racial fixity and hierarchy.[84] In some ways, McCune Smith's understanding of race hearkens back to eighteenth-century environmental and climatic thinking. As Greta LaFleur shows in *The Natural History of Sexuality*, climate theory enfolded Euro/American anxieties about race and racialization in an age of increasing global movement.[85] Concerns over "impressibility" continued to shape the racial-evolutionary imaginary over the course of the nineteenth century, as we saw in chapter 4.[86] McCune Smith's adaptation of such theories under the newer and more active sign of "geology" replaced anxiety with anticipation, touting environmentally guided racial malleability as the key to Black social advancement.

In the first of the *Anglo-African* essays, McCune Smith derides physiologically based arguments for Black inferiority as primitive thinking; he calls them the "Great Idol of the Tribe" and appeals to renowned geologists to counter the so-called evidence in which they were based.[87] The British paleontologist Richard Owen, whom he names the "most distinguished of British naturalists," is a key source, as his research on the distinctions between ape and human skulls formed part of the "sublime argument for the unity of the human race."[88] But geology, in McCune Smith's hands, was more than a means of checking the errors of white supremacist biologists. It also formed part of his contrasting theory of human development, Lamarckian in nature and oriented toward the social mingling of different races as a means toward the advancement of civilizations. Against beliefs in racial fixity that argued for the "innate superiority of any portion of the human race," human bodies were decidedly plastic in McCune Smith's view; they took form in response to "physical circumstances," including climate and topography.[89] These affected their physical development and consequently their characters, sometimes on a microlevel: "The opposite banks of the same river, owing to some peculiarity in geological or climactic feature, will produce a greater diversity ... than can be afforded by one thousand times the distance in a plain but level country."[90]

McCune Smith's attention to geological and climatological factors as producing greater diversity, as well as possibilities for intrahuman contact, folds earth systems into the project of overcoming the spatial arrangements that McKittrick, following Sylvia Wynter, identifies as "Man's geographies."[91] On a global level, these conspire to keep populations apart and unequal. Yet those spaces, McKittrick reminds us, remain "life-filled and poetic," countering Man's fixed geographies with lived relationships that make visible alternate worldviews and new ways of being human.[92] In McCune Smith's assessment, geologic life actively participated in these exchanges. What McKittrick, reading with Édouard Glissant, terms a "poetics of landscape" is developed here as planetary poetics, allying geology, climate, and topography in a system that shapes the possibilities of intrahuman social exchange and, consequently, the modes of relation humans can sustain.⁹³ The geologic impact on human history formed a crucial part of McCune Smith's thinking, since both the existence of human diversity and the frequency with which human differences came into nonviolent contact were central factors in the advancement, stasis, or retrogression of civilizations.⁹⁴ A lack of physical access, he argued, had inhibited the spread of Asian and European civilizations to the interior of Africa, and not, as biological racists claimed, an immutable racial hierarchy. He denied that the so-called Anglo-Saxon race was in fact a distinct race, describing it rather as an "admixture of all the Indo-European races" because of its position on the globe. It was this mixture, along with a favorable climate, that accounted for "its great energy"—not purity or innate superiority.⁹⁵ Both malleability and hybridity were central to McCune Smith's theory of race as the product of material and social influences and the geologico-cultural interplay between these.

McCune Smith's thinking about both the isolation of Africans and the heredity and "energy" of Anglo Saxons here partly resembles Georges Cuvier's theory of the impact on race of the last global catastrophe, which was discussed in chapter 1. But unlike Cuvier, who flattened all Africans into a single type, McCune Smith detailed ethnic and regional differences among them. Though Cuvier acknowledges some environmental influence on human development, he insisted on "intrinsic" factors that "halt[ed] the progress of certain races, even in the most favourable circumstances."⁹⁶ It was precisely this kind of biological fixity that McCune Smith sought to challenge. To demonstrate that the human frame is remarkably susceptible to geological factors, McCune Smith points, in "On the Fourteenth Query," to evidence provided by skeletal changes among the African American population. The idea that "climate, or more properly speaking, geological position, has a powerful influence upon the bony structure of man" is, he asserts, "a proposition which numerous facts in our own sphere of observation tend to support." Among these he cites the skeletal similarities of African American men living in Maryland and Virginia, clear markers of their birthplaces. Since "only two hundred years have passed since their ancestors, made up of every of the many diversities of the African tribes, first landed at Jamestown," the melding of these diverse types into similarity "could only be the result of geological influences."⁹⁷ The osteological synthesis of enslaved people stolen from different regions of the African continent into uniform, locally inflected groups of African Americans not only demonstrates the rapidity with which "geological influences" can act but also the way geology can create new cultural forms.[98] Whereas Jeffersonian thinking sought to reinforce scientifically what Hortense Spillers identifies as slavery's "theft of the body," imprisoning Blackness not only within American captivity but biological stasis, McCune Smith's theory of race, as it materializes in the "philosophy of human progress," asserts that the descendants of those forced onto the ships that docked at Jamestown (and elsewhere) retain sufficient vitality to be geologically reconstructed as African Americans.[99]

Even as geology underscores the imbrication of humans and their surroundings, it also condemns the slave system and its effects. Near the end of "Civilization," McCune Smith identifies that system as the greatest obstacle to the propitious synthesis of geology and liberty that, he contends, distinguishes the United States as a nation. The same environmental conditions that homogenized African American skeletons, in his view, also guaranteed physical health and contributed to physical diversity among the population as a whole. And insofar as American democracy sponsored "the largest, the most frequent and freest intercourse of the most variously endowed men that the world has yet seen assembled together," its synthesis with that health and diversity promised the nation an exceptional future.[100] Yet the "retrograde movement" of the slave states, in contrast to the "advancement" visible in free states, showed that that future could not be realized without the removal of "the caste which slavery has thrown into our midst, and which is chief minister to the continuance of slavery."[101] McCune Smith's theory depicts slavery and antiblackness, insofar as they disrupt the flows of material and social energy circulating through American bodies, as not simply *un-* but *anti-*natural, reversing the progress the human species would otherwise enjoy.

Geology is thus intimately involved with the possibility of human freedom in McCune Smith's writing. Not only did the inorganic world impress itself on malleable bodies, but bodies themselves, through their tireless labors, made and remade the material and social world. Under slavery, bodies and land were both worn out and depleted, but positioning geology in the service of Black freedom could also transform Black relationships to land, as McCune Smith would argue in support of the Black agrarian community in upstate New York with which he became involved. McCune Smith was one of 3,000 African American men given a tract of land in 1846 by Gerrit Smith, a wealthy white abolitionist, who sought both to enable Black men to vote (at the time, only those who owned at least $250 worth of freehold property held the franchise)[102] and to establish a community based on democratic principles, which he believed would further the cause of freedom. McCune Smith was initially ambivalent about the project, angered as he was by the property-owning requirement, which did not apply to white men. As he complained in an 1846 letter to Gerrit Smith, "It is established by the solemnity of an oath, that the vile earth has rights superior to manhood!... Is it right to be party to such blasphemy?"[103] Yet he came to support the farming effort enthusiastically, recruiting participants to the project and fundraising to buy them farming equipment. A manifesto he coauthored, aimed at members of the community, associated the earth with freedom: "In a climate in which labour is a means for the full and free development of the energies of mankind—in the heart of an almost free state—protected by nearly equal laws—with an equal right to common school education—amidst the friction of advancing civilization—and at a time when the light of science falling upon it has made almost any soil productive—the earth, a free gift, beckons us to come and till it."[104] The beckoning earth, allied with Black labor and the "light of science," took an active role in healing the fractures of an *almost* free, *nearly* equal state. Along with his insistence on the distinctive benefits provided by US climate and topology, his vision of land and Black labor as co-agential transformed the African American relationship to land from a position of bondage to an intimate alliance.[105]

McCune Smith's attention to the imbrication of (Black) bodies and land, animated by the "light of science," proceeds from an initial consideration of North American land as in essence *terrus nullius*, preemptively cleared of Indigenous people and their own modes of intimacy with land. (Indeed, he refers, evidently without irony, to the Black Adirondack farmers as "pioneers.")[106] In this sense, McCune Smith's theory of malleability reflects how, as Jodi Byrd (Chickasaw) notes, "arrivants and other peoples forced through empire use indigeneity as a transit to redress, grieve, and fill the fractures created through diaspora and exclusion."[107] His negotiation with race, a formation of the settler state, was undertaken with the explicit intent, as he noted in "On the Fourteenth Query," of overcoming one such fracture, undermining claims about those "physical differences... alleged to constitute a bar in the way of incorporating the black men into the American state."[108] McCune Smith's insistence on incorporation reflects his opposition to the colonization movement; like Douglass, he argued that African Americans should remain in the United States to work for justice there.[109] The transit Byrd describes comes to play a part in this project when he situates the Indigenous body as a form through which the "American people" must pass on their way to embodying Americanness: "Two centuries have been sufficient to stamp upon the people of these United States physical and mental peculiarities which the world readily recognizes as American. Nor is this all. The American people, descended from early emigrants, are typically assuming the physical type of the Aboriginal inhabitants of this continent."[110] This transformation doesn't distinguish between Black and white Americans; as we have seen, McCune Smith also maintained that African-descended people were gradually transforming into an American type. The mutual transformation of Black and white people toward Indigeneity, here reframed as a physical typology, undermines the differences keeping the former from full inclusion. At the same time, that reframing would reduce the complex organization of Indigenous social life in relation to land to a single vector: the geological impress of a distinctive physical type.

Like Douglass's rebellious volcano, from which issued forth a revolutionary African American manhood, or Martin's, which regenerated the nation as a whole, McCune Smith's geological theory of race upended Man's stratification without unsettling its ground. But geologic avocations of freedom by those "forced through" empire do not inevitably need to reproduce the terms of the settler state. The alternate reading of Douglass's volcanism as a magmatic evocation of Black connectedness reminiscent of subterranean modes of association among the enslaved reflects a mode of relating to land that does not need to claim it. When considered in this light, fugitive geology holds the potential to envision a form of Black sociality not oriented toward the settler state. That reorientation, moving away from state-recognized political forms and toward collectivity, recalls Shanya Cordis's (Black/Warau/Lakono) caution against the overdetermination of race as the condition of Blackness in settler-colonial theory. As Cordis observes, the distinction between sovereign Indigeneity and racial Blackness maintained in many critiques of the settler state can flatten the understanding of the latter in a way that limits the ability to comprehend Black politics as something other than "an extension of the settler state."[111] Geologic models of Blackness as a mode of sociality, rather than of embodiment or identity, lend themselves more readily to this possibility.

McCune Smith's move toward collectivity at the close of "Civilization" may serve to point us toward this type of model, as he moves his geologic thinking offshore through the then-popular figure of the coral insect. For McCune Smith, that figure aligned collective Black labor, sustained over long periods of time, with transgenerational social connectedness. This coralline Blackness possesses the potential to loosen the essay's hold on race as physical typology—a loosening that was, after all, the essay's ultimate goal, as geologic influences operated to undermine racial divisions. Nineteenth-century popular and scientific interest in coral islands was linked to a fascination with the means of their creation. A lively debate among geologists centered on how these came to rise above sea level, since it was generally understood that coral polyps could only live in relatively shallow water. Until the mid-1830s, many geologists held that coral-based islands and deep-water reefs had been constructed upon the rims of underwater volcanoes that came near enough to the surface for corals to survive and grow. This theory, which appeared in early editions of Lyell's *Principles of Geology*, was countered by Charles Darwin's 1836 proposal that the reefs had initially been constructed above sea level, atop volcanic masses that had since subsided below the surface so that only their coral peaks were visible. Lyell was soon persuaded by Darwin's theory, although other geologists took longer to come around to it, in part because Darwin developed the theory without observing coral islands firsthand.[112]

Popular writings about coral, however, clung tenaciously to the earlier theory. Corals were imagined as battling the waves to build their structures upward toward the surface, persisting over ages to create islands that stood in for worlds. Numerous paeans to coral centered on the astonishing contrast between the size of the islands and the infinitesimally small polyps (commonly envisioned as an insect), which indexed at once a persistent, tireless dedication, since reefs and atolls take tens or hundreds of thousands of years to form, and collective cooperation. For nineteenth-century writers, Michelle Elleray explains, "coral figures the sublimation of the individual to the social, rendering what is ordinary, small, and unprepossessing into a structure renowned for its beauty and purpose."[113] McCune Smith took up this vision as he positioned the coral insect as a figure for "the immense and often unacknowledged labors of a slow and piecemeal racial uplift," in Juliana Chow's apt phrasing.[114] As Chow has shown, McCune Smith was probably aware of Darwin's account of atoll formation from a series of lectures Lyell gave in New York in 1842, which had been published. McCune Smith may well have read the lectures, since, in "Civilization," he references the craniological racism of Dr. John Augustine Smith, whose essay had been appended to the second edition of Lyell's lectures.[115] Yet he continued to embrace the popular trope, using the insect as an analogy for the decisive part African Americans would play in the nation's "advancement":

> Let us toil on, then, and with hope. Away down in the depths of the ocean, scarcely reached by the light of the sun, the coral insect toils on through years and years. The insect perishes, but its labors live, and pile on pile its tiny successors lay, whilst the years roll on. At length, uncounted ages having glided by, the tiny laborers reach the surface of the sea. The waves joyfully caress the visitant, and the birds bring their offerings to the suc-

cessful laborer. At length, the ships of the sea come, and find a refuge from the tempest. Men erect their dwellings, society is organized, and the Great Father of all is glorified;—and all this has come from the noiseless persevering toil of the little laborer, only gifted with instinct, in the depths of the ocean.[116]

Moving from the "pile[s] upon pile[s]" laid down by countless generations of coral insects to oceanic, animal, and human labor, this sequence culminates in the arrival of religious worship—a common destination for coral stories, which, as Elleray notes, were particularly popular in Christian publications; these framed the insects—toiling toward something they could not see—as theolo-geological figures troping faith as well as labor. McCune Smith foregrounds the relationship between religion and intellectual labor by following the coral insects passage with another evocative instance of dispersed, seemingly endless toil: that of early medieval monks, isolated in hundreds of "stony cells," whose "unwearied pens," transcribing and illustrating Greco-Roman texts, toiled for centuries against the Dark Ages' "ocean of ignorance and superstition, damned up by the iron walls of caste" and culminating in the "glory of modern letters and the light of modern science."[117] This geo-biological synthesis, made up of directed energy pulsing across animate and inanimate matter—the waves, the corals, and the birds all playing their part alongside the monks' pens—is responsible for all human achievement, material, social, intellectual, and spiritual.

The ammonite fossil, as we earlier saw, permitted McCune Smith to connect Frederick Douglass's drive for freedom to a long-ago lifeworld. Similarly, in the trope of the coral insect, McCune Smith roots values he associates with African American worldmaking deep in the history of the planet even as he points to their ongoingness in the present tense. Coral itself, as Michelle Navakas astutely argues, undermined biological racism, as its intriguing, inhuman strangeness "served as everyday encouragement to remain skeptical toward the very divisions of nature that made it possible to imagine race as a fixed biological fact in the first place."[118] Beyond loosening the grip of race, the focus on coral also gestured to the possibility of social life on other grounds, though ambivalently. As a wholly new world, the coral island may exist on other terms than that of the "New World" constituted by the 1492-event, which reinscribed previously inhabited land and imported captives to work it. Like the subterranean force suggested by the antislavery volcano, corals can invent Black futures beneath the surface, then build these into alternate ecologies. McCune Smith's transfer of the possibility of Black life offshore anticipates, in some ways, Tiffany Lethabo King's figuration of the shoal, an ever-shifting formation proposed as a model for Black thought. The shoal, King specifies, is an improvisational space, "a small, uncovered spot of sand, coral, or rock where one must quickly gather, lose oneself, or proceed in a manner not yet known."[119] For King, the shoal complicates and unsettles the division between the habitual linkage of Black studies with the oceanic alongside an Indigenous studies singularly associated with land, to the exclusion of water. The latter association, as we have seen, marks McCune Smith's geologic theory of race, as the land of North America imprints Indigenous typology on bodies located thereon. But the coral island, land arising from ocean, stone from biotic life, departs from this opposition, aligning this juncture with an idea of Black collective life that underscores vitality as it de-emphasizes racial typology, a redirection that might unsettle the constraints of politics waged on the terms of the nation-state.

Ultimately, though, the latter is the ground where McCune Smith's deployment of the coral trope is headed. The island is not an improvisational gathering-space but a permanent landed "refuge"; indeed, the ships that arrive there recall the romance of the Mayflower, carrying religious refugees to a distant shore. This idealized refuge may likewise beckon to those brought to the shores on slave ships, though they are not yet delivered from the "tempest." McCune Smith drives home the analogy by comparing the work of island/worldmaking to "the work allotted to the man of color in these United States... doomed to toil, but he toils with a reward constantly in his grasp... [as] he knows that the progress of mankind is entrusted to his keeping."[120] "Toil," here, is not a reference to slavery, but to the voluntary, if prolonged, labor of Black people, "for the first time... placed within the pale of civilization, with the chances of becoming part and parcel thereof," as they fight their way past white American obstructionism.[121] The profound energies unleashed by this human-animal-vegetable-mineral-spiritual alliance, forced, as Byrd reminds us, through empire, would transform the nation, though necessarily on its terms.

A queerer, cross-species version of the coral insect trope emerges, however, in a version McCune Smith included in an 1848 letter to his friend Gerrit Smith.[122] McCune Smith confessed himself frustrated by the results of Gerrit Smith's land grant, as a number of African-American men enfranchised by the grant had voted for candidates who failed to oppose slavery. Education, he decided, was the missing link in the movement from land to labor to social transformation, and he promised to "fling whatever I have into the cause of colored children" in the hope of preventing such outcomes in the future.[123]

He joked to Smith that his commitment to such causes pointed to his own theolo-geological ancestry: "This kind of work suits me because it is very hard, and somewhat noiseless: in the series of metamorphoses, I must have had a coral insect for a millo-millo grandfather, living to work beneath the tide in a superstructure, that some day, when the labourer is long dead & forgotten, may rear itself above the waves & afford rest & habitation for the Creatures of his Good, Good Father of All."[124] As it segues from scientific to domestic and spiritual frames, the passage corresponds to the synthesis of science and religion that Elleray calls the "moral economy of coral" in the nineteenth century.[125] Yet McCune Smith's identification of himself here as a deep-temporal descendant (a "millo-millo" grandchild) of coral, rather than analogous to the creatures, also anticipates the queer synthesis that characterizes his depiction of Douglass's evolution. The epochal imbrication of fleshy and stony matter conveys the possibility of a form of the human other than the self-possessed individual—something more diffuse, at once less assertive and more enduring. The coral's labor, here, is more loosely directed, culminating only in a scene of collective rest and worship rather than the "civilized" forms developed elsewhere in his work. In this sense, his fantasy of coralline descent at once parallels and queers the geological/environmental theories of race he developed over the course of his career: alternate accounts highlighting social and material forces dispersed and ordinary enough to be overlooked but that collectively suggest and spawn other ways of being.

The forms of geological fantasy appearing in the writing of Douglass, Martin, and McCune Smith generated energetic affirmations of the necessity of justice and freedom for African Americans. Occasionally they also gestured toward variant inflections of the human and modes of connectedness, intimating worlds that might emerge from Black sociality. In the oscillation between the two, though, they notably omit any consideration of Black women or femininity. Indeed, some of these manifestations of the geologic have a decidedly masculine cast. Douglass's channeling of the volcanic toward exemplary masculinity, as we have seen, resisted the sentimental spectacularization of Black suffering but replicated individualist ideas founded on the subjection of African Americans. And while McCune Smith's depictions of masculinity departed from the heroic ideal favored in Douglass's writing, his assertion that the future of humankind lay in the hands of "the *man* of color in these United States" may have intended the specificity.[126] Radiclani Clytus and Derrick Spires both emphasize McCune Smith's investment in a form of "escritorial manhood," in Clytus's phrasing, that, as Spires documents, deployed "misogynoir nineteenth-century style" to circumscribe the boundaries of Black print publics.[127] Whether or not Black womanhood itself is being intentionally crowded out of these models, the emphasis on Black subjects as formed from geologic matter sidesteps the social arrangements that surround biological reproduction. Hence, just as we saw in chapter 4, these new forms of geologic life remain underequipped to address the natal alienation and sexual violence central to the slave system, and the consequent de-formation of Black gender and sexuality emphasized by Spillers.[128] The consequences of this gap are significant, since it both limits these forms' ability to respond critically to the structures of antiblackness and partly obfuscates the way enslaved Black bodies operate within the settler state—in Cordis's phrasing, as "the body dispossessed of itself that produces the plantation as the grounds through which the settler self-actualizes and facilitates the ongoing process of settlement."[129]

Even as they muddy the gendered histories of this dispossession, though, some aspects of the fantasies considered here—magmatic socialities, electric ecologies, coralline genealogies—hint at possibilities for redress beyond the pursuit of self-possession in the mode of Man. Proposing alternatives to Man's projection of the human, they complicate and unsettle the masculinist forms they elsewhere uphold. Those possibilities resonate against recent models developed by Black feminist scholars—Hartman's subterranean practices, Sharpe's counterecologies, McKittrick's enlivened geographies, King's shoals—which open political pathways unglimpsed in the shadow of that projection. Attuning the African American imagination to "those ruptures that our planet delivers now and again," the reverberations of these fugitive geologies reinvent the human in relation to the earth, aligning their energies in the service of a reimagined Black freedom.

coda

ishmael's anthropocene: geological fantasy
in the twenty-first century

MOST STUDIES OF THE LITERARY HISTORY of the Anthropocene, the proposed new geological epoch that would be distinguished by significant and long-term anthropogenic damage to earth systems, go back, at most, a few decades—to the post-1945 period, in view of the geochronological moment recently put forth as the epoch's starting date, or to the late 1980s, when anthropogenic climate change first gained widespread public attention.[1] The term was introduced around the turn of the twenty-first century; in 2008, a working group was formed to consider whether it would officially become part of the International Chronostratigraphic Chart, a process that has not, as of this writing, concluded. But the affective resonance of the concept can be traced much farther back. We can see Melville presciently plotting out two common reactions to the Anthropocene within the space of a paragraph in the middle of *Moby-Dick*. The paragraph in question occurs in the midst of that most deliriously geological of chapters, "The Fossil Whale," which muses on the paleontological record of the species. Ishmael's recollection of his encounters with various whale fossils opens onto an awed meditation on the vastness of geological time: "When I stand among these mighty Leviathan skeletons, skulls, tusks, jaws, ribs, and vertebrae, all characterized by partial resemblances to the existing breeds of sea-monsters; but at the same time bearing on the other hand similar affinities to the annihilated antechronical Leviathans, their incalculable seniors; I am, by a flood, borne back to that wondrous period, ere time itself can be said to have begun; for time began with man."[2] The long history of mutation and differentiation that the fossil whale opens to view offers a point of entry to the fascinations of the deep geological past. In that "wondrous period" before man's time, historical time, the world and time were both constituted otherwise. Yet when Ishmael puts himself—or rather, man—back into the picture, wonder turns to terror. As he visualizes the "Polar eternities" (his own take on the Ice Age, a theory that had been debated since the late 1830s) when the whale was "king of creation," Ishmael imagines a glaciated planet inhospitable to and devoid of humans and then speculates on the possibility that this world might come around again. The initially seductive fascination of the geological past segues into a meditation on finitude as he invokes the prospect of human extinction: "Here Saturn's grey chaos rolls over me.... I am horror-struck at this antemosaic, unsourced existence of the unspeakable terrors of the whale, which, having been before all time, must needs exist after all humane ages are over."[3] As an index of planetary time, the whale once again eclipses the human, Leviathan's fantastic longevity—legible in the rock record—underscoring Man's imminent, inevitable endpoint.

Ishmael's astonishment in the face of that "wondrous period" is the first of those common reactions to the Anthropocene. What David Farrier terms the "peculiar intimacy of the Anthropocene," which points humans to their emplotment within geochronology, produces a kind of awestruck reflection on our necessarily changed perception of time. The geological perspective enables humans to see beyond their own time—to see themselves as "fossils in the making," to cite one oft-used phrase.[4] As that phrase itself might suggest, though, the amazement unleashed by the prospect of geological humanity is shadowed by more negative sentiments in view of the lithification of the human. Like the whale, the Anthropocene activates the thought of human extinction, materializing the conceptual obliteration of Man that so often accompanies the invocation of geological time—recall McPhee's nail file, illustrating human history in the act of wiping it out. While it has historically been the "heroic" work of stratigraphy to de-emphasize that obliteration by highlighting Man's understanding of the planetary past, the Anthropocene proposal ironically reverses that function: its compelling contribution to the geological timescale is to mark out the self-annihilating capacity of the species Man claims as his own.

The Anthropocene materializes geologic inhumanity as lithic mortality, humanity's ultimate inscription into the very rock record geology has taught it to read. The scientific quest to find a boundary marker, a material index of humanity's planetary footprint, to inaugurate the epoch inverts modernity's fort-da game with the planetary past; instead of the usual look backward, this search relies on what Elizabeth Kolbert, discussing the writing of Jan Zalasiewicz, founder of the International Commission on Stratigraphy's Anthropocene Working Group (AWG), evocatively terms "stratigraphy of the future": looking back at the present across deep time, a hundred thousand or a million years from now, to discern which piece of geological evidence will definitively index that epoch-making turn toward anthropogenic alteration and, perhaps, self-obliteration.[5] This potentially annihilative effect serves as the source of the concept's political power. It is intended to operate, as Will Steffen, a member of the AWG asserts, as a "wake-up call for humanity."[6] In its Anthropocenic rendition, the geochronological fort-da game does not simply stabilize the human intellectually, but catalyzes a desire to preserve it materially: the speculative swing forward to the deep future, looping around the terror of nonexistence, brings its spirit back to the present, where it is transformed into a determination to alter the course of the pendulum.

Melville's ability to outline these common reactions to the Anthropocene concept a century and a half before it was proposed reveals its conformity to long-established conventions surrounding the invocation of geology. The Anthropocene, in this light, constitutes the twenty-first century's most prominent example of geological fantasy; it revisits geology's primal scene—the positing of a world apart from humans—in order to interrupt it, to develop new modes of geologically inflected humanity that might navigate and repair the damage. The concept relies, like any well-told story, on conscious plotting. Despite the AWG's stated desire for professional neutrality, the quest for a boundary marker has become a highly symbolic endeavor, narrated with interest in the popular as well as scientific press. Two especially evocative proposals are plastic rocks, pieces of lithified trash which would indicate the massive and long-lasting environmental impact of human waste production since the mid-twentieth century, and fossilized chicken skeletons, which would reveal both the enormous rise in poultry consumption over the course of that century (the chicken is now the planet's most common bird) and the genetic manipulation of the species, making birds larger and heavier, to satisfy consumer demand.[7] These markers of the Great Acceleration—the massive, rapid and concurrent upswing in numerous measures of human activity, from consumption to population growth to the production of trash—are tangentially recognized in the AWG's selection of the mid-twentieth century as the epoch's inaugural point.[8] But the boundary marker favored (as of this writing) is the radionucleides from atomic bombs exploded between 1945 and 1963.[9] This anthropogenic trace has been most compelling to the AWG insofar as it offers a boundary marker in line with stratigraphic convention: aboveground nuclear explosions left radioactive isotopes that can be detected in bedrock around the globe, producing a lasting, rock-based signal of human interference with planetary systems.

Beyond its stratigraphic clarity, the nuclear Anthropocene also brims with symbolic significance as it illuminates, perhaps better than any other symbol, the tragedy of modern self-cancellation. (Though climate change likely poses a greater threat to the planet at present, it is harder to encapsulate in a single apocalyptic image.) Michel Foucault uses the same symbol to identify that modern tragedy as an irony inherent to biopower, remarking, with respect to the "atomic situation," that "modern man is an animal whose politics places his existence as a living being in question."[10] This conundrum marks what Foucault identifies as the biopolitical "threshold of modernity": the point at which "the life of the species is wagered on its own political practices."[11] If, as I argued in chapter 1 of this book, the recognition of species extinction marked a foundational moment in the installation of biopower by securing the form of "life" that it administers, so the active capacity to execute the extinction of our own species constitutes biopower's full manifestation. The substitution of the Anthropocene epoch for the "atomic situation" in this equation underscores the persistent presence of geological fantasy, both as aid to and index of biopower; here, it proves itself capable of measuring Man's deadliness as well as helping to support its administration of life and death.

As numerous critics have pointed out, however, the epoch's proposed name wrongly universalizes, under the sign of "Anthropos," the largely Western source of the planetary damage it illuminates, reproducing what Wynter calls Man's overrepresentation as the human by conflating overlapping global histories of extraction, dispossession, and toxification into a generalized gesture at "human" causality. In this sense, the epoch obscures, as Rob Nixon succinctly points out, the "unequal human impacts, unequal human agency, and unequal human vulnerabilities" that characterize the conditions to which it points.[12] Already those areas least responsible for the rise in atmospheric CO_2 are experiencing the worst effects, including crop disruption and sea level rise. Millions of climate refugees have fled central Africa, Southeast Asia, and Central America in the last couple of decades, and by 2050, more than a billion people—the majority of them from the global South—may be displaced.[13] Against the false universalism and relatively shallow historical perspective of the Anthropocene, several alternative frameworks have been proposed which would situate climate crisis in relation to these unequal impacts and the histories behind them. What Macarena Gómez-Barris names the "colonial Anthropocene" (or the variant "colonialocene") recognizes the epoch as "a spatial and temporal structure with accelerating consequences ... span[ning] more than five centuries of colonial domination."[14] The Plantationocene, a term proposed by Donna Haraway and Anna Tsing in 2015, though anticipated in earlier work by Katherine McKittrick and other scholars of African diasporic studies, underscores the impact on the biosphere of the global relocation of human populations tethered to the forced production of monocrops.[15] And the Capitalocene, a term coined by Jason Moore, dates the epoch back to the fifteenth century, tying it to the emergence of capitalism and its modes of organizing and commodifying nature (including humans).[16] Taken together, these complementary frameworks identify the interlocking roots of contemporary environmental crisis in a range of materially exploitative practices—of humans, other biotic life, and planetary matter, all of which, in the modern era, are remade as "resources" and wrongly treated as if they were endlessly renewable. The rendering of the Anthropocene as an ironic drama framed around Man's self-undoing is countered with a specific set of historical concerns, producing an account of the epoch as a concrete political problem to be solved rather than a philosophical conundrum.

Of the three alternative frameworks discussed above, only one, a version of the colonial Anthropocene, has been rendered stratigraphically. That proposal, named the "Orbis hypothesis" by its authors, Simon Lewis and Mark Maslin, finds, in the declining levels of atmospheric carbon detected in Arctic ice cores from the sixteenth and early seventeenth centuries, geologic evidence of the death of over 50 million Indigenous residents of the Americas in the first century after European contact, conveyed by the decline in human carbon-producing activities and by the mass reforestation of the continents.[17] The Orbis hypothesis reconfigures the "rock record" not simply as a passive archive but as an active witness, rendering it compatible with other cosmologies that grant land a certain agency in testifying to acts of violence committed upon it.[18] (Indeed, it may have been these qualities that led to the proposal's resounding rejection by the Anthropocene Working Group, which insisted that the boundary marker "should simply be pragmatically and dispassionately chosen, by the same manner in which all earlier stratigraphic boundaries were chosen."[19]) As testimonial geology, like Hitchcock's revision of Babbage, the Orbis hypothesis takes its place alongside the minor geologies examined in chapters 4 and 5—geologies that speak to the need to alter or interrupt the fantasies that sustain Man. At the same time, the authors' decision to privilege a geologically legible signal of the violent history of modernity renders the Orbis hypothesis partial, isolated from the other critical frameworks addressed above, insofar as these have not (yet) been formally linked to geological markers that can stand in for the histories they chart. And like stratigraphy in general, it is fundamentally necropolitical; its reading of mass Indigenous death as a geologically legible lesson for the present, as Matt Hooley has shown, suspends Indigeneity in the space of death, signifying only as traces to be read by settlers—in a sense, replicating the very logic of the "fossil other" even in the attempt to unsettle what geology can bear witness to.[20]

If even the perceptive Orbis hypothesis runs into such problems, we are left with the question: What exactly do we need a geological Anthropocene for? The relative speed with which the AWG has undertaken their labor (as is often pointed out, the nineteenth-century debate over the naming of the Holocene, the epoch in which we still officially reside, took several decades) indicates that the scientists driving the effort consider it a matter of some urgency. But what it will accomplish is less clear. Part of the epoch's appeal is its buttressing of the scientific authority behind climate change; the formal ratification of a new geological epoch, it is hoped, will drive home this reality for those who continue to be misled by the denial industry.[21] If the epoch is officially adopted—the AWG's proposal would first need to be ratified by several larger geological societies—science textbooks around the world would enshrine the profound and lasting impact of anthropogenic activity as settled fact. But the epoch became a popular concept long before the AWG was ready to decide on a proposal. Indeed, as Carlos Santana observes, the "breathless enthusiasm for the Anthropocene" outside the geological profession outstrips that within it.[22] That enthusiasm has been particularly marked among humanists, who often cite the Anthropocene as a methodologically transformative moment.[23] Dipesh Chakrabarty, for instance, insists that the epoch demands that historians abandon "the age-old humanist distinction between natural history and human history." [24] Environmental historians have done this for quite some time, of course, but Chakrabarty seems to want them, and everyone else, to scale up; insofar as "the geologic now of the Anthropocene has become entangled with the now of human history," historians must learn to think in relation to the "deep history of humanity," a species perspective imposed by our collective vulnerability to extinction.[25] This sort of emphasis on the need to think across scale and substance—to think in far larger and more material terms than humanists are used to doing—demonstrates that geological inflections remain active even when the Anthropocene concept is removed from geological circles.

Despite the appeal of "stratigraphy of the future," there remains some debate over whether the undeniably disastrous anthropogenic impacts on planetary systems being considered actually constitute geological markers—signals, that is, that will remain legible over the geological longue durée.[26] If the Anthropocene proposal does not pass, it will likely be for this reason, not because geologists do not recognize the catastrophic implications of those impacts on the biosphere. (They do.)[27] Of course, many people have come to use the term as simply a convenient shorthand, an easy means of inflecting the present with a sense of urgency, without being especially invested in the stratigraphic debate. Yet the geologic aura of the name still informs that inflection. In the assertion of humanity as geological agent or force, geology is positioned, once again, as a source of moral education, though the "rock record" has now become a mirror held up to humanity, an attempt to force self-confrontation through a kind of shock therapy impelled by the distorted size of our reflection. The Anthropocene, in this sense, feels like modernity turned inside out, no longer protected by its geological exoskeleton. The claim that humans have become a geologic force reflects an anxiety that we are, like earthquakes or volcanic eruptions, a destructive and irresistible power, that we may no longer be able to catch up to ourselves, as mounting evidence of the acceleration of climate change and the imminence of the point at which it will become catastrophic continues to be met with inaction, obstructionism, and denial.[28]

But the epoch need not be framed as exomodernity's existential crisis. In an analysis of the Anthropocene that traces the extension of settler colonialism into contemporary petrocapitalism, Heather Davis and Zoe Todd (Métis) pursue a more located analysis, identifying the underlying cause of the conditions gathered under the epochal sign as "a severing of relations between humans and the soil, between plants and animals, between minerals and our bones."[29] Accordingly, the starting point for the global metamorphoses necessary to reverse contemporary environmental crisis—exiting petrocapitalism, demilitarization, economic restructuring and redistribution, the transformation of food systems—must be understood as the work of remaking and maintaining those relations. Davis and Todd's emphasis on *relation*, drawing upon Indigenous thought, refuses the narcissistic account of the epoch that would frame it as a geologic memento mori. What is needed, they insist, is not simply awareness, the wake-up call that the Anthropocene may or may not issue, but transformative intimacies—a "tending once again to relations, to kin, to life, longing, and care," those forms of connection that can intensify in the interstices of catastrophe.[30]

What might this intensification look like when imagined geologically? How might it alter how we think of the geologic itself? The reestablishment of noncoercive relations between rocks and bones, flesh and land, fossils and living creatures reshapes not only how we can conceive of "geologic life" but also how we comprehend and move through geological time.[31] Understood in terms of intensified connection and responsible relation, time takes on the form that Kyle Powys Whyte (Citizen Potawatomi) calls "time as kinship," measured through the "duration, span and movement of kinship relations," imbricating present relations with past and future ones in other-than-linear connections. The strictly linear model that stratigraphy marks out, which now looms over the anxious Anthropocene as a "ticking clock," can "obscure responsibility," as Whyte explains; indeed, it is partly responsible for the severed relations that Todd and Davis emphasize. Time told through kinship, on the other hand, centers interdependence and shared responsibility while shifting the sense of urgency, focusing not on the apocalyptic future but the damaged relationships of the present.[32] Elizabeth Freeman's reflections on the centrality of an embodied "sense of timing" to sociality are also important here, even as social relations are extended beyond the domain of the human. Departing from the objective, distanced mode favored by Western science, Freeman engages time as "a visceral, haptic, proprioceptive mode of apprehension—a way of feeling and organizing the world through and with the individual body often in concert with other bodies" (and, we might add, other matter).[33] These ways of seeing and experiencing time depart from those conventionally associated with the geological, but this doesn't have to be the case. As geologist Marcia Bjornerud explains, the long-standing emphasis on the immensity and slow progression of geological time—which, she contends, is alienating and disempowering—does not exhaust the possibilities offered by planetary time. What Bjornerud calls timefulness involves "a feeling for distances and proximities in the geography of deep time," a recalibrated time-sense that would better illuminate "our deep roots and permanent entanglement with Earth's history."[34]

Approaching the Anthropocene through transformative intimacies and responsive, responsible relations would mean abandoning the geochronological fort-da game, comprehending planetary time as multidirectional, capacious, and sensual—an understanding of the "geologic 'Now'" that enfolds distant pasts and far-off futures into a present understood as multidimensional. This Anthropocene eschews shock and awe. It avoids plotting itself as tragedy; although it encompasses a great deal of suffering and acknowledges the violent histories behind that suffering, it does not ascribe these to humanity's "tragic flaw," its ironic orientation toward self-cancellation, a diagnosis that serves only to obscure the usurpation of the human by Man. This Anthropocene—if it remains an Anthropocene at all—changes shape. Avoiding the tendency to scale up, expand outward, abstract, and universalize that the epochal concept currently inspires, it makes room for more creative responses to the crisis; for as Jayna Brown reminds us, the dimensional present can be "the place of great improvisations."[35] If, as Elizabeth Ellsworth and Jamie Kruse contend, the "turn toward the geologic" is inspired by a search for "explanation, motivation, and inspiration for ... responses to conditions of our present moment," both that moment and the times, geologic and otherwise, that it imbricates must be recalibrated, harnessing the forms of material liveliness operating under the sign of the "geologic" against the biopolitical administration of "life" that takes shape against extinction.[36]

Elsewhere, Todd develops an alternate reading of the "rock record," speculating on the nonhuman resistance that might, undetectable to a conventional geological gaze, reside in rocks: "What if the rocks refuse the classifications imposed upon them by white supremacist geontopower? What if the rocks are performing their own renewal ceremonies, and the renewal is the refusal to allow white supremacy to claim the fossils, the atoms, the waters, and time as its heritage? What if the rocks are working in concert with those residence times of those who were violated by the nightmares that white supremacy has summoned?"[37] Alluding to Christina Sharpe's consideration of "residence time," the time it takes for salt to leave the ocean—260 million years—as a material memorial to the blood of African captives tossed overboard during the Middle Passage, Todd joins this memorial to a decolonizing activation of the rocks claimed by settler science in a planetary refusal of white supremacy.[38] For all its devastation, Todd reminds us, white supremacy is merely a "blip in time" from the perspective of the rocks—a brilliant revision of the obliterative deployment of deep time that seeks not to diminish or humiliate the human as such but to provincialize the history of Man falsely operating in its name. Todd's improvisation resembles some of the geophantasmatic evocations of material memory we have seen in these pages, from Hitchcock's material echoes of the groans of Black bodies abandoned to the ocean to Lewis and Maslin's reading of Arctic carbon levels encoding histories of Indigenous genocide. Crucially, though, Todd's emphasis on the activity of *renewal* avoids framing material memory in necropolitical terms. The time of the rocks is expansive, building intimate, animating connections with other histories and temporalities, connections at once reparative and speculative as they advise us that other worlds are possible.

The rhythms of lithic refusal and renewal remind us not only of "what we have in common with rocks and mountains and other nonliving historical structures" but also of what these commonalities might accomplish conjointly.[39] It is this kind of intimacy that should inform the (s)cene of the present, vitalizing new life, pointing toward the possibility of a more habitable world beyond the one that the geology of Man sought to make its own.

notes

INTRODUCTION

1. On the origins of the Anthropocene proposal, see Kolbert, *Sixth Extinction*.
2. See, for example, Wood, *Deep Time, Dark Times*, 34.
3. De Landa, *Thousand Years of Nonlinear History*, 27.
4. Metcalf, "Interest and Importance," 227.
5. O'Connor, *Earth on Show*, 33.
6. Hutton, "Theory of the Earth," 304.
7. Playfair, "Biographical Account."
8. Denton, *Our Planet*, 66.
9. For explorations of the cultural significance of these events in the eighteenth and nineteenth centuries, see McCallam, *Volcanoes in Eighteenth-Century Europe*, and Gardner Coates et al., *Last Days of Pompeii*.
10. Ansted, *Great Stone Book of Nature*.
11. Rozet, quoted in Hitchcock, "Preface," vi.
12. Metcalf, "Interest and Importance," 227.
13. Foucault, *History of Sexuality*.
14. Puar, "'I Would Rather Be,'" 63.
15. Playfair, "Biographical Account."
16. Berlant, "Intensity Is a Signal," 114.
17. Berlant, *Cruel Optimism*, 2.
18. McPhee, *Basin and Range*, 126. For reflections on the power of thinking with, beyond, and against extinction, see Grusin, *After Extinction*.
19. McGurl, "New Cultural Geology," 382.
20. Buckland, quoted in O'Connor, *Earth on Show*, 279.
21. O'Connor, *Earth on Show*, 1–2.

22. B. Noble, *Articulating Dinosaurs*.
23. Denton, *Our Planet*, 41, 51.
24. As I discuss in chapter 4, some of Denton's own research literalizes this technique. He was a believer in psychometry, a form of mediumship that involved the sensing of residues of past experience, and along with his wife, Elizabeth Denton, and sister, Annie Denton Cridge, he used this technique to conduct research from the first-person perspective of geological and astronomical artifacts (stones, meteorites, and so forth).
25. Wynter, "Unsettling the Coloniality"; Foucault, *Order of Things*.
26. Agassiz, "America, the Old World," 375. See also Agassiz, "Silurian Beach," "Fern Forests," "Mountains and Their Origin," "Growth of Continents," "Geological Middle Age," "Tertiary Age."
27. Buckland, "'Inhabitants of the Same World.'"
28. Hutton, *Theory of the Earth*, 271. Hutton argued that the history of the earth could be inferred from causes now in operation, a forerunner of what would come to be known as "uniformitarian" or steady-state theory, against what was often called "catastrophism," the belief that the sudden, violent changes that were primarily responsible for the state of the earth had been more intense in the prehistoric past and were gradually diminishing in force. This argument permitted some "catastrophists" to remain within the biblical time frame, then established at 6,000 years, though not all did. For instance, Georges Cuvier is often deemed to be a biblical literalist because of his catastrophist leanings, but as we will see in chapter 1, he actually accepted then-current geological thinking about the earth's age.
29. Rudwick, *Meaning of Fossils*.
30. Hitchcock, *Religion of Geology*.
31. Denton, *Our Planet*, 296.
32. Denton, *Our Planet*, 123.
33. Denton, here, is an exception; as I discuss in chapter 4, his geology aligned with Modern Spiritualism rather than Christianity. Overall, though, the presence of Christianity within the field, as Bowler shows, was pronounced, though it declined by the end of the century. See Bowler, *Fossils and Progress*; see also Klaver, *Geology and Religious Sentiment*.
34. Bowler, *Fossils and Progress*, 29.
35. Asad, *Formations of the Secular*, 13; quoted in Ogden, *Credulity*, 6. For other important recent studies of secularism in the nineteenth-century US, see Modern, *Secularism in Antebellum America*, and Coviello, *Make Yourselves Gods*.
36. Holbrook, "Family Cabinets of Nature."
37. Holbrook, "Family Cabinets of Nature."
38. Ellsworth and Kruse, "Introduction," 6.
39. Wood, *Deep Time, Dark Times*.
40. Fecht, "Urban Geology."
41. Gould, *Time's Arrow, Time's Cycle*, 1.

42 Chakrabarty, "Anthropocene Time," 6.
43 Grusin, "Introduction," vii.
44 Meillassoux, *After Finitude*, 5.
45 Morton, *Hyperobjects*, 61.
46 Morton, *Hyperobjects*, 59–60.
47 Bennett, "Systems and Things," 232.
48 McGurl, "New Cultural Geology," 380.
49 On ecocentrism, see Buell, *Environmental Imagination*.
50 Bjornerud, *Timefulness*, 16.
51 Povinelli, *Geontologies*, 76. A noteworthy exception to this tendency is Jussi Parikka's *Geology of Media*. Observing that "a deep time of the planet is inside our machines, crystallized as part of the contemporary political economy," Parikka tracks the global peregrinations of rare earth minerals—from toxic sites of extraction through computers and other techno-toys to the ever-growing piles of e-waste disproportionately dumped on the non-Western world, proposing that these reveal the geologic underpinnings of sped-up consumerism and exploitation of cheap labor. See Parikka, *Geology of Media*, 57–58.
52 Z. I. Jackson, "Animal," 671. See also Z. I. Jackson, "Outer Worlds." For related critiques of the obfuscation of race in new materialist thought, see Tompkins, "On the Limits and Promise"; Leong, "Mattering of Black Lives."
53 Morton, *Hyperobjects*, 58. Wynter's analysis of overrepresented Man, which I discuss in more detail below, is contained in Wynter, "Unsettling the Coloniality."
54 Morton, *Realist Magic*, 82.
55 Morton, *Realist Magic*, 101.
56 As Neel Ahuja has recently outlined, for instance, oil is the very material of globalization, insofar as petroleum production played a central role in the spread of racial capitalism from the Atlantic world across Asia. See Ahuja, *Planetary Specters*.
57 Morton, for instance, frequently mocks Marxist critics for trying to explain everything. New materialist philosopher Jane Bennett, similarly, affirms without explanation that within the nonhuman turn, "'historical materialisms' are not perceived as offering [a] ... satisfying response to ... those [trends] described roughly as ecological: the growing awareness of climate change and the possibility that Earth may have entered the geo-political epoch of the Anthropocene." See Bennett, "Systems and Things," 232. For powerful historical materialist analyses that do provide responses to ecological crisis, see Moore, *Capitalism in the Web of Life*; Malm, *Fossil Capital*. For Marxist responses to the nonhuman turn itself, see Rosenberg, "Molecularization of Sexuality"; Nealon, "Infinity for Marxists."
58 Coole and Frost, "Introducing the New Materialisms," 9.
59 Deleuze, *Difference and Repetition*, 2. See also Cohen, *Stone*. Deleuzoguattarian thought is a key influence on new materialist thought, though not the only

one. See Coole and Frost, "Introducing the New Materialisms"; also Dolphijn and Tuin, *New Materialism*.
60 De Landa, *Thousand Years of Nonlinear History*, 20.
61 Bennett, *Vibrant Matter*, 122; Yusoff, "Geologic Life," 779. See also Bob Johnson's fine *Mineral Rites*, which excavates the experience and meanings of geologic life in the era of fossil fuels.
62 Barad, *Meeting the Universe Halfway*, 91.
63 Deleuze and Guattari, *Thousand Plateaus*, 19.
64 Deleuze, "What Children Say," 64; partially quoted in Byrd, *Transit of Empire*, 14.
65 Byrd, *Transit of Empire*, 14.
66 Todd, "Indigenous Feminist's Take." See also TallBear, "Indigenous Reflection on Working"; Ravenscroft, "Strange Weather." As a white scholar educated and operating within settler contexts and theoretical frames, I don't, as yet, have sufficient knowledge of Indigenous thought to do justice to its breadth and complexity within this book, although I have tried to engage Indigenous views of place and land in relation to settler-geological ones. My purpose in citing Todd's critique is to observe that settler scholars at minimum need to be conscious of the limitations of Euro/American theories in relation to Indigenous and decolonial thought and to call attention to the way histories of Indigenous displacement are bound up with the subjects they address.
67 Todd, "Indigenous Feminist's Take," 16.
68 See O'Brien, *Firsting and Lasting*. In an earlier study, *Dispossession by Degrees*, O'Brien asserts that the myth of extinction was itself a way of understanding land, predicated on certain assumptions about the "connection between land and identity" that associated landlessness with disappearing (10).
69 Todd, "Indigenous Feminist's Take," 15.
70 Ellsworth and Kruse, "Introduction," 6. One example of such situated responses is *Geologic City*, created by Ellsworth and Kruse, collaborating under the name Friends of the Pleistocene. The project narrates the structures that organize and enable life in New York City in geological terms. (Brownstone buildings, for instance, are labeled "Dinosaur Houses," referencing the contemporaneity of their sandstone exteriors with the iconic Triassic/Jurassic creatures, leading to the renaming of Brooklyn as "Brownstone National Park.") See Friends of the Pleistocene, *Geologic City*.
71 Coulthard, *Red Skin, White Masks*, 13. See also Simpson, "Land as Pedagogy," 9–10.
72 Vanessa Watts similarly identifies the ongoing abstraction and anthropocentrism attached to recent moves in settler scholarship that seek to recognize the agency of nonhumans. See Watts, "Indigenous Place-Thought."
73 Rifkin, *Settler Common Sense*, 3.
74 In *The Birth of Energy*, Cara New Daggett examines what she terms the "energy-work nexus ... the intertwining of energy and the Western ethos of

dynamic, productive work ... produced as cosmic truth." Geology made this entanglement possible; as she observes, the geological emphasis on the earth as historical rendered it "a duration in time, and thus ... a potential reservoir for work." Yet in this view, geological matter (fossil fuels) and the solar energy system remain passive in themselves; humans must release energy from this reservoir, must put the earth to work. See Daggett, *Birth of Energy*, 5, 25.

75 Goeman in Aikau et al., "Indigenous Feminisms Roundtable," 94.
76 Rifkin, "Geo into Bio and Back Again," 876.
77 De Landa, *Thousand Years of Nonlinear History*, 21.
78 Bennett, "Powers of the Hoard," 239–40.
79 I make this claim at greater length in "How the Earth Feels," 7.
80 Brown, *Black Utopias*, 124. On the racialization of matter see especially Chen, *Animacies*, and Z. I. Jackson, *Becoming Human*.
81 King, *Black Shoals*; Cram, *Violent Inheritance*. See also Savoy, *Trace*, and LeMenager, "Sediment."
82 Yusoff, *Billion Black Anthropocenes*, 14.
83 Foucault, *History of Sexuality*, 136.
84 Povinelli, *Geontologies*.
85 Povinelli, *Geontologies*, 5.
86 Gómez-Barris, *Extractive Zone*, 5.
87 Wynter, "Unsettling the Coloniality," 290.
88 Quoted in Robins, *Mercury, Mining, and Empire*, 69. After the Spanish Crown took over Indigenous silver mining sites in South and Central America, it expanded both the scale and the danger of mine work through the introduction of techniques such as the use of mercury to amalgamate silver. The adoption of this process led to the acceleration of silver mining in Bolivia and the establishment of mercury mines at Huancavelica in what is now Peru. (Both sites remain profoundly contaminated by mercury to this day.) Robins asserts that initially, enslaved Africans were not used as mine laborers at Potosí because enslavers regarded them as capital investments and did not want to risk losing them to the horrific conditions in the mines. This was not the case in Brazil and elsewhere, however.
89 Schoolcraft, *Summary Narrative*, 185.
90 McKittrick, "On Plantations," 948.
91 McKittrick, "Plantation Futures," 8.
92 Allewaert, *Ariel's Ecology*.
93 K. Adams, "DuBois, Dirt Determinism."
94 Simpson's account of "land as pedagogy," a framework within Nishnaabeg thought, requires knowing with, not simply about, land: understanding oneself as "ultimately dependent on intimate relationships of reciprocity, humility, honesty and respect with all elements of creation, including plants and animals." Simpson, "Land as Pedagogy," 9–10. The mapping practices

developed by enslaved and self-emancipated Black subjects, McKittrick contends, navigated land in terms of material relations and sensory connections: "fugitive and maroon maps, literacy maps, food-nourishment maps, family maps, [and] music maps... assembled alongside 'real' maps (those produced by black cartographers and explorers who document landmasses, roads, routes, boundaries, and so forth)." McKittrick, "On Plantations," 949. Forms of resistant recollection like Jennifer C. James's "ecomelancholia," which emphasizes how "memory permeates black landscape... becom[ing] a part of the natural world," demonstrate the survival of these alternate modes of land knowledge in and as modes of critical memory. James, "Ecomelancholia," 163.

95 Schoolcraft, *Memoir on the Geological Position*, 3.
96 O'Brien, *Firsting and Lasting*, 107.
97 O'Brien, *Firsting and Lasting*, 119. In an earlier study, O'Brien asserts that the myth of extinction was itself a way of understanding land, predicated on certain assumptions about the "connection between land and identity" that associated landlessness with disappearing. See O'Brien, *Dispossession by Degrees*, 10.
98 Coulthard, *Red Skin, White Masks*, 152; quoted in Schuller, "Fossil and the Photograph," 232.
99 Pandian, *Anthropology and the Western Tradition*, 57.
100 Barker, "For Whom Sovereignty Matters." See also Morgensen, "Biopolitics of Settler Colonialism"; Rifkin, *When Did Indians Become Straight?*
101 Mbembe, "Necropolitics," 40.
102 Byrd, *Transit of Empire*, xxiii. Wynter's account of the emergence of overrepresented Man identifies these two processes as stages, which she differentiates with the terms Man1 and Man2. I have chosen not to use these terms in order to avoid the implication that Man2, the figure organizing modern racialization, displaces Man1 insofar as these processes, as Byrd stresses, are entangled but not identical. See Mark Rifkin's discussion of Wynter along these lines in Rifkin, *Fictions of Land and Flesh*, 20–25.
103 On the rhetoric of the images produced in postbellum geological surveys, see Trachtenberg, "Naming the View"; Sandweiss, *Print the Legend*; Berger, "Overexposed." For perspectives on Indigenous photography as it counters the alliance between photography and settler colonialism, see Tsinhnahjinnie and Passalacqua, *Our People, Our Land, Our Images*. On the "bone wars," see Jaffe, *Gilded Dinosaur*. For a brilliant consideration of settler photography of Western subjects in tandem with paleontology, see Schuller, "Fossil and the Photograph." On dinosaurs as cultural objects, see especially B. Noble, *Articulating Dinosaurs*, and W. J. T. Mitchell, *Last Dinosaur Book*.
104 On dinosaurs and empire, see W. J. T. Mitchell, *Last Dinosaur Book*.
105 Schoolcraft, *Memoir on the Geological Position*, 9–10.
106 Allen, *Republic in Time*, 152.
107 On the structures of feeling that suture settler kinship and land ownership, see Rifkin, *Settler Common Sense*.

108 See Allen, *Republic in Time*; Arsić, *On Leaving* and *Bird Relics*; Cadava, *Emerson and the Climates of History*; Jonik, *Herman Melville and the Politics*; Dimock, *Through Other Continents*; Farmer and Schroeder, *Ahab Unbound*; Morgan, "Transcendental Geologies"; R. Martin, "Fossil Thoughts"; Nurmi, *Magnificent Decay*; Windolph, *Emerson's Nonlinear Nature*; Guthrie, *Above Time*.

109 For a fine exploration of what a nineteenth-century Black feminist minor geology might look like, see Samantha Pinto's reading of three nineteenth-century Black women whose narratives make visible the imbrication of sexual and scientific violence. Pinto's "unnatural history" speculates on how the fossil form might generate an alternate framework for the imagination of Black women's sexual agency. Pinto, "Objects of Narrative Desire."

CHAPTER ONE. "THE INFINITE GO-BEFORE OF THE PRESENT"

1 Emerson, "Poet," 329.
2 Whitman, "Slang in America," 431.
3 Whitman, "Slang in America," 435.
4 A similar analogy is made by Richard Chenevix Trench in his widely read *On the Study of Words*: "You know how the geologist is able from the different strata and deposits, primary, secondary, or tertiary, succeeding one another ... to conclude the successive physical changes through which a region has passed.... Now with such a composite language as English before us, we may carry on moral and historical researches precisely analogous to his." Trench, *On the Study of Words*, 73–74.
5 Metcalf, "Interest and Importance," 229.
6 For readings of Emerson and Whitman that foreground their resonance with the nonhuman turn, see Arsić, *On Leaving*; Arsić and Wolfe, *Other Emerson*; Allen, *Republic in Time*; Bennett, *Influx and Efflux*.
7 Emerson, "Fate," 201.
8 Emerson, "Fate," 202.
9 Though this paragraph is sometimes taken as an expression of Emerson's own racist opinions, within the context of an essay that excoriates the positing of limits, whether of fate or nature, as obstacles to freedom, one that Eduardo Cadava identifies as "perhaps Emerson's most profound and searching engagement of the idea of manifest destiny in terms of questions of race," the deliberate failure of the pretended continuity between natural, prehuman history and the unnatural violence of American history becomes clearer. Cadava, "Guano of History," 106. For a nuanced reading of how Emerson's revision of geological time surfaces to disrupt the sedimentation of racial violence in his 1844 antislavery address, see Morgan, "Transcendental Geologies."
10 Goffe, "'Guano in Their Destiny,'" 30. On the composition and location of various types of guano, see Schnug et al., "Guano."

11 LeMenager, *Manifest and Other Destinies*, 222.
12 Whewell, "Address to the Geological Society"; quoted in Todhunter, *William Whewell, D.D.*, 145.
13 Agassiz, "Mountains and Their Origin," 748. Contemporary historians of the science often replicated these tendencies. The Anglophone world's version locates Scottish naturalist James Hutton as the "father," or founder, of modern geology, crediting him with a singularly bold refutation of the 6,000-year creationist timescale said to have guided his predecessors. In fact, the secular recalibration of planetary time was not, in fact, Hutton's alone; over the course of the eighteenth century, most European natural historians came to situate the earth's development within longer time spans than the handful of millennia recognized in the Bible. Yet instead of appearing as one participant in a gradual scaling-up of the planetary past, Hutton has often been positioned by latter-day historians as the discoverer of deep time: a visionary figure who, departing from the security of the known world, came upon the temporal equivalent of *terrus nullius*: enormous swaths of time available for the plotting of new geochronologies. See, e.g., Repcheck, *Man Who Found Time*.
14 See Rudwick, *Earth's Deep History*, 159–61.
15 Scrope, *Memoir on the Geology*, 165.
16 Lyell, *Principles of Geology*, 16.
17 Lyell, *Principles of Geology*, 16.
18 Scrope, *Memoir on the Geology*, 165.
19 Agassiz, "Silurian Beach," 460; quoted in Gould, *Time's Arrow, Time's Cycle*, 94.
20 Rudwick, *Earth's Deep History*.
21 Cuvier, "Preliminary Discourse," 185.
22 Cuvier, "Preliminary Discourse," 185.
23 Cuvier, "Preliminary Discourse," 185.
24 W. Smith, *Stratigraphical System*, x.
25 W. Smith, *Stratigraphical System*, vi.
26 W. Smith, *Stratigraphical System*, vi.
27 Whewell, "Address to the Geological Society," 96.
28 Ogden, *Credulity*. On secularism as the management of belief, see also Asad, *Formations of the Secular*; Modern, *Secularism in Antebellum America*.
29 Coviello, *Make Yourselves Gods*; Schuller, *Biopolitics of Feeling*.
30 Buckland, *Novel Science*, 111. The distinctiveness of Lyell's anti-narrative approach accounts for his influence on Henry David Thoreau's innovative geological thought. According to Branka Arsić, Lyell's comprehension of the earth as a "continuity of mutability" permitted Thoreau's more radical inclusion of "the earth and the elements among living beings partaking in universal life." Arsić, *Bird Relics*, 188, 187.
31 Rudwick, *Earth's Deep History*, 171.
32 Bowler, *Fossils and Progress*.
33 Davis, *Principles of Nature*, 223.

34 Grimes, *Phreno-Geology*.
35 Train, *Facts*, 125; quoted in M. Mitchell, "'Lower Orders,'" 133.
36 Foucault, *History of Sexuality*, 142.
37 Foucault, *Order of Things*, 265.
38 Foucault, *Order of Things*, 274.
39 Foucault, *Order of Things*, 270.
40 With respect to Cuvier's disbelief in evolution, Foucault argues that what really matters is not what he thought, but the way his research inaugurates the conception of an energetic interplay between life and death, which laid the foundation for the modern understanding of evolution. Foucault, *Order of Things*, 156.
41 Foucault, *"Society Must Be Defended,"* 80; quoted in Mader, "Modern Living and Vital Race," 105.
42 Mader, "Modern Living and Vital Race," 108.
43 Foucault also recognizes that the geological timescale—its vast secular understanding of time—is necessary to the formation of the modern episteme. He asserts that the "discontinuity of living forms [in the guise of extinction] made it possible to conceive of a great temporal current"—geological time—which "replace[d] natural history with a 'history' of nature." Foucault, *Order of Things*, 275.
44 Foucault, *Order of Things*, 275. As Foucault goes on to point out, that current in turn came to provide the (exomodern) basis for the ontological understanding of time with which modern philosophy would wrestle.
45 Schuller, *Biopolitics of Feeling*, 35. Indeed, in the 1975–76 lectures, Foucault concedes that a largely Lamarckian linear-developmental time line, supported by nineteenth-century evolutionism, constructed the modern conception of race. Lamarckian understandings of evolution, and the models of race these spawned, remained, moreover, importantly open to lifeworlds, enfolding exterior influences into processes of improvement or degeneration—an enfolding that would ensure that racialized bodies and populations remained open to geological forces and events.
46 Cuvier, "Preliminary Discourse," 192–93.
47 See Brantlinger, *Dark Vanishings*.
48 Lyell, *Principles of Geology*, 291.
49 For an overview of the complex and overlapping histories of "Indian" and "tribal" blood, see TallBear, *Native American DNA*.
50 On the belated and incomplete state enfolding of Indigenous people into biopolitics, see Morgensen, "Biopolitics of Settler Colonialism."
51 Cuvier, "Preliminary Discourse," 239.
52 Cuvier, "Preliminary Discourse," 242, 244.
53 Cuvier, "Preliminary Discourse," 246.
54 See Jackson and Weidman, *Race, Racism, and Science*.
55 Rudwick, *Georges Cuvier*, xi.

56 Rudwick, *Georges Cuvier*, 246n150.
57 Pinto, "Objects of Narrative Desire," 359.
58 Rudwick, *Georges Cuvier*, 246n150.
59 Usher, in Nott et al., *Types of Mankind*.
60 See Fabian, *Skull Collectors*; see also Winsor, "Louis Agassiz and the Species Question."
61 Lyell to Ticknor, 1860; quoted in Wool, *Milestones in the Evolving Theory*, 127.
62 Allen, *Republic in Time*, 151.
63 Agassiz, "America, the Old World," 373.
64 Agassiz, "America, the Old World," 373.
65 Quoted in Allen, *Republic in Time*, 162.
66 Ansted, *Gold-Seeker's Manual*, 162.
67 Ansted, *Gold-Seeker's Manual*, 170–71.
68 Morgensen, "Biopolitics of Settler Colonialism." Mark Rifkin contends that Indigenous governance practices negotiated with biopower rather than simply acceding to it, remaking biopolitical forms to access land- and place-based understandings of community. See Rifkin, "Geo into Bio and Back Again."
69 For an insightful reading of settler land inheritance in the North American West, see Cram, *Violent Inheritance*.
70 Winslow, *Preparation of the Earth*, 8, 15.
71 Winslow, *Preparation of the Earth*, 23.
72 Winslow, *Preparation of the Earth*, 38, 41, 51.
73 Winslow, *Preparation of the Earth*, 53–54.
74 Winslow, *Preparation of the Earth*, 50.
75 Winslow, *Preparation of the Earth*, 37.
76 Winslow, *Preparation of the Earth*, 47.
77 Winslow, *Preparation of the Earth*, 41, 53.
78 Ansted, *Gold-Seeker's Manual*, 25.
79 Winslow, *Preparation of the Earth*, 25.
80 Lindsey, *Murder State*.
81 Burnett, "State of the State Address."
82 Nor did Burnett's effort to set California aside for Anglo-Americans end there; the speech also devoted several paragraphs to justifying the legal exclusion of free African Americans from the state, claiming that this would be in their best interest, since law and custom would prevent them from rising socially, as well as insisting (against the state constitution) that English alone should be the state's official language. The race that Ansted declared "inclined to make the most of [California's] natural advantages" (170) was provided with an abundance of legal advantages in order to facilitate that inclination. Burnett, "State of the State Address."
83 Goodrich, *Wonders of Geology*, 25.
84 "Review of *Professor Hitchcock's Report*," 425.

85 Cooper, *Crater*, 5.
86 Cooper, *Crater*, 101.
87 I am drawing on Stephanie LeMenager's discussion of Cooper's *The Prairie: A Tale* (1827), published two decades before *The Crater*; LeMenager observes that the novel's setting on lands deemed untillable—the so-called Great American Desert of the Great Plains—prevents the growth of national fantasy; the "American desert" appears as a "scene of the impossible" rather than a site for the secure production of the American future. LeMenager, *Manifest and Other Destinies*, 32.
88 See Barnard, "Empire."
89 LeMenager, *Manifest and Other Destinies*, 75; James, "'Buried in Guano,'" 122.
90 James, "'Buried in Guano,'" 116. See also James in Newman and Finley, "Race and Nature."
91 Cooper, *Crater*, 213.
92 In addition to the aforementioned violence of compelled Black and Chinese labor in guano mining in the nineteenth century, James points out that guano was also synonymous with the soil exhaustion caused by slavery, and it was Southern slaveholders, in large part, who pushed the United States to pass the Guano Islands Act in 1856, which proclaimed the US's ability to take possession of any "unclaimed" islands on which guano deposits were uncovered.
93 Cooper, *Crater*, 342.
94 Richardson, *American Literature*, 309. For latter-day critical responses to the ending, see Gates, "A Defense of the Ending of Cooper's *The Crater*"; McWilliams, "Crater and the Constitution"; Scudder, "Cooper's *The Crater*"; Grossman, *James Fenimore Cooper*.
95 For an analysis of Lyell's writing on Graham Island and its significance in his own career, see Dean, "Graham Island."
96 For discussions of Lyell's influence on Cooper, see Scudder, "Cooper's *The Crater*," and C. H. Adams, "Uniformity and Progress," 206.
97 Cooper, *Crater*, 161–62.
98 Cooper, *Crater*, x.
99 Cooper, *Crater*, 4.
100 Cooper, *Crater*, 6.
101 Cooper, quoted in L. L. Noble, *Course of Empire*, 225.
102 Cooper, *Crater*, 479.
103 Cooper, *Crater*, 481.
104 Prince, *Earthquakes*, 12.
105 Cooper, *Crater*, 142.
106 Muir-Wood, *Dark Side of the Earth*, 3.
107 Metcalf, "Interest and Importance," 227.

CHAPTER TWO. UNSETTLED GROUND

Earlier versions of material in chapter 2 appeared in "Unsettled Ground: Indigenous Prophecy, Geological Fantasy, and the New Madrid Earthquakes," *American Quarterly* 74, no. 4 (December 2022): 821-43.

1. Flint, *Recollections*, 226.
2. Num. 16:30: "If the LORD make a new thing, and the earth open her mouth, and swallow them up, with all that *appertain* unto them, and they go down quick into the pit; then ye shall understand that these men have provoked the LORD."
3. "Extracts from a Letter," *Lexington Reporter*, 3.
4. The most comprehensive history of these events and their aftermath is Valencius, *Lost History*. See also Penick, *New Madrid Earthquakes*; Feldman, *When the Mississippi Ran Backwards*.
5. Valencius, *Lost History*.
6. The phrase builds on Naomi Klein's "disaster capitalism." See Klein, *Shock Doctrine*.
7. Coulthard, *Red Skin, White Masks*.
8. Simpson, "Land as Pedagogy." See also Simpson, *As We Have Always Done*.
9. Wynter, "Unsettling the Coloniality."
10. Pandian, *Anthropology and the Western Tradition*, 57.
11. Dowd, *Spirited Resistance*, 128-29.
12. Edmunds, *Shawnee Prophet*. See also Edmunds, *Tecumseh and the Quest*.
13. Edmunds, *Shawnee Prophet*, 117.
14. Sami Lakomäki notes that this idea was a revival of one held by the "Indian Confederacy"—a collection of regional alliances and kinship networks that came together to resist US incursions on Indigenous territory in the wake of the Treaty of Paris, and in which Shawnee leaders were especially active. The alliance also had a spiritual dimension, drawing on prophetic tradition to encourage unity. See Lakomäki, *Gathering Together*, 120-31. See also Dowd, *Spirited Resistance*.
15. Edmunds, *Shawnee Prophet*, 38.
16. Edmunds, *Shawnee Prophet*, 38.
17. Watts, "Indigenous Place-Thought and Agency."
18. Norton-Smith, *Dance of Person and Place*, 63. See also Deloria, *God Is Red*.
19. Goeman, *Mark My Words*, 19-20.
20. Edmunds, *Tecumseh*, 98.
21. Coulthard, *Red Skin, White Masks*, 13.
22. Quoted in Dowd, *Spirited Resistance*, 142.
23. Goeman, in Aikau et al., "Indigenous Feminisms Roundtable," 94.
24. Goeman, in Aikau et al., "Indigenous Feminisms Roundtable," 94.
25. Quoted in Fixico, *Call for Change*, 66.
26. Nichols, *Theft Is Property!*, 115.

27 Quoted in Lakomäki, *Gathering Together*, 148.
28 "Indian Affairs," 2.
29 Quoted in Hancock, *Convulsed States*, 1.
30 "Indian Affairs," 2.
31 "Indian Affairs," 2.
32 Hancock, *Convulsed States*, 82–83.
33 Gambold to Simon Peter, March 21, 1812; quoted in Hancock, *Convulsed States*, 83.
34 Quoted in Yang, "Cherokee and Moravian Relations," 34.
35 Quoted in Yang, "Cherokee and Moravian Relations," 34.
36 Hancock, *Convulsed States*, 78.
37 Quoted in Yang, "Cherokee and Moravian Relations," 34.
38 Quoted in Pesantubbee, "When the Earth Shakes," 310. As Pesantubbee points out, the recorded versions of these prophecies are found in the mission diaries, and the missionaries did not speak Cherokee. In this light, references to "God" may be a translation or imposition rather than evidence of Christian belief.
39 Quoted in Pesantubbee, "When the Earth Shakes," 307.
40 Quoted in Pesantubbee, "When the Earth Shakes," 307.
41 Rifkin, *Beyond Settler Time*. The temporality of the Nativist movement from which the prophecies issued was also complex. Because of their insistence on the necessity of returning to tradition, such prophecies are often linked to an understanding of "nativism" associated with "conservatism and regression," as Gregory Dowd points out. And yet, he argues, rather than comprehending the movement through temporal stages—as situating "a native past *against* a modern present"—it might rather be viewed in terms of "people in a landscape (a native adaptation to the pressures of an encroaching power)." The movements he designates *nativist*, especially Tenskwatawa and Tecumseh's pan-Indigeneity, mix times as well as places: participants in these movements "identified with other native inhabitants of the continent [and] self-consciously proclaimed that selected traditions and new (sometimes even imported) modes of behavior held keys to earthly and spiritual salvation." Dowd, *Spirited Resistance*, xxii.
42 "Extracts from a Letter," 3.
43 Quoted in Valencius, *Lost History*, 150–51.
44 Eliza Bryan to Lorenzo Dow, March 22, 1816; reproduced in Dow, *History of Cosmopolite*, 344.
45 Pierce, *To the Editor*, December 25, 1811.
46 Flint, *Recollections*, 227.
47 See Kanon, "Scared from Their Sins."
48 Anonymous, "A Call to the People of Louisiana," 1812; reprinted in Hudson, "Ballad of New Madrid Earthquake," 150.
49 *Louisiana Gazette and Daily Advertiser*, December 21, 1811.

50 General Assembly of the Missouri Territory, *Resolution ... for the Relief of the Inhabitants*.

51 Joseph Ficklin, February 1812; quoted in Mitchill, "Detailed Narrative of the Earthquakes," 294–95.

52 See Valencius, *Lost History*.

53 See, e.g., Eliza Bryan's letter to Lorenzo Dow (1816), later published in Dow, *History of Cosmopolite*, 344–46. Bryan's letter was read into the *Congressional Record* to mark the 100th anniversary of the first earthquake. Russell, "Remarks on the Centennial."

54 James McBride to Mary McRoberts, April 1, 1812; reprinted in *The Quarterly Publication of the Historical and Philosophical Society of Ohio* 5, no. 1 (1910): 27–31.

55 William Leigh Pierce, quoted in Valencius, *Lost History*, 23.

56 Hunter's is the only written report of Tecumseh visiting the Osage. Lewis Cass, who would later serve as Andrew Jackson's Secretary of War, took pains to discredit Hunter's report of Tecumseh's visit to the Osage in his scathing 1826 denunciation of the narrative as a fabrication. For more on the controversy over Hunter's narrative, see Drinnon, *White Savage*. John Sugden supports the possibility that Tecumseh did visit the Osage during the early part of the quake series, in which case he would likely have discussed them, since the Missouri Osage lived not far from their epicenter. See Sugden, "Early Pan-Indianism."

57 Fixico, *American Indian Mind*, 76–77.

58 Hunter, *Memoirs of a Captivity*, 39, 47.

59 McHenry, "The Indian Prophet," letter to the *Georgia Journal*, n.d.; reproduced in *Halcyon Luminary and Theological Repository*, June 1, 1812, 275. As Sayre notes, whites sometimes conflated Tenskwatawa and Tecumseh and/or assumed that the latter was the leader known as the Shawnee Prophet.

60 Stiggins, *Creek Indian History*, 87.

61 Stiggins, *Creek Indian History*, 85–86.

62 Gunn, *Ethnology and Empire*, 118.

63 Gunn, *Ethnology and Empire*, 117.

64 McKenney, *History of the Indian Tribes*, 64.

65 McKenney, *History of the Indian Tribes*, 64–65.

66 McKenney, *History of the Indian Tribes*, 65.

67 A similar account was given in *Life and Times of Gen. Sam. Dale* (1860) by John F. H. Claiborne, who claimed to have been present at the speech: "When the white men approach you the yawning earth shall swallow them up.... I will stamp my foot at Tippecanoe, and the very earth shall shake" (61).

68 Sayre, *Indian Chief as Tragic Hero*.

69 Sayre, *Indian Chief as Tragic Hero*, 277.

70 Hough and Bilham, *After the Earth Quakes*, 84.

71 Bringier, "Notices of the Geology," 30.

72 Bringier, "Notices of the Geology," 21

73 Bringier, "Notices of the Geology," 20.
74 Bringier, "Notices of the Geology," 32.
75 Bringier, "Notices of the Geology," 40.
76 Bringier, "Notices of the Geology," 40, 41.
77 On quake-related damages, see R. A. Myers, "Cherokee Pioneers in Arkansas."
78 Bringier, "Notices of the Geology," 22.
79 Schuller, "Fossil and the Photograph," 238.
80 A biographical account of Bringier stresses his experience with Indigenous tribes in the region, though without specifying tribal affiliation: "He is said to have lived among the Indians, was adopted by a tribe and became its chief, and crossed the continent westward with Indian trading parties." See Williams, "Louis Bringer and His Description." The claim that he became chief of a tribe may be specious, but his praise of Osage hospitality in the report— "their hospitality exceeds all bounds; they act as if nothing was their own, and the best way to please them, is to refuse nothing from them"—suggests his own experience thereof. Bringier, "Notices of the Geology," 31.
81 Bringier, "Notices of the Geology," 35.
82 Wynter, "Unsettling the Coloniality," 266.
83 See Morgensen, "Biopolitics of Settler Colonialism."
84 Schoolcraft, *Summary Narrative*, 185.
85 Schoolcraft, *Summary Narrative*, 185.
86 Schoolcraft, "Transallegania," reprinted in Schoolcraft, *Journal of a Tour*.
87 Schoolcraft, "Transallegania," 23.
88 Schoolcraft, "Transallegania," 24.
89 Schoolcraft, *Personal Memoirs*, 53.
90 Rafferty, *Rude Pursuits and Rugged Peaks*, 9; Penick, *New Madrid Earthquakes*, 127.
91 As Virginia Jackson has argued, the formal qualities that contemporary critics associate with lyric poetry—the genre through which they view all poems—are not, at this point in the nineteenth century, dominant; many poetic genres, with different uses, proliferate, including the genres Schoolcraft mixes. See V. Jackson, *Dickinson's Misery*.
92 R. H. Stoddard, "Henry Rowe Schoolcraft."
93 I draw this phrase from Mark Rifkin, *Settler Common Sense*.
94 Schoolcraft, *Memoir on the Geological Position*, 9–10.
95 Lyell, *Second Visit*, 238.
96 Volney, *View of the Climate and Soil*, 65.
97 Lyell, *Second Visit*, 238.
98 Lyell, *Second Visit*, 85, 65.
99 Lyell, *Travels in North America*, 29.
100 US Geological Survey, *Tecumseh's Prophecy*.
101 US Geological Survey, *Tecumseh's Prophecy*.
102 The source of the woodcut is given on the inside cover as "Woodcut of the Great Earthquake in the West," in Devens, *Our First Century*, 220.

103   The source is given as Penick, *New Madrid Earthquakes*.
104   A previous USGS report on New Madrid, published in 1912, included a sentence citing Lyell's report of the "Indian tradition" about the previous earthquake, though it asserted that Lyell's calculation that many centuries had elapsed since the previous quakes was mistaken, citing "conclusive" geological evidence for "shocks long antedating that of 1811." The report also cites other settler reports of Indigenous testimony about the magnitude and effects of the 1811–12 series. See Fuller, *New Madrid Earthquake*.
105   See Coulthard, *Red Skin, White Masks*, 152.
106   Whyte, "Indigenous Food Sovereignty," 361.

CHAPTER THREE. ROMANCING THE TRACE

Earlier versions of material in chapter 3 appeared in "Romancing the Trace: Edward Hitchcock's Speculative Ichnology," in *Anthropocene Reading: Literary History in Geologic Times*, edited by Tobias Menely and Jesse Oak Taylor (University Park: Penn State University Press, 2017).

1   See Dean, "Hitchcock's Dinosaur Tracks," for a review of some of these. The noteworthy impact of the prints on New England–based writers points to a certain regionalist cast retained in the popular view of the tracks.
2   Hitchcock, "Report on Ichnolithology."
3   Metcalf, "Interest and Importance of Geology," 230.
4   Metcalf, "Interest and Importance of Geology," 235.
5   In the 1840s, Deane fought to gain credit for the idea, and the resulting squabble left its mark on both men's writing. See Herbert and Doyle, "Dr. James Deane of Greenfield."
6   See especially Cohen, *Stone*; Bennett, *Vibrant Matter*. Gilles Deleuze and Felix Guattari propose *matter* as a term for "the plane of consistency or Body without Organs, in other words, the unformed, unorganized, nonstratified, or destratified body and all its flows: subatomic and submolecular particles, pure intensities, prevital and prephysical free singularities." Deleuze and Guattari, "10,000 B.C.," 43.
7   Heringman, *Romantic Rocks, Aesthetic Geology*.
8   In classifying Hitchcock's period as Romantic rather than Victorian, I am referencing the fact that both geology and Romanticism operate according to different chronologies in the US, as opposed to the UK.
9   Mayor's *Fossil Legends*, an impressive compilation of Indigenous accounts of geologic phenomena on the continent now known as North America, seeks to recognize Indigenous contributions to modern science, pushing back against the defensive assertion that Indigenous discoveries are, in the words of the mid-twentieth-century paleontologist George Gaylord Simpson, "causal finds without scientific sequel" (quoted in Mayor, *Fossil Legends*, xxiv). Unlike the US Geological Survey's 1990 report discussed in chapter 2,

Mayor actively resists the consignment of Indigenous knowledge and people to the past. Still, the desire to legitimate Indigenous knowledge in the eyes of settler scientists like Simpson (who, Mayor acknowledges, is "the imaginary scientific reader I would most hope to convince of the worthiness of this project" [xxviii]) leads her to privilege Indigenous understandings of fossils that resemble geology—when they "anticipate the development of modern theories of geological ages and life-forms in the deep past, the relationships among species, changes over time, and extinctions" (xxxv). Geological time (indexed in the geological time chart that prefaces Mayor's book) constitutes the standard against which modernity is measured. On the coincidence between Indigenous narrative and geological history, see also Bruchac, "Geology and Cultural History of the Beaver Hill Story."

10 "Review of *Professor Hitchcock's Report*," 425.
11 "Review of *Professor Hitchcock's Report*," 443.
12 See, e.g., Winslow, *Preparation of the Earth*.
13 Quoted in Bedell, *Anatomy of Nature*, 5.
14 Spivak, "Translator's Preface," xvii.
15 Spivak, "Translator's Preface," xv.
16 Shaviro, "Specters of Marx."
17 A. J. Martin, *Dinosaurs without Bones*, 9.
18 Buckland, *Novel Science*.
19 See, for example, Pemberton et al., "Edward Hitchcock and Roland Bird," 49: "I find Hitchcock's inaugural 1836 monograph awe-inspiring."
20 Hitchcock, *Reminiscences of Amherst College*, 87, 88.
21 Hitchcock, "Ornithichnology," 312.
22 Hitchcock, "Ornithichnology," 322.
23 Untitled headnote, *Knickerbocker* 8, no. 6 (December 1836): 750.
24 Untitled headnote, *Knickerbocker*, 750.
25 Though its classical Latinate form had begun to decline by the time geology took modern form, Anglophone adaptations of scientific-didactic poetry flourished through the nineteenth century. See Hazen, *Poetry of Geology*.
26 *Knickerbocker* 8, no. 6 (December 1836): 752.
27 See Marché, "Edward Hitchcock's Poem, *Sandstone Bird* (1836)." A more recent analysis of this poem is given in Reiter, "'New Knowledge of Lost Worlds'?"
28 *Knickerbocker* 8, no. 6 (December 1836): 751.
29 See Baker, "Dead Bones and Honest Wonders."
30 Though the history Longfellow's poem contains is scant, it was enfolded in a later account of Omaha displacement coauthored by an Omaha woman and a settler: the 1898 history of Omaha City, highlighting Indigenous history, story, and art, composed by Fannie Reed Giffen and Inshta Theumba/Susette La Flesche Tibbles (Omaha), in which a narrative of the 1854 treaty that displaced the Omahas is followed by a biographical account of the Omaha

leaders who signed the treaties and then a reprinting of "To the Driving Cloud" illustrated with a portrait of its subject by Tibbles. Giffen, *Oo-ma-ha Ta-wa-tha*.

31 A. Jackson, "Annual Message to Congress."
32 Willis, *Environmental Evasion*, 63. It is precisely this orientation toward nature, Willis suggests, that has caused Longfellow to be dropped from the canon—because his extensive "physical and terrestrial" descriptions of nature resist absorption into the "naturalistic Whitmanian personality" (73) that twentieth-century literary critics favored.
33 Willis's target here is what he terms the "canonical erasure of material nature" in the American literary tradition. Longfellow's dynamic understanding of the matter of nature holds the potential, Willis suggests, to activate a less anthropocentric relation to the world, one that impresses humans with the claims of the nonhuman rather than abstracting and absorbing these, as Willis claims that writers like Emerson and Whitman do. Willis, *Environmental Evasion*, 55.
34 Greyser, *On Sympathetic Grounds*.
35 For a reading of the Lenape account of mammoth fossils against settler takes on that story by Jefferson and others, see Sweet, *Extinction and the Human*.
36 Indeed, even as Mathews admits that he has "taken the liberty of transferring an Indian tradition [about megafauna] to the credit of their predecessors, the Mound-Builders," he also suggests that those stories may have originally derived from the supposedly earlier peoples. Mathews, *Behemoth*, 162.
37 In linking this poem to the Anthropocene, I have in mind the so-called Orbis proposal, which dates the start of the epoch to 1610 based on the material traces of settler destruction of Indigenous peoples of the Americas. See Luciano, "Inhuman Anthropocene."
38 Willis, *Environmental Evasion*, 66. Following Walter Benjamin, Willis asserts that the ruin still possesses some critical and creative potential; yet, I argue, that potential is here circumscribed by the form of the poem.
39 V. Jackson, "Longfellow in His Time."
40 See Dean, "Hitchcock's Dinosaur Tracks." Dean observes that the tracks were, by 1838, already the subject of scientific controversy, to which Longfellow's professional proximity to Hitchcock may have permitted him access.
41 V. Jackson, "Longfellow in His Time."
42 This sort of reabsorption is on display, for instance, in Shira Wolosky's reading of Longfellow's footprint allusions (in both "A Psalm of Life" and "To the Driving Cloud") as references to poetry itself, "characteristic pun[s] on poetic meter." The substitution of metric for geologic referentiality reads poems as always about poetry, where "poetry" indexes, at once, the spontaneous overflow and transmission of feeling and the self-conscious and formally complex mimicry of that spontaneity. Wolosky, "Poetic Languages," 257.

43 On nineteenth-century depictions of the US interior as a desert, see LeMenager, *Manifest and Other Destinies*.
44 Babbage and Herschel, *Ninth Bridgewater Treatise*, 115.
45 Liu, *Local Transcendence*; Choi, "Natural History's Hypothetical Moments," 283.
46 Hitchcock, "Report on Ichnolithology," 320–21.
47 Hitchcock, "Report on Ichnolithology," 321.
48 Hitchcock, "Report on Ichnolithology," 321.
49 Hitchcock, "Report on Ichnolithology," 321–22.
50 Hitchcock, *Ichnology of New England*, 173.
51 Hitchcock, *Ichnology of New England*, 173–74.
52 Iovino and Oppermann, "Introduction," 4.
53 Bennett, *Vibrant Matter*.
54 Hitchcock, *Religion of Geology*, 413.
55 Hitchcock, *Religion of Geology*, 413.
56 The citation of Babbage's text is one of only two citations of the slave system in the book, the other of which is a fleeting citation of slavery as a manifestation of evil. Hitchcock, instead, follows this extended quotation by further developing his speculations on the endless chain of impressibility. Returning to his earlier suggestion that a "higher sphere" might be able to discern such traces, he hypothesizes that they might well affect that sphere as well—that they could transcend the material realm to produce a further reaction, transmuted but still resonant in the celestial afterlife. The suggestion that temporal deeds did not simply determine what one's posthumous fate would be but continued to act upon the afterlife implicitly extended Babbage's contention still further, suggesting that the slave trade has done damage not only to the planet, but to eternity.
57 Many thanks to Tavia Nyong'o for clarifying this point.
58 In "Unsettling the Coloniality" and elsewhere, Wynter refers to the supposedly secular frameworks of law and science, as they participated in Man's overrepresentation as the human, as "de-godded," though "only partly." The continued presence of religion in these frameworks, as I have shown with respect to geology, does not inherently challenge (indeed, largely upholds) this overrepresentation, though in some deployments—particularly those emphasizing the materialization of spirit—a speculative re-godding may possess the potential to do so. Wynter, "Unsettling the Coloniality," 263.
59 Higginson, "Emily Dickinson's Letters," 444.
60 See V. Jackson, *Dickinson's Misery*, 17.
61 W. J. T. Mitchell, *Last Dinosaur Book*. Mitchell observes that while public interest in dinosaurs picked up in the US after the Civil War, mass interest initially centered on the frontier adventures of bone collectors in the west; the creatures themselves emerged as figures for empire and white racial "purity" after the century's turn. See also B. Noble, *Articulating Dinosaurs*.

CHAPTER FOUR. MATTERS OF SPIRIT

Earlier versions of material in chapter 4 appeared in "Geological Fantasies, Haunting Anachronies: Eros, Time, and History in Harriet Prescott Spofford's 'The Amber Gods,'" *ESQ* 55, nos. 3–4 (2009): 269–303, and "Sacred Theories of Earth: Matters of Spirit in *The Soul of Things*," *American Literature* 86, no. 4 (December 2014): 713–36.

1. Spofford, "Amber Gods," 42.
2. Spofford, "Amber Gods," 42. For an intriguing analysis of the musical dimension of geology as it traveled from Lyell to Transcendental circles, see Katopodis, "Music of the Spheres."
3. Buckland, quoted in O'Connor, *Earth on Show*, 279.
4. E. Stoddard, *Morgesons*, 37. On the geologics of Stoddard's writing, see Goldberg, "Elizabeth Stoddard's Geologic Form," and Davoudi, "Creeping in the Crevices."
5. E. Stoddard, *Morgesons*, 38.
6. Spofford, "Amber Gods," 43.
7. Phelps, *Lectures to Young Ladies*, 218. On Phelps and other nineteenth-century women who wrote about geology, often for the young, see Larson, *Women Who Popularized Geology*.
8. Penn, *Conversations on Geology*. The book follows (and references) the Conversations model popularized by Jane Marcet. For background on Marcet, see G. Myers, "Fictionality, Demonstration, and a Forum."
9. Penn, *Conversations on Geology*, 5.
10. Schuller, *Biopolitics of Feeling*, 19.
11. Schuller, *Biopolitics of Feeling*, 19.
12. Emily Dickinson to Abiah Root, May 7, 1845. In Franklin, "Emily Dickinson to Abiah Root," 11.
13. See Peel, "Emily Dickinson and Transatlantic Geology"; Wry, "Deep Mapping"; Uno, "Geology in Emily Dickinson's Poetry."
14. Cohen, *Stone*, 27.
15. Bowler, *Fossils and Progress*.
16. De Landa, *Thousand Years of Nonlinear History*, 20.
17. Bennett, *Vibrant Matter*, 122.
18. Foucault, *Order of Things*, 274.
19. Schuller, *Biopolitics of Feeling*, 17–18.
20. Gould, *Time's Arrow, Time's Cycle*, 3. The trope continues into the present. An article in *Scientific American* asserts that "the human brain may not be hardwired to comprehend the billions of years of history that have shaped the modern environment." Fecht, "Urban Geology."
21. Darwin, *Voyage of the Beagle*, 529.
22. Deleuze and Guattari, "10,000 B.C.," 43.
23. See "Obituary: William Denton." For Denton's research on the LaBrea Tar Pits, see Denton, "On an Asphalt Bed."

24 Powell, *William Denton*.
25 Davis, *Principles of Nature*, 223.
26 Denton, *Our Planet*, 296.
27 Denton, *Our Planet*, 301.
28 Buchanan, *Manual of Psychometry*, 73. Though he sneered at Buchanan's system, the phrenologist J. Stanley Grimes also linked the human mind and the rock record in his "phreno-geology," the belief that the progressive development of the earth paralleled the progressive development of the human mind. See Grimes, *Phreno-Geology*.
29 Rochelle Raineri Zuck has documented another case of the geological use of psychometry—in this instance, the "oil wizard" Abraham James's supposed ability to uncover crude oil deposits. See Zuck, "Wizard of Oil."
30 Denton and Denton, *Soul of Things*, 1:287. On gendered understandings of psychometry, see Strang, "Measuring Souls."
31 On the sexual politics of mediums, see Braude, *Radical Spirits*; McGarry, *Ghosts of Futures Past*; and Tromp, *Altered States*.
32 Buchanan, *Manual of Psychometry*, 19.
33 Buchanan, *Manual of Psychometry*, 70, 19.
34 I discuss the feminized form of the human more extensively in Luciano, *Arranging Grief*, and in Luciano and Chen, "Introduction."
35 Denton and Denton, *Soul of Things*, 1:126.
36 Denton and Denton, *Soul of Things*, 1:285.
37 Denton and Denton, *Soul of Things*, 1:55.
38 Denton and Denton, *Soul of Things*, 1:115.
39 Denton, *Soul of Things*, 2:29, 27–28.
40 Denton, *Soul of Things*, 2:117.
41 Denton, *Soul of Things*, 2:75.
42 Denton, *Soul of Things*, 2:76.
43 Denton, *Soul of Things*, 2:117.
44 Denton, *Soul of Things*, 2:116.
45 Denton, *Soul of Things*, 2:38–39.
46 Denton, *Soul of Things*, 2:74.
47 Morton, "Here Comes Everything," 165.
48 Denton and Denton, *Soul of Things*, 1:114.
49 Denton and Denton, *Soul of Things*, 1:114.
50 The white explorer trope returns in the second volume, where he declares that the psychometer "drops upon island or continent, watches the wild tribes of Africa, explores the desert interior of Australia, or solves the problem of the poles." Denton, *Soul of Things*, 2:29.
51 Racialized hierarchies of cultivation and cognition are more explicitly outlined in the psychometric explorations of prehistoric early humans that dominate the second volume of *The Soul of Things*, while volume 3's psychometric exploration of Mars by Sherman, Elizabeth, and Annie charts the alien races

observed there according to white-supremacist hierarchy. Volume 3 in particular underscores what Christine Ferguson has identified as Spiritualism's increasing investment in racial eugenicism across the latter part of the nineteenth century. See Ferguson, *Determined Spirits*.
52 Bennett, "Powers of the Hoard," 246.
53 Bennett, "Powers of the Hoard," 259. The term *geo-affect* appears in Bennett, *Vibrant Matter*, 122.
54 Bennett, "Powers of the Hoard," 269.
55 Bennett, "Powers of the Hoard," 259.
56 Buchanan, *Manual of Psychometry*, 19.
57 See Foucault, *History of Sexuality*. Siobhan Somerville has outlined the way racial and sexual deviance were entwined in the nineteenth century. See Somerville, *Queering the Color Line*.
58 Spofford, "Amber Gods," 39.
59 Spofford, "Amber Gods," 59.
60 Spofford, "Amber Gods," 58.
61 Spofford, "Amber Gods," 55.
62 Rudwick, *Meaning of Fossils*.
63 See, e.g., Lawrence, "Edward Hitchcock."
64 I develop this account of sacred time, adapted from Mircea Eliade, further in Luciano, *Arranging Grief*.
65 Bataille, *Death and Sensuality*, 61, 40.
66 Spofford, "Amber Gods," 55.
67 Clark and Yusoff, "Queer Fire," 21.
68 Spofford, "Amber Gods," 55.
69 Spofford, "Amber Gods," 43.
70 Spofford, "Amber Gods," 55.
71 Spofford, "Amber Gods," 56.
72 Spofford, "Amber Gods," 54.
73 Spofford, "Amber Gods," 56.
74 Spofford, "Amber Gods," 56.
75 Spofford, "Amber Gods," 52, 46.
76 Deleuze and Guattari, *Anti-Oedipus*, 296.
77 Spofford, "Amber Gods," 56.
78 In his *Principles of Geology*, Charles Lyell also speculated that geological time might contain a cyclical dimension, although he does not seem to desire it as ardently as Yone does. Illustrating the correspondence between the earth's surface and the temperature of the globe, he described the changes a cooling earth had seen and speculated on the possibility that a return to prehistoric climates would extinguish present-day life-forms and revive past ones: "Then might those genera of animals return, of which the memorials are preserved in the ancient rocks of our continents. The huge iguanodon might reappear in the woods, and the ichthyosaur in the sea,

while the pterodactyle might flit again through umbrageous groves of tree-ferns" (67).
79 Day, *Alien Capital*, 36, 7.
80 Spofford, "Amber Gods," 53.
81 Spofford, "Amber Gods," 53.
82 R. J. Ellis, "'Latent Color' and 'Exaggerated Snow,'" 268.
83 Spofford, "Amber Gods," 44.
84 For an extended reading of this possibility, see R. J. Ellis, "'Latent Color' and 'Exaggerated Snow.'"
85 Spofford, "Amber Gods," 45.
86 Spillers, "Mama's Baby, Papa's Maybe," 66.
87 Derrida, *Specters of Marx*, 6.
88 Spofford, "Amber Gods," 45.
89 Derrida, *Specters of Marx*, xviii.
90 Spofford, "Amber Gods," 79, 83.
91 Freeman, *Beside You in Time*, 8.
92 Bennett, "Powers of the Hoard," 240.
93 Bennett, "Powers of the Hoard," 241.

CHAPTER FIVE. THE NATURAL HISTORY OF FREEDOM

1 J. M. Smith, "Introduction," 18.
2 Interestingly, McCune Smith does not mention Miller's attacks on Douglass in the *Witness*, the newspaper of the Free Church of Scotland, which Miller edited. In chapter 24 of *My Bondage and My Freedom*, Douglass notes that his participation, during his tour of Scotland in 1846, in public condemnations of the Free Church's acceptance of donations from US slaveholders resulted in "aspersions cast upon me through [Church] organs," though he does not cite Miller by name. For an overview of this conflict see Shepperson, "Frederick Douglass and Scotland."
3 H. Miller, *Autobiography: My Schools and Schoolmasters*, 153.
4 J. M. Smith, "Introduction," 25–26. In a footnote to this passage, McCune Smith clarifies that "organic life also encompasses 'vegetable matter' according to a recent scientific paper." J. M. Smith, "Introduction," 32n4.
5 Rusert, *Fugitive Science*, 60, 59. See also C. Ellis, *Antebellum Posthuman*.
6 Metcalf, "Interest and Importance of Scientific Geology," 235.
7 Agassiz, "Silurian Beach," 460.
8 Clark, Gormally, and Tuffen, "Speculative Volcanology," 274.
9 M. A. Miller, *Natural History of Revolution*, 148. For a broader overview of European volcanic imagery in this century, see McCallam, *Volcanoes in Eighteenth-Century Europe*.
10 Gleason, "Volcanoes and Meteors."
11 Sale, *Slumbering Volcano*, 63.
12 Cited in "Mr. Lincoln's Forebodings."

13 "Garrison on Slavery."
14 Douglass, "Decision of the Hour," 515.
15 See, e.g., Lyell, *Principles of Geology*, vol. 1, chap. 26, "Causes of Earthquakes and Volcanoes," 162–79.
16 Gleason, "Volcanos and Meteors," 111.
17 J. M. Smith, "Lecture on the Haytien Revolutions," 35. For the influence of the Haitian Revolution in the US, see Hunt, *Haiti's Influence on Antebellum America*. Mirabeau's statement was also cited in numerous works published outside the US; see, e.g., "Past and Present State of Hayti," 436.
18 "Letters from the West Indies."
19 Installed in the wake of formal emancipation in 1834, the unpaid "apprenticeship" system was supposed to end after four to six years; however, as the "Letters" author noted, rumors that agricultural laborers would be forced to endure the full six years significantly increased unrest. The apprenticeship system did legally end in 1838, but Montserrat's white planters continued to wield disproportionate power, putting in place what was in effect a sharecropper system. "Letters from the West Indies."
20 *Liberator*, May 12, 1832, 75.
21 Gleason, "Volcanos and Meteors," 132n25. The quoted passage, attributed to the *US Telegraph*, was reprinted in the *Liberator* on December 19, 1835. The reprinted article went on to argue that the main threat to slavery's continuance was not the possibility of insurrection but the operations of "conscience" in response to antislavery arguments, a position that corresponded to the Garrisonian *Liberator*'s embrace of moral suasion and disavowal of violence.
22 Holbrook, "Family Cabinets of Nature and Art."
23 Fraser, *Star Territory*, 52.
24 "Terrific Theory," *North Star*, February 2, 1849.
25 "Terrific Theory," *North Star*, February 2, 1849. The same article appears in *Gazette of the Golden Rule*, 98, and *London Journal and Weekly Record*, 62.
26 "Is the Center of the Earth a Mass of Fire?"
27 "The Force of Volcanoes," *Christian Recorder*, April 13, 1861.
28 "What a Volcano Can Do," *Christian Recorder*, November 2, 1861.
29 "EARTHQUAKES."
30 "Use of Earthquakes."
31 "Use of Earthquakes."
32 Douglass, "What to the Slave?," 66. I discuss this speech further in Luciano, *Arranging Grief*, 183–87.
33 Douglass, "What to the Slave?," 72; Douglass, "Revolution of 1848," 129; Douglass, "What of the Night?," 120.
34 *Liberator*, June 2, 1832, 87.
35 The inert cavities left by the incinerated victims of this eruption were the subject of much attention in the first half of the nineteenth century, though

successful reproductions—the plaster casts that now stand in for the disaster in the popular imagination—were not made until 1863. See Gardner Coates, "On the Cutting Edge."
36 Hartman, *Scenes of Subjection*, 22.
37 Hartman, *Scenes of Subjection*, 34.
38 Hartman, *Scenes of Subjection*, 35.
39 *Life and Times of Frederick Douglass*, quoted in Hartman, *Scenes of Subjection*, 47.
40 Hartman, *Scenes of Subjection*, 47.
41 Bernier, "From Fugitive Slave."
42 Douglass, quoted in "Great Anti-Colonization Meeting."
43 Douglass, quoted in "Great Anti-Colonization Meeting."
44 For an overview of Douglass's evolution from pacifism to advocate of armed confrontation, see Wallace, "Violence, Manhood, and War."
45 Douglass, "Tyrants' Jubilee!," in Gleason, "Volcanos and Meteors," 130.
46 Douglass, "Tyrants' Jubilee!," in Gleason, "Volcanos and Meteors," 129, 130.
47 Douglass, "Tyrants' Jubilee!," in Gleason, "Volcanos and Meteors," 129.
48 M. A. Miller, *Natural History of Revolution*, 169, 170.
49 Z. I. Jackson, *Becoming Human*, 50.
50 Z. I. Jackson, *Becoming Human*, 50.
51 See Ferreira da Silva, *Toward a Global Idea of Race*.
52 Frederick Douglass, "John Brown and the Slaveholders' Insurrection," January 30, 1860; quoted in Gleason, "Volcanos and Meteors."
53 Insko, *History, Abolition, and the Ever-Present Now*, 129–30.
54 "Great Anti-Colonization Meeting."
55 "Great Anti-Colonization Meeting."
56 "Cingues," *Colored American*, October 10, 1839, 1; quoted in Sale, *Slumbering Volcano*, 92.
57 Sale, *Slumbering Volcano*, 180.
58 Z. I. Jackson, *Becoming Human*, 47. For nuanced critical considerations of Douglass's vision of masculinity in relation to white gendered ideals, see Yarborough, "Race, Violence, and Manhood," and Wallace, *Constructing the Black Masculine*.
59 Hartman, *Scenes of Subjection*, 152.
60 Sale, *Slumbering Volcano*, 195.
61 Hartman, *Scenes of Subjection*, 64, 66.
62 Hartman, *Scenes of Subjection*, 65, 64.
63 Hartman, *Scenes of Subjection*, 70.
64 For a biography of Martin, see Blackett, "John Sella Martin."
65 J. Sella Martin, "Speech of Rev. J. S. Martin," reprinted in "Great Meeting in Boston," 194.
66 National Aeronautics and Space Administration Advisory Council, *Earth System Science*, 2.
67 Sharpe, *In the Wake*, 106.

68 Sharpe, *In the Wake*, 106.
69 "The Sentinel of Freedom," a poem Martin published the previous month in the *Anglo-African Magazine* (where it immediately followed a lengthy report on Brown's rebellion and trial), outlines the change in the weather in greater detail, troping every aspect of the natural world as it participates in revolt, including "lightnings of truth," "volcanic speech," and earthquakes shattering the prisons of truth and reason, until finally "truth's great sunlight" and "earth renovated by fire and blood" appear as the storm fades. J. S. Martin, "Sentinel of Freedom."
70 Blackett, "John Sella Martin," 190.
71 Neimanis, "Sea and the Breathing."
72 Fraser, *Star Territory*, 48.
73 McKittrick, *Demonic Grounds*, 6. See also Sylvia Wynter's reflections in "Novel and History" on how the enslaved used the plots of land allotted them as a place to nurture not only food but communal values and forms of social connection as well.
74 Biographies of James McCune Smith include Blight, "In Search of Learning"; Stauffer, *Black Hearts of Men*; Duane, *Educated for Freedom*.
75 Peterson, "Untangling Genealogy's Tangled Skeins."
76 Ansted, *Science, Scenery and Art*, 307, 308.
77 J. M. Smith, "Heads of the Colored People"; reprinted in Stauffer, *Works of James McCune Smith*, 230.
78 Stauffer, *Works of James McCune Smith*, 230.
79 Lyell's consideration of the slavery question in those books was "pained," as Richard Huzzey has observed; though he firmly opposed the institution, he opposed immediate abolition, professing himself sympathetic to the plight of the southern slave-owner. Huzzey, *Freedom Burning*, 25.
80 J. M. Smith, "Heads of the Colored People," 230.
81 "Communipaw," February 20, 1851, in *Frederick Douglass' Paper*; reprinted in Stauffer, *Works of James McCune Smith*, 88.
82 Spires, *Practice of Citizenship*, 114.
83 "Communipaw," February 20, 1851; reprinted in Stauffer, *Works of James McCune Smith*, 88.
84 As Britt Rusert and Gene Andrew Jarrett have pointed out, a number of antebellum African American writers criticized Jefferson's claims, although McCune Smith's, Jarrett asserts, "stands as one of the most sustained critiques of a racial premise in *Notes* and of Jefferson's specter over the black presence in American 'civilization.'" See Jarrett, "'To Refute Mr. Jefferson's Arguments,'" 308; "The Banneker Age," in Rusert, *Fugitive Science*, 33–64.
85 LaFleur, *Natural History of Sexuality*.
86 See Schuller, *Biopolitics of Feeling*.
87 J. M. Smith, "Civilization," *Anglo-African Magazine* 1, no. 1 (January 1859); reprinted in Stauffer, *Works of James McCune Smith*, 252.

88   J. M. Smith, "On the Fourteenth Query," *Anglo-African Magazine* 1, no. 8 (August 1859): 268, 289. Owen's research on apes was in part intended to refute arguments for evolution, which he, like Lyell, opposed at the time. See Desmond, "Richard Owen's Reaction."
89   James McCune Smith's celebration of corporeal plasticity and racial malleability intervenes in a long and problematic history of the concept. As Zakiyyah Iman Jackson demonstrates, plasticity has long been bound up with antiblackness, exemplified in the "coerced formlessness" of the enslaved. Z. I. Jackson, *Becoming Human*, 71. Similarly, Kyla Schuller and Jules Gill-Peterson point out that ideas about corporeal plasticity "emerged hand in hand with biopolitics." However, as they acknowledge with respect to C. Riley Snorton's work, "racial plasticity serves as both the vector of biopower and a site of critical maneuver." Schuller and Gill-Peterson, "Introduction," 5, 10; Snorton, *Black on Both Sides*. McCune Smith's optimism about geological optimization marks the biopolitical cast of his thinking; however, his embrace of plasticity as a counter to racial fixity positions it critically as a means of undoing a whiteness predicated on sociobiological permanence.
90   J. M. Smith, "Civilization," 258.
91   McKittrick, *Demonic Grounds*, 124.
92   McKittrick, *Demonic Grounds*, 133.
93   McKittrick, *Demonic Grounds*, 133. In her reading of Glissant's *Une Nouvelle Région du Monde*, which opens with a view of an uninhabited volcanic island off the coast of Martinique, Carine M. Mardossian assesses Glissant's thinking as explicitly extending to the geologic. See Mardossian, "'Poetics of Landscape,'" 991.
94   J. M. Smith, "Civilization," 257–58.
95   J. M. Smith, "Civilization," 260.
96   Cuvier, quoted in Douglas, "Climate to Crania," 41.
97   J. M. Smith, "On the Fourteenth Query," 270.
98   Though James McCune Smith here depicts the captives, somewhat neutrally, as "landing" on North American shores, he elsewhere highlights their theft. For instance, in his biographical sketch on Henry Highland Garnet, he describes the journey thus: "His grandfather was stolen by slave-traders from the coast of Africa, survived the horrors of the middle-passage ... landed on the James River, and was thence transferred to the estate of Colonel William Spencer at New Market, doomed to perpetual slavery, himself and his heirs forever." See Garnet, *Memorial Discourse*, 17.
99   Spillers, "Mama's Baby, Papa's Maybe," 67; J. M. Smith, "Civilization," 280.
100   J. M. Smith, "Civilization," 262.
101   J. M. Smith, "Civilization," 262.
102   See Liebman, "Quest for Black Voting Rights."
103   James McCune Smith to Gerrit Smith, December 28–31, 1846; reprinted in Stauffer, *Works of James McCune Smith*, 304.

104 Rev. Theodore S. Wright et al., *Address to the Three Thousand*, n.p.; quoted in D. Miller, "At Home in the Great Northern Wilderness," 130. James McCune Smith praised the hard work of those who had established themselves on the land yet also privately acknowledged the difficulty of raising enough money to buy the oxen and equipment needed to clear the forested tracts. See, e.g., James McCune Smith to Gerrit Smith, July 7, 1848, and James McCune Smith to Gerrit Smith, February 6, 1850, both reprinted in Stauffer, *Works of James McCune Smith*, 310–11, 314–15.

105 J. M. Smith, "Civilization," 262.

106 J. M. Smith to Gerrit Smith, July 7, 1848, 310.

107 Byrd, *Transit of Empire*, 39.

108 J. M. Smith, "On the Fourteenth Query," 279.

109 See Fisher, "Antebellum Black Climate Science."

110 J. M. Smith, "Civilization," 256.

111 Cordis, "Settler Unfreedoms," 20.

112 According to Dobbs, the coral debate among geologists became a flashpoint for tensions between empiricism and theory in nineteenth-century science. See Dobbs, *Reef Madness*.

113 Elleray, *Victorian Coral Islands*, 41.

114 Chow, *Nineteenth-Century American Literature*, 100.

115 Lyell, *Lectures on Geology*. An earlier (1842) edition of the lectures did not carry the appendix by McCune Smith, and the reason it was appended to the later edition is unclear.

116 J. M. Smith, "Civilization," 262–63.

117 J. M. Smith, "Civilization," 263.

118 Navakas, "Antebellum Coral," 265.

119 King, *Black Shoals*, 9.

120 J. M. Smith, "Civilization," 263.

121 J. M. Smith, "Civilization," 262.

122 James McCune Smith notes in "On the Fourteenth Query" that "Civilization" was composed in 1844, and the version published in 1859 was "slightly amended." It is possible, then, that the version of the coral story contained in the 1848 letter to Smith may be a revision of the one in the 1844 draft of the essay; conversely, it may have inspired McCune Smith to write a new ending when readying "Civilization" for publication. J. M. Smith, "On the Fourteenth Query," 280.

123 James McCune Smith to Gerrit Smith, May 12, 1848, reprinted in Stauffer, *Works of James McCune Smith*, 308.

124 James McCune Smith to Gerrit Smith, May 12, 1848, 308.

125 Elleray, "Little Builders," 228.

126 On disabled masculinities in James McCune Smith's writing see Crane, "'Razed to the Knees.'"

127 Clytus, "Visualizing in Black Print," 31; Spires, "Aliened Americans," 42.

128 See Spillers, "Mama's Baby, Papa's Maybe."
129 Cordis, "Settler Unfreedoms," 17.

CODA

Earlier versions of material in the coda appeared in *Timelines of American Literature*, edited by Cody Marrs and Christopher Hager (Baltimore: Johns Hopkins University Press, 2019).

1 Some fine examples of Americanist Anthropocene literary studies include Marshall, "What Are the Novels?," 529; Ronda, *Remainders*; Farrier, *Anthropocene Poetics*; Trexler, *Anthropocene Fictions*.
2 Melville, *Moby-Dick*, 350.
3 Melville, *Moby-Dick*, 350.
4 Farrier, *Anthropocene Poetics*, 16; Nijhuis, "When Did the Human Epoch Begin?"
5 Kolbert, "Lost World"; Zalasiewicz, *Earth after Us*.
6 Steffen, "Anthropocene."
7 See Corcoran et al., "Anthropogenic Marker Horizon"; Carrington, "How the Domestic Chicken Rose." I have written more extensively on plastigomerates as boundary markers elsewhere; see Luciano, "Speaking Substances."
8 "Results of Binding Vote by AWG, Released 21st May 2019." On the Great Acceleration, see McNeill and Engelke, *Great Acceleration*.
9 Brazile, "Marking the Anthropocene."
10 Foucault, *History of Sexuality*, 137, 143.
11 Foucault, *History of Sexuality*, 143. Foucault's notion of the "threshold of modernity" was actually introduced much earlier, in relation to the modern episteme as such rather than modern political practices. In *The Order of Things*, Foucault asserts that the moment "[Western] culture crossed the threshold beyond which we recognize our modernity" is the moment when "finitude was conceived in an eternal cross-reference with itself" (275). In *The Order of Things*, the threshold is posited as epistemic, a moment of perception central to Man's self-recognition as modern; in the *History of Sexuality*, however, Foucault renders the biopolitical "threshold of modernity" marked by the threat of global nuclear war ontologically: it is not a perception but an existential risk, a material threat to the "life of the species." In the context of the Anthropocene, a geological epoch illuminated by the looming threat of biological extinction, the difference between these two figurations of modernity's threshold is especially striking.
12 Nixon, "Anthropocene." For similar critiques of the Anthropocene, see Malm and Hornberg, "Geology of Mankind?"; Ahuja, *Planetary Specters*; Haraway, *Staying with the Trouble*; Yusoff, *Billion Black Anthropocenes*.
13 Lustgarten and Kohut, "Great Climate Migration."
14 Gómez-Barris, "Colonial Anthropocene."

15 Haraway et al., "Anthropologists Are Talking"; Davis et al., "Anthropocene, Capitalocene,... Plantationocene?"
16 See Moore, *Capitalism in the Web of Life*.
17 Lewis and Maslin, "Defining the Anthropocene." The article actually contains two proposals for boundary markers, the other of which is a version of the nuclear Anthropocene, but the Orbis hypothesis has drawn far more attention because of the expansiveness of its critique.
18 I have made this argument earlier; see Luciano, "Inhuman Anthropocene." See also A. Mitchell, "Decolonising the Anthropocene." For an astute consideration of the land as witness to colonial violence, see Greyser, *On Sympathetic Grounds*.
19 Zalasiewicz et al., "Colonization of the Americas," 7.
20 Hooley, "Reading Vulnerably."
21 On the sources of climate change denial, see Oreskes and Conway, *Merchants of Doubt*. Oreskes is a member of the AWG.
22 Santana, "Waiting for the Anthropocene," 1075.
23 According to John McNeill, an environmental historian and a member of the AWG, Google Scholar hits for the term are highest for humanities scholars. Presentation at "Anthropocene Impacts" panel, Georgetown University, November 28, 2017.
24 Chakrabarty, "Climate of History," 201.
25 Chakrabarty, "Climate of History," 212, 213. Timothy Clark also frames the Anthropocene as a demand for changes in the scale of humanist analysis, arguing that it "entails the realization of how deeply [ordinary perceptions of 'everyday' experience] may be misleading, underlining how (worryingly) our 'normal' scales of space and time must be understood as contingent projections of a biology which may be relatively inexorable." T. Clark, *Ecocriticism on the Edge*, 30.
26 See Gibbard and Walker, "Term 'Anthropocene'"; Santana, "Waiting for the Anthropocene."
27 Geological Society of America, "Climate Change."
28 Intergovernmental Panel on Climate Change, "Climate Change 2021."
29 Davis and Todd, "Importance of a Date," 770.
30 Davis and Todd, "Importance of a Date," 775.
31 Yusoff, "Geologic Life."
32 Whyte, "Time as Kinship," 49, 42, 48.
33 Freeman, *Beside You in Time*, 11, 8.
34 Bjornerud, *Timefulness*, 17, 16.
35 Brown, *Black Utopias*, 17. On care across deep time, see also Lifetimes Research Collective, "Fossilization."
36 Ellsworth and Kruse, "Introduction," 6.
37 Todd, "On Time."
38 See Sharpe, *In the Wake*, 41.
39 De Landa, *Thousand Years of Nonlinear History*, 20.

bibliography

Adams, Charles H. "Uniformity and Progress: The Natural History of *The Crater*." In *James Fenimore Cooper: New Historical and Literary Contexts*, edited by W. M. Verhoeven, 203-13. Amsterdam: Rodopi, 1993.
Adams, Katherine. "DuBois, Dirt Determinism, and the Reconstruction of Global Value." *American Literary History* 31, no. 4 (2019): 715-40.
Agassiz, Louis. "America the Old World." *Atlantic Monthly* 11, no. 65 (March 1, 1863): 373-81.
Agassiz, Louis. "The Fern Forests of the Carboniferous Period." *Atlantic Monthly* 11, no. 67 (May 1, 1863): 615-25.
Agassiz, Louis. "The Geological Middle Age." *Atlantic Monthly* 12, no. 70 (August 1, 1863): 212-24.
Agassiz, Louis. "The Growth of Continents." *Atlantic Monthly* 12, no. 69 (July 1, 1863): 72-81.
Agassiz, Louis. "Mountains and Their Origin." *Atlantic Monthly* 11, no. 68 (June 1, 1863): 747-56.
Agassiz, Louis. "The Silurian Beach." *Atlantic Monthly* 11, no. 66 (April 1, 1863): 460-71.
Agassiz, Louis. "The Tertiary Age, and Its Characteristic Animals." *Atlantic Monthly* 12, no. 71 (September 1, 1863): 333-42.
Ahuja, Neel. *Planetary Specters: Race, Migration, and Climate Change in the Twenty-First Century*. Chapel Hill: University of North Carolina Press, 2021.
Aikau, Hokulani K., Maile Arvin, Mishuana Goeman, and Scott Morgensen. "Indigenous Feminisms Roundtable." In "Transnational Feminisms," ed. Karen J. Leong, Roberta Chevrette, Ann Hibner Koblitz, Karen Kuo, and Heather Switzer, special issue, *Frontiers: A Journal of Women Studies* 36, no. 3 (2015): 84-106.
Allen, Thomas M. *A Republic in Time: Temporality and Social Imagination in Nineteenth-Century America*. Chapel Hill: University of North Carolina Press, 2008.

Allewaert, Monique. *Ariel's Ecology: Plantations, Personhood, and Colonialism in the American Tropics*. Minneapolis: University of Minnesota Press, 2013.
Ansted, David T. *The Gold-Seeker's Manual*. London: John Van Voorst, 1849.
Ansted, David T. *Science, Scenery and Art, Being Extracts from the Note-book of a Geologist and Mining Engineer*. London: John Van Voorst, 1854.
Ansted, David T. *The Great Stone Book of Nature*. Philadelphia: George S. Childs, 1863.
Anthropocene Working Group. "Results of Binding Vote by AWG: Released May 21, 2019." *Subcommission on Quaternary Stratigraphy*. http://quaternary.stratigraphy.org/working-groups/anthropocene/.
Arsić, Branka. *Bird Relics: Grief and Vitalism in Thoreau*. Cambridge, MA: Harvard University Press, 2016.
Arsić, Branka. *On Leaving: A Reading in Emerson*. Cambridge, MA: Harvard University Press, 2010.
Arsić, Branka, and Cary Wolfe, eds. *The Other Emerson*. Minneapolis: University of Minnesota Press, 2010.
Asad, Talal. *Formations of the Secular: Christianity, Islam, Modernity*. Stanford, CA: Stanford University Press, 2003.
Babbage, Charles, and John F. W. Herschel. *The Ninth Bridgewater Treatise: A Fragment*. 2nd ed. London: John Murray, 1837–38.
Baker, Jennifer J. "Dead Bones and Honest Wonders: The Aesthetics of Natural Science in *Moby-Dick*." In *Melville and Aesthetics*, edited by Samuel Otter and Geoffrey Sanborn, 85–101. New York: Palgrave Macmillan, 2011.
Barad, Karen. *Meeting the Universe Halfway: Quantum Physics and the Entanglement of Matter and Meaning*. Durham, NC: Duke University Press, 2007.
Barker, Joanne. "For Whom Sovereignty Matters." In *Sovereignty Matters: Locations of Contestation and Possibility in Indigenous Struggles for Self-Determination*, edited by Joanne Barker, 1–33. Lincoln: University of Nebraska Press, 2005.
Barnard, John Levi. "Empire." In *American Literature in Transition, 1820–1860*, edited by Justine S. Murison, 37–53. Cambridge: Cambridge University Press, 2022.
Bataille, Georges. *Death and Sensuality: A Study of Eroticism and the Taboo*. New York: Walker, 1962.
Bedell, Rebecca. *The Anatomy of Nature: Geology and American Landscape Painting, 1825–75*. Princeton, NJ: Princeton University Press, 2002.
Bennett, Jane. *Influx and Efflux: Writing Up with Walt Whitman*. Durham, NC: Duke University Press, 2020.
Bennett, Jane. "Powers of the Hoard: Further Notes on Material Agency." In *Animal, Vegetable, Mineral: Ethics and Objects*, edited by Jeffrey Jerome Cohen, 237–69. Washington, DC: Oliphaunt Books, 2012.
Bennett, Jane. "Systems and Things: On Vital Materialism and Object-Oriented Philosophy." In *The Nonhuman Turn*, edited by Richard Grusin, 223–39. Minneapolis: University of Minnesota Press, 2015.
Bennett, Jane. *Vibrant Matter: A Political Ecology of Things*. Durham, NC: Duke University Press, 2010.

Berger, Martin. "Overexposed: Whiteness and the Landscape Photography of Carleton Watkins." *Oxford Art Journal* 26, no. 1 (2003): 1–23.
Berlant, Lauren. *Cruel Optimism*. Durham, NC: Duke University Press, 2011.
Berlant, Lauren. "Intensity Is a Signal, Not a Truth: An Interview with Lauren Berlant," by Nicholas Manning. *Revue Française d'Études Américaines* 154, no. 1 (2018): 113–20.
Bernier, Celeste-Marie. "From Fugitive Slave to Fugitive Abolitionist: The Oratory of Frederick Douglass and the Emerging Heroic Slave Tradition." *Atlantic Studies* 3, no. 2 (October 2006): 201–24.
Bjornerud, Marcia. *Timefulness: How Thinking like a Geologist Can Help Save the World*. Princeton, NJ: Princeton University Press, 2018.
Blackett, R. J. M. "John Sella Martin: The Lion from the West." In *Beating against the Barriers: Biographical Essays in Nineteenth Century Afro-American History*, 184–285. Baton Rouge: Louisiana State University Press, 1986.
Blight, David W. "In Search of Learning, Liberty, and Self Definition: James McCune Smith and the Ordeal of the Antebellum Black Intellectual." *Afro-Americans in New York Life and History* 9, no. 2 (1985): 7–25.
Bowler, Peter J. *Fossils and Progress: Paleontology and the Idea of Progressive Evolution in the Nineteenth Century*. New York: Science History Publications, 1976.
Brantlinger, Patrick. *Dark Vanishings: Discourse on the Extinction of Primitive Races, 1800–1930*. Ithaca, NY: Cornell University Press, 2003.
Braude, Ann. *Radical Spirits: Spiritualism and Women's Rights in Nineteenth-Century America*. Boston: Beacon, 1989.
Brazile, Rachel. "Marking the Anthropocene." *Chemistry World*, January 29, 2021. https://www.chemistryworld.com/features/marking-the-anthropocene/4012969.article.
Bringier, Louis. "Notices of the Geology, Mineralogy, Topography, Productions, and Aboriginal Inhabitants of the Regions around the Mississippi and Its Confluent Waters." *American Journal of Science and Arts* 3, no. 1 (1821): 15–46.
Brown, Jayna. *Black Utopias: Speculative Life and the Music of Other Worlds*. Durham, NC: Duke University Press, 2021.
Bruchac, Margaret. "The Geology and Cultural History of the Beaver Hill Story." In *Raid on Deerfield: The Many Stories of 1704*. University of Pennsylvania Department of Anthropology Papers, 2005. https://repository.upenn.edu/anthro_papers/144.
Buchanan, Joseph Rodes. *Manual of Psychometry: The Dawn of a New Civilization*. 4th ed. Boston: Published by the author, 1885.
Buckland, Adelene. "'Inhabitants of the Same World': The Colonial History of Geological Time." *Philological Quarterly* 97, no. 2 (2018): 219–40.
Buckland, Adelene. *Novel Science: Fiction and the Invention of Nineteenth-Century Geology*. Chicago: University of Chicago Press, 2013.
Buell, Lawrence. *The Environmental Imagination: Thoreau, Nature Writing, and the Formation of American Culture*. Cambridge, MA: Harvard University Press, 1995.

Burnett, Peter. "State of the State Address to the California State Legislature," January 6, 1851.

Byrd, Jodi A. *The Transit of Empire: Indigenous Critiques of Colonialism*. Minneapolis: University of Minnesota Press, 2011.

Cadava, Eduardo. *Emerson and the Climates of History*. Stanford, CA: Stanford University Press, 1997.

Cadava, Eduardo. "The Guano of History." In *The Other Emerson*, edited by Branka Arsić and Cary Wolfe, 101–30. Minneapolis: University of Minnesota Press, 2010.

Carrington, Damian. "How the Domestic Chicken Rose to Define the Anthropocene." *Guardian*, August 31, 2016. https://www.theguardian.com/environment/2016/aug/31/domestic-chicken-anthropocene-humanity-influenced-epoch.

Chakrabarty, Dipesh. "Anthropocene Time." *History and Theory* 57, no. 1 (2018): 5–32.

Chakrabarty, Dipesh. "The Climate of History: Four Theses." *Critical Inquiry* 35, no. 2 (2009): 197–222.

Chen, Mel Y. *Animacies: Biopolitics, Racial Mattering, and Queer Affect*. Durham, NC: Duke University Press, 2012.

Choi, Tina Young. "Natural History's Hypothetical Moments: Narratives of Contingency in Victorian Culture." *Victorian Studies* 51, no. 2 (2009): 275–97.

Chow, Juliana. *Nineteenth-Century American Literature and the Discourse of Natural History*. Cambridge: Cambridge University Press, 2021.

Claibourne, John F. H. *Life and Times of Gen. Sam. Dale, the Mississippi Partisan*. New York, Harper and Brothers, 1860.

Clark, Nigel, Alexandra Gormally, and Hugh Tuffen. "Speculative Volcanology: Time, Becoming, and Violence in Encounters with Magma." *Environmental Humanities* 10, no. 1 (2018): 273–94.

Clark, Nigel, and Kathryn Yusoff. "Queer Fire: Ecology, Combustion, and Pyrosexual Desire." *Feminist Review* 118, no. 1 (2018): 7–24.

Clark, Timothy. *Ecocriticism on the Edge: The Anthropocene as a Threshold Concept*. New York: Bloomsbury, 2015.

Clytus, Radiclani. "Visualizing in Black Print: The Brooklyn Correspondence of William J. Wilson aka 'Ethiop.'" *J19: The Journal of Nineteenth-Century Americanists* 6, no. 1 (2018): 29–66.

Cohen, Jeffrey J. *Stone: An Ecology of the Inhuman*. Minneapolis: University of Minnesota Press, 2015.

Coole, Diana, and Samantha Frost. "Introducing the New Materialisms." In *New Materialisms: Ontology, Agency, Politics*, edited by Diana Coole and Samantha Frost, 1–43. Durham, NC: Duke University Press, 2010.

Cooper, James Fenimore. *The Crater, or, Vulcan's Peak: A Tale of the Pacific*. 1847. Edited by Thomas Philbrick. Cambridge, MA: Harvard University Press, 1962.

Corcoran, Patricia L., Charles J. Moore, and Kelly Jazvac. "An Anthropogenic Marker Horizon in the Future Rock Record." *GSA Today* 24, no. 6 (June 2014): 4–6. https://www.geosociety.org/gsatoday/archive/24/6/article/i1052-5173-24-6-4.htm.

Cordis, Shanya. "Settler Unfreedoms." *American Indian Culture and Research Journal* 43, no. 2 (2019): 9–23.

Coulthard, Glen Sean. *Red Skin, White Masks: Rejecting the Colonial Politics of Recognition*. Minneapolis: University of Minnesota Press, 2014.

Coviello, Peter. *Make Yourselves Gods: Mormons and the Unfinished Business of American Secularism*. Chicago: University of Chicago Press, 2019.

Cram, E. *Violent Inheritance: Sexuality, Land, and Energy in Making the North American West*. Oakland: University of California Press, 2022.

Crane, Jacob. "'Razed to the Knees': The Anti-Heroic Body in James McCune Smith's 'The Heads of Colored People.'" *African American Review* 51, no. 1 (Spring 2018): 7–21.

Cuvier, Georges. "Preliminary Discourse." In *Georges Cuvier, Fossil Bones, and Geological Catastrophes: New Translations and Interpretations of the Primary Texts*, edited by Martin J. S. Rudwick, 183–252. Chicago: University of Chicago Press, 1997.

Daggett, Cara New. *The Birth of Energy: Fossil Fuels, Thermodynamics, and the Politics of Work*. Durham, NC: Duke University Press, 2019.

Darwin, Charles. *The Voyage of the* Beagle*: Darwin's Five-Year Circumnavigation*. Santa Barbara, CA: Narrative Press, 2000.

Davis, Andrew Jackson. *The Principles of Nature, Her Divine Revelations, and a Voice to Mankind*. Boston: Colby and Rich, 1847.

Davis, Heather, and Zoe Todd. "On the Importance of a Date, or, Decolonizing the Anthropocene." *ACME: An International Journal for Critical Geographies* 16, no. 4 (2017): 761–80.

Davis, Janae, Alex A. Moulton, Levi Van Sant, and Brian Williams. "Anthropocene, Capitalocene, . . . Plantationocene?: A Manifesto for Ecological Justice in an Age of Global Crises." *Geography Compass* 13, no. 5 (2019): e12438/n.p. https://compass-onlinelibrary-wiley-com.proxy.libraries.rutgers.edu/doi/full/10.1111/gec3.12438.

Davoudi, Dalia. "Creeping in the Crevices: Geology and the Re-scaling of Women's Mobility in Elizabeth Stoddard's *The Morgesons*." *Legacy: A Journal of American Women Writers* 37, no. 2 (2020): 213–34.

Day, Iyko. *Alien Capital: Asian Racialization and the Logic of Settler Colonial Capitalism*. Durham, NC: Duke University Press, 2016.

Dean, Dennis. R. "Graham Island, Charles Lyell, and the Craters of Elevation Controversy." *Isis* 71, no. 4 (December 1980): 571–88.

Dean, Dennis R. "Hitchcock's Dinosaur Tracks." *American Quarterly* 21, no. 3 (Autumn 1969): 639–44.

De Landa, Manuel. *A Thousand Years of Nonlinear History*. Brooklyn, NY: Zone, 1997.

Deleuze, Gilles. *Difference and Repetition*. Translated by Paul Patton. New York: Columbia University Press, 1994.

Deleuze, Gilles. "What Children Say." In *Essays Critical and Clinical*, translated by Daniel W. Smith and Michael A. Greco, 61–67. Minneapolis: University of Minnesota Press, 1997.

Deleuze, Gilles, and Felix Guattari. "10,000 B.C.: The Geology of Morals (Who Does the Earth Think It Is?)." In *A Thousand Plateaus: Capitalism and Schizophrenia*, translated by Brian Massumi, 39–74. Minneapolis: University of Minnesota Press, 1987.

Deleuze, Gilles, and Felix Guattari. *Anti-Oedipus: Capitalism and Schizophrenia*. Translated by Robert Hurley, Mark Seem, and Helen R. Lane. New York: Viking, 1977.

Deleuze, Gilles, and Felix Guattari. *A Thousand Plateaus: Capitalism and Schizophrenia*. Translated by Brian Massumi. Minneapolis: University of Minnesota Press, 1987.

Deloria, Vine. *God Is Red: A Native View of Religion*. New York: Putnam, 1973.

DeLoughrey, Elizabeth M. *Allegories of the Anthropocene*. Durham, NC: Duke University Press, 2019.

de Man, Paul. "The Rhetoric of Temporality." In Paul de Man, *Blindness and Insight: Essays in the Rhetoric of Contemporary Criticism*, 2nd revised edition, edited by Wlad Godzich, 187–228. Minneapolis: University of Minnesota Press, 1983.

Denton, William. "On an Asphalt Bed Near Los Angeles, Cal., and Its Contained Fossils." *Proceedings of the Boston Society of Natural History* 18 (1875): 185–86. https://www.biodiversitylibrary.org/item/130607#page/8/mode/1up.

Denton, William. *Our Planet, Its Past and Future: or, Lectures on Geology*. 1868. Reprint. Wellesley, MA: Mrs. E. M. F. Denton, 1881.

Denton, William. *The Soul of Things; or, Psychometric Researches and Discoveries*. Vol. 2. Wellesley, MA: Mrs. E. M. F. Denton, 1873.

Denton, William. *The Soul of Things; or, Psychometric Researches and Discoveries*. Vol. 3. Boston: W. Denton, 1874.

Denton, William, and Elizabeth Foote Denton. *The Soul of Things; or, Psychometric Researches and Discoveries*. Vol. 1. Boston: W. Denton, 1863.

Derrida, Jacques. *Specters of Marx: The State of the Debt, the Work of Mourning, and the New International*. Translated by Peggy Kamuf. New York: Routledge, 1994.

Desmond, Adrian. "Richard Owen's Reaction to Transmutation in the 1830's." *British Journal for the History of Science* 18, no. 1 (March 1985): 25–50.

Devens, R. M. *Our First Century: Being a Popular Descriptive Portraiture of the One Hundred Great and Memorable Events of Perpetual Interest in the History of Our Country*. Springfield, MA: C. A. Nichols and Co., 1876.

Dimock, Wai Chee. *Through Other Continents: American Literature across Deep Time*. Princeton, NJ: Princeton University Press, 2006.

Dobbs, David. *Reef Madness: Charles Darwin, Alexander Agassiz, and the Meaning of Coral*. New York: Doubleday, 2005.

Dolphijn, Rick, and Iris Van Der Tuin, eds. *New Materialism: Interviews and Cartographies*. Ann Arbor, MI: Open Humanities Press, 2012.

Douglas, Bronwen. "Climate to Crania: Science and the Racialization of Human Difference." In *Foreign Bodies: Oceania and the Science of Race 1750–1940*, edited by Bronwen Douglas and Chris Ballard, 33–96. Canberra: Australian National University Press, 2008.

Douglass, Frederick. "The Decision of the Hour." In *Frederick Douglass: Selected Speeches and Writings*, edited by Philip S. Foner, 514-18. Chicago: Lawrence Hill Books, 1999.

Douglass, Frederick. *My Bondage and My Freedom*. New York: Miller, Orton and Mulligan, 1855.

Douglass, Frederick. "The Revolution of 1848." In *Frederick Douglass: Selected Speeches and Writings*, edited by Philip S. Foner, 128-36. Chicago: Lawrence Hill Books, 1999.

Douglass, Frederick. "What of the Night?" In *Frederick Douglass: Selected Speeches and Writings*, edited by Philip S. Foner, 120-21. Chicago: Lawrence Hill Books, 1999.

Douglass, Frederick. "'What to the Slave Is the Fourth of July?' An Address Delivered in Rochester, New York, 5 July 1852." In *The Speeches of Frederick Douglass: A Critical Edition*, edited by John R. McKivigan, Julie Husband, and Heather L. Kaufman, 55-92. New Haven, CT: Yale University Press, 2018.

Dow, Lorenzo. *History of Cosmopolite: or, The Writings of Rev. Lorenzo Dow: Containing His Experience and Travels, in Europe and America, up to Near His Fiftieth Year: Also His Polemic Writings*. Cincinnati: H. S. and J. Applegate, 1848.

Dowd, Gregory Evans. *A Spirited Resistance: The North American Indian Struggle for Unity, 1745-1815*. Baltimore: Johns Hopkins University Press, 1992.

Drinnon, Richard. *White Savage: The Case of John Dunn Hunter*. New York: Schocken, 1972.

Duane, Anna Marie. *Educated for Freedom: The Incredible Story of Two Fugitive Schoolboys Who Grew Up to Change a Nation*. New York: NYU Press, 2020.

"EARTHQUAKES: Their Volcanic Origin and Their Function in Nature. The Earth in a Continual State of Perturbation. Possible Methods of Rendering Earthquakes Harmless." *New York Times* (September 19, 1868): 1.

Edmunds, R. David. *The Shawnee Prophet*. Lincoln: University of Nebraska Press, 1985.

Edmunds, R. David. *Tecumseh and the Quest for Indian Leadership*. Boston: Little, Brown, 1984.

Elleray, Michelle. "Little Builders: Coral Insects, Missionary Culture, and the Victorian Child." *Victorian Literature and Culture* 39, no. 1 (2011): 223-38.

Elleray, Michelle. *Victorian Coral Islands of Empire, Mission, and the Boys' Adventure Novel*. New York: Routledge, 2020.

Ellis, Cristin. *Antebellum Posthuman: Race and Materiality in the Mid-Nineteenth Century*. New York: Fordham University Press, 2018.

Ellis, R. J. "'Latent Color' and 'Exaggerated Snow': Whiteness and Race in Harriet Prescott Spofford's 'The Amber Gods.'" *Journal of American Studies* 40, no. 2 (August 2006): 257-82.

Ellsworth, Elizabeth, and Jamie Kruse. "Introduction." In *Making the Geologic Now: Responses to Material Conditions of Contemporary Life*, edited by Elizabeth Ellsworth and Jamie Kruse, 5-12. New York: Punctum, 2012.

Emerson, Ralph Waldo. "Fate." In *Emerson: Political Writings*, edited by Kenneth S. Sacks, 195–216. Cambridge: Cambridge University Press, 2008.

Emerson, Ralph Waldo. "The Poet." In *The Complete Essays and Other Writings of Ralph Waldo Emerson*, edited by Brooks Atkinson, 319–36. New York: Modern Library, 1950.

"Extracts from a Letter to a Gentleman in Lexington, from His Friend at New Madrid, (U.L.) Dated 16th December, 1811." *Lexington Reporter*, February 1, 1812, 3. http://history.hanover.edu/texts/1811/index.

Fabian, Ann. *The Skull Collectors: Race, Science, and America's Unburied Dead*. Chicago: University of Chicago Press, 2010.

Farmer, Meredith, and Jonathan D. S. Schroeder, eds. *Ahab Unbound: Melville and the Materialist Turn*. Minneapolis: University of Minnesota Press, 2022.

Farrier, David. *Anthropocene Poetics: Deep Time, Sacrifice Zones, and Extinction*. Minneapolis: University of Minnesota Press, 2019.

Fecht, Sarah. "Urban Geology: Artists Investigate Where Cities and Natural Cycles Intersect." *Scientific American*, September 22, 2011. https://www.scientificamerican.com/article/urban-geology/.

Feldman, Jay. *When the Mississippi Ran Backwards: Empire, Intrigue, Murder, and the New Madrid Earthquakes*. New York: Free Press, 2005.

Ferguson, Christine. *Determined Spirits: Eugenics, Heredity, and Racial Regeneration in Anglo-American Spiritualist Writing, 1848–1939*. Edinburgh: Edinburgh University Press, 2012.

Ferreira da Silva, Denise. *Toward a Global Idea of Race*. Minneapolis: University of Minnesota Press, 2007.

Fisher, Colin. "Antebellum Black Climate Science: The Medical Geography and Emancipatory Politics of James McCune Smith and Martin Delany." *Environmental History* 26, no. 3 (2021): 461–83.

Fixico, Donald L. *The American Indian Mind in a Linear World: American Indian Studies and Traditional Knowledge*. New York: Routledge, 2003.

Fixico, Donald L. *Call for Change: The Medicine Way of American Indian History, Ethos, and Reality*. Lincoln: University of Nebraska Press, 2013.

Flint, Timothy. *Recollections of the Last Ten Years, Passed in Occasional Residences and Journeyings in the Valley of the Mississippi, from Pittsburg and the Missouri to the Gulf of Mexico, and from Florida to the Spanish Frontier, in a Series of Letters to the Rev. James Flint, of Salem, Massachusetts*. Boston: Cummings, Hilliard, and Co., 1826.

"The Force of Volcanoes." *Christian Recorder*, April 13, 1861.

Foucault, Michel. *The History of Sexuality, Volume 1: An Introduction*. Translated by Robert Hurley. New York: Vintage, 1990.

Foucault, Michel. *The Order of Things: An Archaeology of the Human Sciences*. New York: Vintage, 1994.

Foucault, Michel. *"Society Must Be Defended": Lectures at the Collège de France, 1975–76*. Translated by David Macey. New York: Picador, 2003.

Franklin, R. W. "Emily Dickinson to Abiah Root: Four Reconstructed Letters." *Emily Dickinson Journal* 4, no. 1 (1995): 1–43.

Fraser, Gordon. *Star Territory: Printing the Universe in Nineteenth-Century America*. Philadelphia: University of Pennsylvania Press, 2021.

Freeman, Elizabeth. *Beside You in Time: Sense Methods and Queer Sociabilities in the American Nineteenth Century*. Durham, NC: Duke University Press, 2019.

Freud, Sigmund. *Beyond the Pleasure Principle*. Translated by C. J. M. Hubback. London: International Psycho-Analytical Press, 1922.

Friends of the Pleistocene. *Geologic City: A Field Guide to the GeoArchitecture of New York*. New York: Smudge Studio, 2011.

Fuller, Myron L. *The New Madrid Earthquake*. Bulletin 494, US Geological Survey. Washington, DC: US Government Printing Office, 1912.

Gardner Coates, Victoria C. "On the Cutting Edge: Pompeii and New Technology." In *The Last Days of Pompeii: Decadence, Apocalypse, Resurrection*, edited by Victoria C. Gardner Coates, Kenneth Lapatin, and Jon L. Seyol, 44–51. Los Angeles: Getty Publications, 2012.

Garnet, Henry Highland. *A Memorial Discourse by Henry Highland Garnet, Delivered in the Hall of the House of Representatives, Washington City, D.C., on Sabbath, February 12, 1865*. Introduction By James McCune Smith, MD. Philadelphia: Joseph M. Wilson, 1865.

"Garrison on Slavery." *National Era*, August 23, 1855.

Gates, W. B. "A Defense of the Ending of Cooper's *The Crater*." *Modern Language Notes* 70, no. 5 (1955): 347–49.

General Assembly of the Missouri Territory. *Resolution . . . for the Relief of the Inhabitants of New Madrid County, Who Have Suffered by Earthquakes*. February 12, 1814. Washington, DC: A. and G. Way, Printers, 1814.

The Geological Society of America, Inc. "Climate Change: Position Statement." *Geological Society of America*, May 2020. https://www.geosociety.org/gsa/positions/position10.aspx.

Gibbard, P. L., and M. J. C. Walker. "The Term 'Anthropocene' in the Context of Formal Geological Classification." *Geological Society London Special Publications* 395 (May 2013): 29–37.

Giffen, Fannie Reed. *Oo-ma-ha Ta-wa-tha (Omaha City) 1854–1898*. Illustrations by Susette La Flesche Tibbles. Lincoln, NE: Published by the Authors, 1898.

Gleason, William. "Volcanoes and Meteors: Douglass, Melville, and the Poetics of Insurrection." In *Frederick Douglass and Herman Melville: Essays in Relation*, edited by Robert S. Levine and Samuel Otter, 110–33. Chapel Hill: University of North Carolina Press, 2008.

Goeman, Mishuana. *Mark My Words: Native Women Mapping Our Nations*. Minneapolis: University of Minnesota Press, 2013.

Goffe, Tao Leigh. "'Guano in Their Destiny': Race, Geology, and a Philosophy of Indenture." *Amerasia Journal* 45, no. 1 (2019): 27–49.

Goldberg, Sylvan. "Elizabeth Stoddard's Geologic Form: Patience, Indifference, Crisis." *ESQ: A Journal of Nineteenth-Century American Literature and Culture* 66, no. 3 (2020): 367–408.

Gómez-Barris, Macarena. "The Colonial Anthropocene: Damage, Remapping, and Resurgent Resources." *Antipode Online*, March 19, 2019. https://antipodeonline.org/2019/03/19/the-colonial-anthropocene/.

Gómez-Barris, Macarena. *The Extractive Zone: Social Ecologies and Decolonial Perspectives*. Durham, NC: Duke University Press, 2017.

Goodrich, Samuel. *The Wonders of Geology, by the Author of Peter Parley's Tales*. Boston: Bradbury, Soden and Co., 1845.

Gould, Stephen Jay. *Time's Arrow, Time's Cycle: Myth and Metaphor in the Discovery of Geological Time*. Cambridge, MA: Harvard University Press, 1988.

"Great Anti-Colonization Meeting in New York." *North Star* 2, no. 20 (May 11, 1849): 2.

"Great Meeting in Boston on the Day of the Execution of Captain John Brown." *Liberator* 29, no. 49 (December 9, 1859): 194–95.

Greyser, Naomi. *On Sympathetic Grounds: Race, Gender, and Affective Geographies in Nineteenth-Century North America*. New York: Oxford University Press, 2017.

Grimes, J. Stanley. *Phreno-Geology: The Progressive Creation of Man, Indicated by Natural History, and Confirmed by Discoveries Which Connect the Organization and Functions of the Brain with the Successive Geological Periods*. Boston: James Monroe and Co., 1851.

Grossman, James. *James Fenimore Cooper*. New York: W. Sloane Associates, 1949.

Grusin, Richard, ed. *After Extinction*. Minneapolis: University of Minnesota Press, 2018.

Grusin, Richard. "Introduction." In *The Nonhuman Turn*. Edited by Richard Grusin, vii–xxix. Minneapolis: University of Minnesota Press, 2015.

Gunn, Robert Lawrence. *Ethnology and Empire: Languages, Literature, and the Making of the North American Borderlands*. New York: NYU Press, 2015.

Guthrie, James R. *Above Time: Emerson's and Thoreau's Temporal Revolutions*. Columbia: University of Missouri Press, 2001.

Hancock, Jonathan Todd. *Convulsed States: Earthquakes, Prophecy, and the Remaking of Early America*. Chapel Hill: University of North America Press, 2021.

Haraway, Donna J. *Staying with the Trouble: Making Kin in the Chthulucene*. Durham, NC: Duke University Press, 2016.

Haraway, Donna, Noboru Ishikawa, Scott F. Gilbert, Kenneth Olwig, Anna L. Tsing, and Nils Bubandt. "Anthropologists Are Talking—About the Anthropocene." *Journal of Anthropology* 81, no. 3 (2016): 535–64.

Hartman, Saidiya V. *Scenes of Subjection: Terror, Slavery, and Self-Making in Nineteenth-Century America*. New York: Oxford University Press, 1997.

Hazen, Robert M. *The Poetry of Geology*. London: Allen and Unwin, 1982.

Herbert, Robert L., and Sarah Doyle. "Dr. James Deane of Greenfield, Edward Hitchcock's Rival Discoverer of Dinosaur Tracks." *Mount Holyoke College Institutional Digital Archive*. Accessed March 17, 2018. https://ida.mtholyoke.edu/xmlui/bitstream/handle/10166/3529/JD%20final.pdf?sequence=1&isAllowed=y.

Heringman, Noah. *Romantic Rocks, Aesthetic Geology*. Ithaca, NY: Cornell University Press, 2004.

Higginson, Thomas Wentworth. "Emily Dickinson's Letters." *Atlantic Monthly*, October 1891, 444–56.
Hitchcock, Edward. *Ichnology of New England: A Report on the Sandstone of the Connecticut Valley, Especially Its Fossil Footmarks, Made to the Government of the Commonwealth of Massachusetts*. Boston: W. White, 1858.
Hitchcock, Edward. "Ornithichnology—Description of the Foot Marks of Birds (Ornithichnites) on New Red Sandstone, in Massachusetts." *American Journal of Sciences and Arts* 29, no. 2 (1836).
Hitchcock, Edward. "Preface." In *Researches in Theoretical Geology*, by Henri de la Beche. New York: F. J. Huntington and Co., 1837.
Hitchcock, Edward. *The Religion of Geology and Its Connected Sciences*. Boston: Phillips, Sampson and Co., 1851.
Hitchcock, Edward. *Reminiscences of Amherst College, Historical, Scientific, Biographical, and Autobiographical, also, of Other and Wider Life Experiences*. Northampton, MA: Bridgeman and Childs, 1863.
Hitchcock, Edward. "Report on Ichnolithology, or Fossil Footmarks." *American Journal of Science and Arts* 47, no. 2 (1844): 292–322.
Holbrook, Josiah. "Family Cabinets of Nature and Art." *Colored American*, May 8, 1841.
Hooley, Matt. "Reading Vulnerably: Indigeneity and the Scale of Harm." In *Anthropocene Reading: Literary History in Geologic Times*, edited by Tobias Menely and Jesse Oak Taylor, 184–201. University Park: Penn State University Press, 2017.
Hough, Susan Elizabeth, and Roger G. Bilham. *After the Earth Quakes: Elastic Rebound on an Urban Planet*. Oxford: Oxford University Press, 2006.
Hudson, Arthur Palmer. "A Ballad of the New Madrid Earthquake." *Journal of American Folklore* 60, no. 236 (1947): 147–50.
Hunt, Alfred N. *Haiti's Influence on Antebellum America: Slumbering Volcano in the Caribbean*. Baton Rouge: Louisiana State University Press, 2006.
Hunter, John Dunn. *Memoirs of a Captivity among the Indians of North America, from Childhood to the Age of Nineteen: With Anecdotes Descriptive of Their Manners and Customs*. London: Longman, Hurst, Rees, Orme, Brown, and Green, 1824.
Hutton, James. "Theory of the Earth; or an Investigation into the Laws Observable in the Composition, Dissolution, and Restoration of Land upon the Globe." *Transactions of the Royal Society of Edinburgh* 1, no. 2 (1788): 209–304.
Hutton, James. *Theory of the Earth, with Proofs and Illustrations*. Edinburgh: Published for the author, 1795.
Huzzey, Richard. *Freedom Burning: Slavery and Empire in Victorian Britain*. Ithaca, NY: Cornell University Press, 2012.
"Indian Affairs." *Louisiana Gazette* (St. Louis, Louisiana Territory), June 13, 1812, 2. http://history.hanover.edu/texts/1811/.
Insko, Jeffrey. *History, Abolition, and the Ever-Present Now in Antebellum American Writing*. New York: Oxford University Press, 2018.
Intergovernmental Panel on Climate Change, "Climate Change 2021: The Physical Science Basis." https://www.ipcc.ch/report/ar6/wg1/.

Iovino, Serenella, and Serpil Oppermann. "Introduction." In *Material Ecocriticism*, edited by Serenella Iovino and Serpil Opperman, 1–18. Bloomington: Indiana University Press, 2014.

"Is the Center of the Earth a Mass of Fire?" *Frederick Douglass' Paper*, August 17, 1855. Reprinted from the *Baltimore American*.

Jackson, Andrew. "Annual Message to Congress," December 6, 1830.

Jackson, John P., and Nadine M. Weidman. *Race, Racism, and Science: Social Impact and Interaction*. New Brunswick, NJ: Rutgers University Press, 2005.

Jackson, Virginia. *Dickinson's Misery: A Theory of Lyric Reading*. Princeton, NJ: Princeton University Press, 2005.

Jackson, Virginia. "Longfellow in His Time." In *The Cambridge History of American Poetry*, edited by Alfred Bendixen and Stephen Burt, 238–58. Cambridge: Cambridge University Press, 2014.

Jackson, Zakiyyah Iman. "Animal: New Directions in the Theorization of Race and Posthumanism." *Feminist Studies* 39, no. 3 (2013): 669–85.

Jackson, Zakiyyah Iman. *Becoming Human: Matter and Meaning in an Antiblack World*. New York: NYU Press, 2020.

Jackson, Zakiyyah Iman. "Outer Worlds: The Persistence of Race in 'Movement Beyond the Human.'" In "Queer Inhumanisms," edited by Mel Y. Chen and Dana Luciano. Special issue, *GLQ* 21, nos. 2–3 (June 2015): 215–18.

Jaffe, Mark. *The Gilded Dinosaur: The Fossil War between E. D. Cope and O. C. Marsh and the Rise of American Science*. New York: Crown, 2000.

James, Jennifer C. "'Buried in Guano': Race, Labor, and Sustainability." *American Literary History* 24, no. 1 (2012): 115–42.

James, Jennifer C. "Ecomelancholia: Slavery, War, and Black Ecological Imaginings." In *Environmental Criticism for the Twenty-First Century*, edited by Stephanie LeMenager, Teresa Shewry, and Ken Hiltner, 163–78. New York: Routledge, 2011.

Jarrett, Gene Andrew. "'To Refute Mr. Jefferson's Arguments Respecting Us': Thomas Jefferson, David Walker, and the Politics of Early African American Literature." *Early American Literature* 46, no. 2 (2011): 291–318.

Johnson, Bob. *Mineral Rites: An Archaeology of the Fossil Economy*. Baltimore: Johns Hopkins University Press, 2019.

Jonik, Michael. *Herman Melville and the Politics of the Inhuman*. Cambridge: Cambridge University Press, 2018.

Kanon, Tom. "Scared from Their Sins for a Season: The Religious Ramifications of the New Madrid Earthquakes, 1811–1812." *Ohio Valley History* 5, no. 2 (2005): 21–38.

Katopodis, Christina. "The Music of the Spheres in Emerson, Fuller, and Thoreau: Lyell's *Principles* and Transcendental Listening." *ISLE: Interdisciplinary Studies in Literature and Environment* 28, no. 3 (Autumn 2021): 839–67.

King, Tiffany Lethabo. *The Black Shoals: Offshore Formations of Black and Native Studies*. Durham, NC: Duke University Press, 2019.

Klaver, Jan M. I. *Geology and Religious Sentiment: The Effect of Geological Discoveries on English Society and Literature between 1829 and 1859*. New York: Brill, 1997.

Klein, Naomi. *The Shock Doctrine: The Rise of Disaster Capitalism*. Toronto: Knopf Canada, 2007.

Kolbert, Elizabeth. "The Lost World: Fossils of the Future." *New Yorker*, December 23/30, 2013. https://www.newyorker.com/magazine/2013/12/23/the-lost-world-3.

Kolbert, Elizabeth. *The Sixth Extinction: An Unnatural History*. New York: Picador, 2014.

LaFleur, Greta. *The Natural History of Sexuality in Early America*. Baltimore: Johns Hopkins University Press, 2018.

Lakomäki, Sami. *Gathering Together: The Shawnee People through Diaspora and Nationhood, 1600–1870*. New Haven, CT: Yale University Press, 2014.

Larson, Kristine M. *The Women Who Popularized Geology in the Nineteenth Century*. New York: Springer International, 2017.

Lawrence, Philip J. "Edward Hitchcock: The Christian Geologist." *Proceedings of the American Philosophical Society* 116, no. 1 (February 15, 1972): 21–34.

LeMenager, Stephanie. *Manifest and Other Destinies: Territorial Fictions of the Nineteenth-Century United States*. Lincoln: University of Nebraska Press, 2005.

LeMenager, Stephanie. "Sediment." In *Veer Ecology: A Companion for Environmental Thinking*, edited by Jeffrey J. Cohen and Lowell Duckert, 168–82. Minneapolis: University of Minnesota Press, 2017.

Leong, Diana. "The Mattering of Black Lives: Octavia Butler's Hyperempathy and the Promise of the New Materialisms." *Catalyst: Feminism, Theory, Technoscience* 2, no. 2 (2016): 1–35.

"Letters from the West Indies." *Colored American* 1, no. 13 (April 1, 1837): 1.

Lewis, Simon L., and Mark A. Maslin. "Defining the Anthropocene." *Nature* 519 (2015): 171–80.

Liebman, Bennett. "The Quest for Black Voting Rights in New York State." *Albany Government Law Review* 11 (2018): 386–421.

Lifetimes Research Collective. "Fossilization, or the Matter of Historical Futures." *History and Theory* 61, no. 1 (March 2022): 4–26.

Lindsey, Brendan C. *Murder State: California's Native Genocide, 1846–1873*. Lincoln: University of Nebraska Press, 2012.

Liu, Alan. *Local Transcendence: Essays on Postmodern Historicism and the Database*. Chicago: University of Chicago Press, 2008.

Lloyd-Smith, Alan. "Race and American Gothic." Paper presented at the Literature Association Symposium on American Gothic, Puerto Vallarta, Mexico, December 5, 2002.

Luciano, Dana. *Arranging Grief: Sacred Time and the Body in Nineteenth-Century America*. New York: NYU Press, 2007.

Luciano, Dana. "How the Earth Feels: A Conversation with Dana Luciano," by Cécile Roudeau. *Transatlantica: Revue d'Etudes Américaines* 1, no. 1 (2015): 1–9.

Luciano, Dana. "The Inhuman Anthropocene." *Avidly*, March 22, 2015. https://avidly.lareviewofbooks.org/2015/03/22/the-inhuman-anthropocene/.

Luciano, Dana. "Speaking Substances: Rock." *Los Angeles Review of Books*, April 12, 2016. https://lareviewofbooks.org/article/speaking-substances-rock/.

Luciano, Dana, and Mel Y. Chen, "Introduction: Has the Queer Ever Been Human?" In "Queer Inhumanisms," edited by Mel Y. Chen and Dana Luciano. Special issue, *GLQ* 21, no. 2 (June 2015): 182–207.

Lustgarten, Abrahm, and Meridith Kohut. "The Great Climate Migration." *New York Times Magazine*, July 23, 2020. https://www.economicsandpeace.org/wp-content/uploads/2020/09/Ecological-Threat-Register-Press-Release-27.08-FINAL.pdf.

Lyell, Charles. *Lectures on Geology, Delivered at the Broadway Tabernacle, in the City of New-York*. New York: Greeley and McElrath, 1843.

Lyell, Charles. *Principles of Geology*. Edited by James A. Secord. New York: Penguin, 1997.

Lyell, Charles. *A Second Visit to the United States*. Vol. 2. London: John Murray, 1849.

Lyell, Charles. *Travels in North America in the Years 1841-42; with geological observations on the United States, Canada, and Nova Scotia*. New York: Wiley and Putnam, 1845.

Mader, Mary Beth. "Modern Living and Vital Race: Foucault and the Science of Life." *Foucault Studies* 12 (October 2011): 97–112.

Malm, Andreas. *Fossil Capital: The Rise of Steam Power and the Roots of Global Warming*. London: Verso, 2016.

Malm, Andreas, and Alf Hornborg. "The Geology of Mankind? A Critique of the Anthropocene Narrative." *Anthropocene Review* 1, no. 1 (2014): 62–69.

Marché, Jordan D., II. "Edward Hitchcock's Poem, *The Sandstone Bird* (1836)." *Earth Sciences History* 10, no. 1 (1991): 5–8.

Mardossian, Carine M. "'Poetics of Landscape': Édouard Glissant's Creolized Ecologies." *Callaloo* 36, no. 4 (Fall 2013): 983–94.

Marshall, Kate. "What Are the Novels of the Anthropocene? American Fiction in Geological Time." *American Literary History* 27, no. 3 (2015): 523–38.

Martin, Anthony J. *Dinosaurs without Bones: Dinosaur Lives Revealed by Their Trace Fossils*. New York: Pegasus, 2014.

Martin, J. Sella. "The Sentinel of Freedom." *Anglo African Magazine* 1, no. 11 (1859): 361–62.

Martin, Ross. "Fossil Thoughts: Thoreau, Arrowheads, and Radical Paleontology." *ESQ: A Journal of Nineteenth-Century American Literature and Culture* 65, no. 3 (2019): 424–68.

Mathews, Cornelius. *Behemoth: A Legend of the Mound-Builders*. New York: J. and H. G. Langley, 1839.

Mayor, Adrienne. *Fossil Legends of the First Americans*. Princeton, NJ: Princeton University Press, 2005.

Mbembe, Achille. "Necropolitics." Translated by Libby Meintjes. *Public Culture* 15, no. 1 (2003): 11–40.

McCallam, David. *Volcanoes in Eighteenth-Century Europe: An Essay in Environmental Humanities*. Liverpool: Liverpool University Press, 2019.

McCune Smith, James. *See* Smith, James McCune.

McGarry, Molly. *Ghosts of Futures Past: Spiritualism and the Cultural Politics of Nineteenth-Century America*. Berkeley: University of California Press, 2008.

McGurl, Mark. "The New Cultural Geology." *Twentieth-Century Literature* 57, nos. 3–4 (2011): 380–90.

McKenney, Thomas L. *History of the Indian Tribes of North America, with Biographical Sketches and Anecdotes of the Principal Chiefs*. Vol. 1. 1836. Philadelphia: D. Rice and Co., 1872.

McKittrick, Katherine. *Demonic Grounds: Black Women and the Cartographies of Struggle*. Minneapolis: University of Minnesota Press, 2006.

McKittrick, Katherine. "On Plantations, Prisons, and a Black Sense of Place." *Social and Cultural Geography* 12, no. 8 (2011): 947–63.

McKittrick, Katherine. "Plantation Futures." *Small Axe* 17, no. 3 (2013): 1–15.

McNeill, John. "Anthropocene Impacts." Paper presented at Georgetown University, Washington, DC, November 28, 2017.

McNeill, John R., and Peter Engelke. *The Great Acceleration: An Environmental History of the Anthropocene since 1945*. Cambridge, MA: Harvard University Press, 2016.

McPhee, John. *Basin and Range*. New York: Farrar, Straus and Giroux, 1981.

McWilliams, John P., Jr. "The Crater and the Constitution." *Texas Studies in Literature and Language* 12, no. 4 (Winter 1971): 631–45.

Meillassoux, Quentin. *After Finitude: An Essay on the Necessity of Contingency*. Translated by Ray Brassier. New York: Continuum, 2008.

Melville, Herman. *Moby-Dick, or, The Whale*. 2nd ed. Edited by Herschel Parker. New York: Norton, 2002.

Metcalf, Samuel L., MD. "The Interest and Importance of Scientific Geology as a Subject of Study." *Knickerbocker: or, New-York Monthly Magazine* 3, no. 4 (1834): 225–35.

Miller, Daegan. "At Home in the Great Northern Wilderness: African Americans and Freedom's Ecology in the Adirondacks, 1846–1859." *Environmental Humanities* 2, no. 1 (2013): 117–46.

Miller, Hugh. *An Autobiography: My Schools and Schoolmasters; or, The Story of my Education*. Boston: Gould and Lincoln, 1857.

Miller, Mary Ashburn. *A Natural History of Revolution: Violence and Nature in the French Revolutionary Imagination, 1789–1794*. Ithaca, NY: Cornell University Press, 2011.

Mitchell, Audra. "Decolonising the Anthropocene." *Worldly*, March 17, 2015. https://worldlyir.wordpress.com/2015/03/17/decolonising-the-anthropocene/.

Mitchell, Michele. "'Lower Orders,' Racial Hierarchies, and Rights Rhetoric: Evolutionary Echoes in Elizabeth Cady Stanton's Thought during the Late 1860s." In *Elizabeth Cady Stanton, Feminist as Thinker: A Reader in Documents and Essays*, edited by Ellen Carol DuBois and Richard Cándida Smith, 128–51. New York: NYU Press, 2007.

Mitchell, W. J. T. *The Last Dinosaur Book: The Life and Times of a Cultural Icon*. Chicago: University of Chicago Press, 1998.

Mitchill, Samuel L. "A Detailed Narrative of the Earthquakes Which Occurred on the 16th Day of December, 1811." *Transactions of the Literary and Philosophical Society of New-York* 1 (1815): 281–307.

Modern, John Lardas. *Secularism in Antebellum America*. Chicago: University of Chicago Press, 2011.

Moore, Jason W. *Capitalism in the Web of Life: Ecology and the Accumulation of Capital*. London: Verso, 2015.

Morgan, Patrick. "Transcendental Geologies: Emerson, Anti-Slavery, and the *Kairos* of Deep Time." In *The Oxford Handbook of Ralph Waldo Emerson*, edited by Christopher Hanlon. Oxford: Oxford University Press, forthcoming 2023.

Morgensen, Scott Lauria. "The Biopolitics of Settler Colonialism: Right Here, Right Now." *Settler Colonial Studies* 1, no. 1 (2011): 52–76.

Morton, Timothy. "Here Comes Everything: The Promise of Object-Oriented Ontology." *Qui Parle* 19, no. 2 (Spring/Summer 2011): 163–90.

Morton, Timothy. *Hyperobjects: Philosophy and Ecology after the End of the World*. Minneapolis: University of Minnesota Press, 2013.

Morton, Timothy. *Realist Magic: Objects, Ontology, Causality*. Ann Arbor, MI: Open Humanities Press, 2013.

"Mr. Lincoln's Forebodings." *Christian Recorder*, June 17, 1865.

Muir-Wood, Robert. *The Dark Side of the Earth*. London: Allen and Unwin, 1985.

Myers, Greg. "Fictionality, Demonstration, and a Forum for Popular Science: Jane Marcet's *Conversations on Chemistry*." In *Natural Eloquence: Women Reinscribe Science*, edited by Barbara T. Gates and Ann Shteir. Madison: University of Wisconsin Press, 1997.

Myers, Robert A. "Cherokee Pioneers in Arkansas: The St. Francis Years, 1785–1813." *Arkansas Historical Quarterly* 56, no. 2 (Summer 1997): 127–57.

National Aeronautics and Space Administration Advisory Council. *Earth System Science: A Closer View*. Washington, DC: National Aeronautics and Space Administration Advisory Council, 1988.

Navakas, Michelle Currie. "Antebellum Coral." *American Literature* 91, no. 2 (June 2019): 263–93.

Nealon, Christopher. "Infinity for Marxists." *Mediations* 28, no. 2 (2015). https://mediationsjournal.org/articles/infinity-for-marxists.

Neimanis, Astrida. "The Sea and the Breathing." *e-flux*, May 2020. https://www.e-flux.com/architecture/oceans/331869/the-sea-and-the-breathing/.

Newman, Lance, and James Finley, eds. "Race and Nature in Nineteenth Century American Literature: A Conversation with Joshua Bennett, Brigitte Fielder, Ian Finseth, Jennifer James, and Others." *Journal of Ecocriticism* 5, no. 2 (July 2013): 1–21.

Nichols, Robert. *Theft Is Property! Dispossession and Critical Theory*. Durham, NC: Duke University Press, 2020.

Nijhuis, Michele. "When Did the Human Epoch Begin?" *New Yorker*, March 11, 2015. https://www.newyorker.com/tech/annals-of-technology/holocene-anthropocene-human-epoch.

Nixon, Rob. "The Anthropocene: The Promise and Pitfalls of a New Epochal Idea." *Edge Effects*, November 6, 2014. http://edgeeffects.net/anthropocene-promise-and-pitfalls/.

Noble, Brian. *Articulating Dinosaurs: A Political Anthropology*. Toronto: University of Toronto Press, 2016.

Noble, Louis Legrand. *The Course of Empire, Voyage of Life, and Other Pictures of Thomas Cole, M.A.* New York: Cornish, Lampart and Co., 1853.

Norton-Smith, Thomas M. *The Dance of Person and Place: One Interpretation of American Indian Philosophy*. New York: SUNY Press, 2010.

Nott, Josiah C., George R. Gliddon, Samuel Morton, Louis Agassiz, William Usher, and Henry S. Patterson. *Types of Mankind: Or, Ethnological Researches, Based upon the Ancient Monuments, Paintings, Sculptures, and Crania of Races, and upon Their Natural, Geographical, Philological, and Biblical History*. 7th ed. Edited by Josiah C. Nott and George R. Gliddon, 327–72. Philadelphia: Lippincott, Grambo and Co., 1854.

Nurmi, Tom. *Magnificent Decay: Melville and Ecology*. Charlottesville: University of Virginia Press, 2020.

"Obituary: William Denton." *Australian Town and Country Journal* (Sydney), October 20, 1883, 25.

O'Brien, Jean M. *Dispossession by Degrees: Indian Land and Identity in Natick, Massachusetts, 1650-1790*. Cambridge: Cambridge University Press, 1997.

O'Brien, Jean M. *Firsting and Lasting: Writing Indians Out of Existence in New England*. Minneapolis: University of Minnesota Press, 2010.

O'Connor, Ralph. *The Earth on Show: Fossils and the Poetics of Popular Science, 1802-1856*. Chicago: University of Chicago Press, 2007.

Ogden, Emily. *Credulity: A Cultural History of US Mesmerism*. Chicago: University of Chicago Press, 2018.

Oreskes, Naomi, and Erik M. Conway. *Merchants of Doubt: How a Handful of Scientists Obscured the Truth on Issues from Tobacco Smoke to Global Warming*. New York: Bloomsbury, 2010.

Pandian, Jacob. *Anthropology and the Western Tradition: Toward an Authentic Anthropology*. Prospect Heights, IL: Waveland Press, 1985.

Parikka, Jussi. *A Geology of Media*. Minneapolis: University of Minnesota Press, 2015.

"Past and Present State of Hayti." *Quarterly Review* 21 (1819): 430–60.

Peel, Robin. "Emily Dickinson and Transatlantic Geology." In *Transatlantic Women: Nineteenth-Century American Women Writers and Great Britain*, edited by Beth Lynne Lueck, Brigitte Bailey, and Lucinda L. Damon-Bach, 232–54. Durham: University of New Hampshire Press, 2012.

Pemberton, S. George, Murray K. Gingras, and James A. MacEachern. "Edward Hitchcock and Roland Bird: Two Early Titans of Vertebrate Ichnology in North America." In *Trace Fossils: Concepts, Problems, Prospects,* edited by William Miller III, 32–51. Amsterdam: Elsevier Science, 2007.

Penick, James Lal, Jr. *The New Madrid Earthquakes.* Columbia: University of Missouri Press, 1981.

Penn, Granville. *Conversations on Geology, Comprising a Familiar Explanation of the Huttonian and Wernerian Systems.* London: S. Maunder, 1828.

Pesantubbee, Michelene E. "When the Earth Shakes: The Cherokee Prophecies of 1811–12." *American Indian Quarterly* 17, no. 3 (1993): 301–17.

Peterson, Carla L. "Untangling Genealogy's Tangled Skeins: Alexander Crummell, James McCune Smith, and Nineteenth-Century Black Literary Traditions." In *A Companion to American Literary Studies,* edited by Caroline F. Levander and Robert S. Levine, 500–16. Malden, MA: Blackwell, 2011.

Phelps, Almira Hart Lincoln. *Lectures to Young Ladies, Comprising Outlines and Applications of the Different Branches of Female Education, for the Use of Female Schools, and Private Libraries.* Boston: Carter, Hendee and Co., 1833.

Pierce, William. *To the Editor of the New-York Evening Post,* Big Prairie (on the Mississippi, 761 miles from N. Orleans), December 25, 1811.

Pinto, Samantha. "Objects of Narrative Desire: An Unnatural History of Fossil Collection and Black Women's Sexuality." *JNT: Journal of Narrative Theory* 49, no. 3 (2019): 351–81.

Playfair, John. "Biographical Account of the Late Dr. James Hutton, F.R.S. Edin.' (read 1803)." *Transactions of the Royal Society of Edinburgh* 5 (1805): 72–73.

Povinelli. Elizabeth A. *Geontologies: A Requiem to Late Liberalism.* Durham, NC: Duke University Press, 2016.

Powell, James Henry. *William Denton, the Geologist and Radical: A Biographical Sketch.* Boston: Colby and Rich, 1870.

Prince, Thomas. *Earthquakes, the Works of God and Tokens of His Just Displeasure: Two Sermons on Psal. xviii. 7. At the Particular Fast in Boston, Nov. 2. and the General Thanksgiving, Nov. 9. Occasioned by the Late Dreadful Earthquake.* Boston: Printed for D. Henchman, 1727, 1–45. http://name.umdl.umich.edu/N02483.0001.001.

Puar, Jasbir K. "'I Would Rather Be a Cyborg Than a Goddess': Becoming-Intersectional in Assemblage Theory." *philoSOPHIA* 2, no. 1 (Spring 2012): 49–66.

Rafferty, Milton D. *Rude Pursuits and Rugged Peaks: Schoolcraft's Ozark Journal, 1818-1819.* Fayetteville: University of Arkansas Press, 1996.

Ravenscroft, Alison. "Strange Weather: Indigenous Materialisms, New Materialism, and Colonialism." *Cambridge Journal of Postcolonial Literary Inquiry* 5, no. 3 (September 2018): 353–70.

Reiter, Geoffrey. "'New Knowledge of Lost Worlds'? Edward Hitchcock's 'Sandstone Bird' and the Poetic Exploration of Science and Faith." *Renascence* 73, no. 2 (Spring 2021): 81–100.

Repcheck, Jack. *The Man Who Found Time: James Hutton and the Discovery of Earth's Antiquity*. New York: Basic Books, 2009.
"Review of *Professor Hitchcock's Report on the Geology, &c. of Massachusetts*." *North American Review* 42, no. 91 (April 1836): 422–48.
Richardson, Charles Francis. *American Literature, 1607–1885*. Vol. 2. New York, G. P. Putnam's Sons, 1887.
Rifkin, Mark. *Beyond Settler Time: Temporal Sovereignty and Indigenous Self-Determination*. Durham, NC: Duke University Press, 2017.
Rifkin, Mark. *Fictions of Land and Flesh: Blackness, Indigeneity, Speculation*. Durham, NC: Duke University Press, 2019.
Rifkin, Mark. "Geo into Bio and Back Again: Tracing the Politics of Race and Sovereignty." *American Quarterly* 71, no. 3 (September 2019): 871–79.
Rifkin, Mark. *Settler Common Sense: Queerness and Everyday Colonialism in the American Renaissance*. Minneapolis: University of Minnesota Press, 2014.
Rifkin, Mark. *When Did Indians Become Straight? Kinship, The History of Sexuality, and Native Sovereignty*. Oxford: Oxford University Press, 2011.
Robins, Nicholas A. *Mercury, Mining, and Empire: The Human and Ecological Cost of Colonial Silver Mining in the Andes*. Bloomington: Indiana University Press, 2011.
Ronda, Margaret. *Remainders: American Poetry at Nature's End*. Stanford, CA: Stanford University Press, 2018.
Rosenberg, Jordy. "The Molecularization of Sexuality: On Some Primitivisms of the Present." *Theory and Event* 17, no. 2 (January 2014): n.p.
Rudwick, Martin J. S. *Earth's Deep History: How It Was Discovered and Why It Matters*. Chicago: University of Chicago Press, 2014.
Rudwick, Martin J. S., ed. *Georges Cuvier, Fossil Bones, and Geological Catastrophes: New Translations and Interpretations of the Primary Texts*. Chicago: University of Chicago Press, 1997.
Rudwick, Martin J. S. *The Meaning of Fossils: Episodes in the History of Palaeontology*. Amsterdam: Elsevier, 1972.
Rusert, Britt. *Fugitive Science: Empiricism and Freedom in Early African American Culture*. New York: NYU Press, 2017.
Russell, Joseph James. "Remarks on the Centennial of the New Madrid Earthquakes," December 16, 1911. Washington, DC. Mss. of congressional speech of Congressional representative from New Madrid's district. 4 pp. typed. Held at Huntington Library, CA.
Sale, Maggie Montesinos. *The Slumbering Volcano: American Slave Ship Revolts and the Production of Rebellious Masculinity*. Durham, NC: Duke University Press, 1997.
Sandweiss, Martha A. *Print the Legend: Photography and the American West*. New Haven, CT: Yale University Press, 2002.
Santana, Carlos. "Waiting for the Anthropocene." *British Journal of the Philosophy of Science* 70, no. 4 (2019): 1073–96.
Savoy, Lauret Edith. *Trace: Memory, History, Race, and the American Landscape*. Berkeley, CA: Counterpoint, 2015.

Sayre, Gordon M. *The Indian Chief as Tragic Hero: Native Resistance and the Literatures of America, from Moctezuma to Tecumseh*. Chapel Hill: University of North Carolina Press, 2005.

Schnug, Ewald, Frank Jacobs, and Kirsten Stöven. "Guano: The White Gold of the Seabirds." In *Seabirds*, edited by Heimo Mikkola. IntechOpen, 2018. Accessed April 8, 2021. Doi: 10.5772/intechopen.79501. https://www.intechopen.com/chapters/62618.

Schoolcraft, Henry R. *Journal of a Tour into the Interior of Missouri and Arkansaw*. London, 1821.

Schoolcraft, Henry R. *A Memoir on the Geological Position of a Fossil Tree, Discovered in the Secondary Rocks of the River des Plaines*. Albany, NY: E. and E. Hosford, 1822.

Schoolcraft, Henry R. *Personal Memoirs of a Residence of Thirty Years with the Indian Tribes on the American Frontiers: With Brief Notices of Passing Events, Facts, and Opinions, A. D. 1812 to A. D. 1842*. New York: Lippincott, Zambo, and Co., 1851.

Schoolcraft, Henry R. *Summary Narrative of an Exploratory Expedition to the Sources of the Mississippi River, in 1820*. Philadelphia: Lippincott, Grambo, and Co., 1855.

Schoolcraft, Henry R. *Transallegania, or, The Groans of Missouri, a Poem*. New York: Printed for the Author by J. Seymour, 1820.

Schuller, Kyla. "The Fossil and the Photograph: Red Cloud, Prehistoric Media, and Dispossession in Perpetuity." *Configurations* 24, no. 2 (Spring 2016): 229–61.

Schuller, Kyla. *The Biopolitics of Feeling: Race, Sex, and Science in the Nineteenth Century*. Durham, NC: Duke University Press, 2017.

Schuller, Kyla, and Jules Gill-Peterson. "Introduction: Race, the State, and the Malleable Body." Special issue, *Social Text* 143, vol. 38, no. 2 (June 2020): 1–17.

Scrope, George Poulett. *Memoir on the Geology of Central France: Including the Volcanic Formations of Auvergne, the Velay, and the Vivarais*. London: Longman, Rees, Orme, Brown, and Green, 1827.

Scudder, Harold H. "Cooper's *The Crater*." *American Literature* 19, no. 2 (1947): 109–26.

Sharpe, Christina. *In the Wake: On Blackness and Being*. Durham, NC: Duke University Press, 2016.

Shaviro, Steven. "Specters of Marx." *Pinocchio Theory*, February 8, 2006. http://www.shaviro.com/Blog/?p=474.

Shepperson, George. "Frederick Douglass and Scotland." *Journal of Negro History* 38, no. 3 (1953): 307–21.

Simpson, Leanne Betasamosake. *As We Have Always Done: Indigenous Freedom through Radical Resistance*. Minneapolis: University of Minnesota Press, 2017.

Simpson, Leanne Betasamosake. "Land as Pedagogy: Nishnaabeg Intelligence and Rebellious Transformation." *Decolonialization: Indigeneity, Education, and Society* 3, no. 3 (2014): 1–25.

Smith, James McCune. "Civilization: Its Dependence on Physical Circumstances." In *The Works of James McCune Smith: Black Intellectual and Abolitionist*, edited by John Stauffer. New York: Oxford University Press, 2006.

Smith, James McCune. "Heads of the Colored People, No. X—The Schoolmaster (continued)." *Frederick Douglass' Paper*, November 17, 1854.

Smith, James McCune. "Introduction." In *My Bondage and My Freedom*, by Frederick Douglass, 17–32. New York: Miller, Orton and Mulligan, 1855.

Smith, James McCune. "A Lecture on the Haytien Revolutions." In *The Works of James McCune Smith: Black Intellectual and Abolitionist*, edited by John Stauffer, 25–47. New York: Oxford University Press, 2006.

Smith, James McCune. "On the Fourteenth Query of Jefferson's Notes on Virginia." In *The Works of James McCune Smith: Black Intellectual and Abolitionist*, edited by John Stauffer. New York: Oxford University Press, 2006.

Smith, William. *A Stratigraphical System of Organized Fossils, with Reference to the Specimens of the Original Geological Collection in the British Museum: Explaining Their State of Preservation and Their Use in Identifying the British Strata*. London: E. Williams, 1817.

Snorton, C. Riley. *Black on Both Sides: A Racial History of Trans Identity*. Minneapolis: University of Minnesota Press, 2017.

Somerville, Siobhan B. *Queering the Color Line: Race and the Invention of Homosexuality in American Culture*. Durham, NC: Duke University Press, 2000.

Spillers, Hortense J. "Mama's Baby, Papa's Maybe: An American Grammar Book." *Diacritics* 17, no. 2 (Summer 1987): 64–81.

Spires, Derrick R. "Aliened Americans: Pseudonymity and Gender Politics in Early Black Social Media." *African American Review* 55, no. 1 (Spring 2022): 33–49.

Spires, Derrick R. *The Practice of Citizenship: Black Politics and Print Culture in the Early United States*. Philadelphia: University of Pennsylvania Press, 2019.

Spivak, Gayatri Chakravorty. "Translator's Preface." In *Of Grammatology*, by Jacques Derrida, ix–lxxxvii. Baltimore: Johns Hopkins University Press, 1976.

Spofford, Harriet Prescott. "The Amber Gods." In *The Amber Gods, and Other Stories*, edited by Alfred Bendixen, 37–83. New Brunswick, NJ: Rutgers University Press, 1989.

Stauffer, John. *The Black Hearts of Men: Radical Abolitionists and the Transformation of Race*. Cambridge, MA: Harvard University Press, 2004.

Stauffer, John, ed. *The Works of James McCune Smith: Black Intellectual and Abolitionist*. New York: Oxford University Press, 2007.

Steffen, Will. "The Anthropocene: The Ultimate Policy Challenge." *Asia and the Pacific Policy Forum*, January 19, 2016. www.policyforum.net / the-anthropocene-the-ultimate- policy-challenge/.

Stiggins, George. *Creek Indian History: A Historical Narrative of the Genealogy, Traditions and Downfall of the Ispocoga or Creek Indian Tribe of Indians by One of the Tribe, George Stiggins (1788–1845)*. Edited by Virginia Pounds Brown. Birmingham: University of Alabama Press, 2003.

Stoddard, Elizabeth. *The Morgesons and Other Writings, Published and Unpublished*. Edited by Lawrence Buell and Sandra A. Zagarell. Philadelphia: University of Pennsylvania Press, 1984.

Stoddard, R. H. "Henry Rowe Schoolcraft." *National Magazine* 6, no. 1 (January 1855): 1–6.
Strang, Cameron B. "Measuring Souls: Psychometry, Female Instruments, and Subjective Science, 1840–1910." *History of Science* 58, no. 1 (2020): 76–100.
Sugden, John. "Early Pan-Indianism: Tecumseh's Tour of the Indian Country, 1811–1812." *American Indian Quarterly* 10, no. 4 (Autumn 1986): 273–304.
Sweet, Timothy. *Extinction and the Human: Four American Encounters*. Philadelphia: University of Pennsylvania Press, 2021.
TallBear, Kim. "An Indigenous Reflection on Working beyond the Human/Not Human." In "Queer Inhumanisms," ed. Mel Y. Chen and Dana Luciano. Special issue, *GLQ* 21, no. 2 (June 2015): 230–35.
TallBear, Kim. *Native American DNA: Tribal Belonging and the False Promise of Genetic Science*. Minneapolis: University of Minnesota Press, 2013.
"Terrific Theory." *Gazette of the Golden Rule: Odd-Fellows Family Companion* 10, no. 6 (1849): 98.
"Terrific Theory." *North Star*, February 2, 1849, 3.
"Terrific Theory." *London Journal and Weekly Record of Science, Literature, and Art* 9, no. 214 (March 31, 1849): 62.
Todd, Zoe. "An Indigenous Feminist's Take on the Ontological Turn: 'Ontology' Is Just Another Word for Colonialism." *Journal of Historical Sociology* 29, no. 1 (March 2016): 4–22.
Todd, Zoe. "On Time." *Speculative Fish-ctions*, November 7, 2018. https://zoestodd.com/2018/11/07/on-time/.
Todhunter, Isaac. *William Whewell, D.D., An Account of His Writings with Selections from His Literary and Scientific Correspondence*. Vol. 1. London: Macmillan and Co., 1876.
Tompkins, Kyla Wazana. "On the Limits and Promise of New Materialist Philosophy." *Lateral: Journal of the Cultural Studies Association* 5, no. 1 (Spring 2016). https://csalateral.org/issue/5-1/forum-alt-humanities-new-materialist-philosophy-tompkins/.
Trachtenberg, Alan. "Naming the View." In *Reading American Photographs: Images as History, Mathew Brady to Walker Evans*, 119–63. New York: Hill and Wang, 1989.
Train, George Francis. *The Facts, or, At Whose Door Does the Sin (?) Lie?* New York: R. M. DeWitt, 1860.
Trench, Richard Chenevix. *On the Study of Words*. 2nd ed. New York: Redfield, 1855.
Trexler, Adam. *Anthropocene Fictions: The Novel in a Time of Climate Change*. Charlottesville: University of Virginia Press, 2015.
Tromp, Marlene. *Altered States: Sex, Nation, Drugs, and Self-Transformation in Victorian Spiritualism*. Albany: SUNY Press, 2006.
Tsinhnahjinnie, Hulleah J., and Veronica Passalacqua, eds. *Our People, Our Land, Our Images: International Indigenous Photographers*. Berkeley, CA: Heyday Books, 2006.

Uno, Hiroko. "Geology in Emily Dickinson's Poetry." *Kobe Jogakuin Daigaku Kenkyujo Yakuin* 48, no. 2 (2001): 1–25.
"The Use of Earthquakes." *Christian Recorder*, October 24, 1868. Reprinted from *The New York Times*.
US Geological Survey. *Tecumseh's Prophecy: Preparing for the Next New Madrid Earthquake, a Plan for an Intensified Study of the New Madrid Seismic Zone*. Edited by Robert M. Hamilton and Arch C. Johnston, 5–7. US Government Printing Office, 1990.
Valencius, Conevery Bolton. *The Lost History of the New Madrid Earthquakes*. Chicago: University of Chicago Press, 2013.
Volney, Constantin-François. *A View of the Climate and Soil of the United States of America*. London, 1804.
Wallace, Maurice O. *Constructing the Black Masculine: Identity and Ideality in African American Men's Literature and Culture, 1775–1995*. Durham, NC: Duke University Press, 2002.
Wallace, Maurice O. "Violence, Manhood, and War in Douglass." In *The Cambridge Companion to Frederick Douglass*, edited by Maurice S. Lee, 73–88. Cambridge: Cambridge University Press, 2009.
Watts, Vanessa. "Indigenous Place-Thought and Agency amongst Humans and Non-humans (First Woman and Sky Woman Go on a European World Tour!)." *Decolonization: Indigeneity, Education and Society* 2, no. 1 (2013): 20–34.
"What a Volcano Can Do." *Christian Recorder*, November 2, 1861.
Whewell, William. "Address to the Geological Society, delivered at the anniversary, on the 15th February, 1839." *Proceedings of the Geological Society of London* 3 (1838–42): 61–98.
Whitman, Walt. "Slang in America." *North American Review* 141, no. 348 (November 1885): 431–35.
Whyte, Kyle Powys. "Indigenous Food Sovereignty, Renewal, and US Settler Colonialism." In *The Routledge Handbook of Food Ethics*, edited by Mary Rawlinson and Caleb Ward, 354–65. New York: Routledge, 2016.
Whyte, Kyle Powys. "Time as Kinship." In *The Cambridge Companion to Environmental Humanities*, edited by Jeffrey Jerome Cohen and Stephanie Foote, 39–55. Cambridge: Cambridge University Press, 2021.
Williams, W. D. "Louis Bringer and His Description of Arkansas in 1812." *Arkansas Historical Quarterly* 48, no. 2 (Summer 1989): 108–36.
Willis, Lloyd. *Environmental Evasion: The Literary, Critical and Cultural Politics of "Nature's Nation."* Albany: SUNY Press, 2011.
Windolph, Christopher J. *Emerson's Nonlinear Nature*. Columbia: University of Missouri Press, 2007.
Winslow, C. F., MD. *The Preparation of the Earth for the Intellectual Races: A Lecture, Delivered at Sacramento, California, April 10, 1854, at the Invitation of the House of Assembly*. Boston: Crosby, Nichols and Co., 1854.
Winsor, Mary Pickard. "Louis Agassiz and the Species Question." *Studies in the History of Biology* 3 (1979): 89–138.

Wolosky, Shira. "Poetic Languages." In *The Cambridge History of American Literature, Vol. 4: Nineteenth-Century Poetry 1800-1910*, edited by Sacvan Bercovitch, 248-323. Cambridge: Cambridge University Press, 1994.

Wood, David. *Deep Time, Dark Times: On Being Geologically Human*. New York: Fordham University Press, 2018.

Wool, David. *Milestones in the Evolving Theory of Evolution*. New York: Taylor and Francis, 2020.

Wright, Theodore S., Rev., Rev. Charles B. Ray, and Dr. J. M'Cune Smith. *An Address to the Three Thousand Colored Citizens of New-York: Who Are the Owners of One Hundred and Twenty Thousand Acres of Land in the State of New York, Given to Them by Gerrit Smith, Esq., of Peterboro, September 1, 1846*. New York: n.p., 1846.

Wry, Joan R. "Deep Mapping in Edward Hitchcock's Writing and Emily Dickinson's Poetry." *Textual Cultures* 12, no. 1 (Spring 2019): 95-119.

Wynter, Sylvia. "Novel and History, Plot and Plantation." *Savacou* 5 (June 1971): 95-102.

Wynter, Sylvia. "Unsettling the Coloniality of Being/Power/Truth/Freedom: Towards the Human, After Man, Its Overrepresentation—An Argument." *CR: The New Centennial Review* 3, no. 3 (2003): 257-337.

Yang, Lucinda. "Cherokee and Moravian Relations during the New Madrid Earthquakes, 1811-1812." *Journal of Moravian History* 19, no. 1 (Spring 2019): 25-44.

Yarborough, Richard. "Race, Violence, and Manhood: The Masculine Ideal in Frederick Douglass's 'The Heroic Slave.'" In *Frederick Douglass: New Literary and Historical Essays*, edited by Eric J. Sundquist, 166-88. New York: Cambridge University Press, 1990.

Yusoff, Kathryn. *A Billion Black Anthropocenes or None*. Minneapolis: University of Minnesota Press, 2019.

Yusoff, Kathryn. "Geologic Life: Prehistory, Climate, Futures in the Anthropocene." *Environment and Planning D: Society and Space* 31 (2013): 779-95.

Zalasiewicz, Jan. *The Earth after Us: What Legacy Will Humans Leave in the Rocks?* New York: Oxford University Press, 2008.

Zalasiewicz, Jan, Colin N. Waters, Anthony D. Barnosky, Alejandro Cearreta, Matt Edgeworth, Erle C. Ellis, and Agnieszka Galuszka et al. "Colonization of the Americas, 'Little Ice Age' Climate, and Bomb-Produced Carbon: Their Role in Defining the Anthropocene." *Anthropocene Review* 2, no. 2 (2015): 1-19.

Zuck, Rochelle Raineri. "The Wizard of Oil: Abraham James, the Harmonial Wells, and the Psychometric History of the Oil Industry." *Journal of American Studies* 46, no. 2 (2012): 313-36.

index

Page numbers in *italics* refer to figures.

Adams, Katherine, 23, 25
aesthetic geology (Heringman), 28
African Americans: in California, 190n82; and coral insect trope, 165-69, 170; geological writing by, 30, 116, 137-40, 158-70; on Jefferson, 160-61, 206n84; newspapers by, 11, 137, 143-45, 155; and volcano trope, 30, 140-58, 165, 167, 204n21, 206n69.
See also antiblackness; slavery
African continent, 22, 44-45, 162, 174
Agamben, Giorgio, 78
Agassiz, Louis, 9, 34-35, 46-47, 56, 87
Ahuja, Neel, 183n56
Allawaert, Monique, 23
Allen, Thomas, 27, 47
American Journal of Science and Arts. See Journal of American Science (prev. *American Journal of Science and Arts*)
American Scientific Association, 88, 94
Amherst College, 87, 94-95, 112
ammonite, 137, 139, 167
Anglo-African Magazine, 160-61, 206n69
Anishnabeeg, 62
Anning, Mary, 14
Ansted, David T.: *The Gold-Seeker's Manual,* 47-50, 160, 190n82; *Science, Scenery and Art . . .,* 159-60
Anthropocene: as geological fantasy, 30, 173-74; geological fantasy in, 12-21; in literature, 30, 104, 171-73, 198n37; proposed epoch, 1, 30, 172, 176-79, 209n11, 210n25; start date of, 173-76, 183n57, 209n11, 210n17
Anthropocene Working Group, 173-76
antiblackness, 30, 39, 45, 156, 159, 163, 170, 207n89
anticolonial resistance, 28, 57, 61-67, 75-76, 192n14. *See also* Indigenous revival movement; pan-Indigenous movements
Anti-Colonization Society, 148, 154
antislavery volcano trope, 30, 140-58, 165, 167, 169-70, 204n21, 206n69
arche-fossil (Meillassoux), 14-15
Arsić, Branka, 27, 188n30
Asad, Talal, 11
Asian continent, 18, 44, 49, 162
Atlantic Monthly, 9, 34, 46-47, 112

Baartman, Sara, 45
Babbage, Charles, 106-11, 175-76, 199n56
Bamewawagezhikaquay, 79
Barad, Karen, 17
Barnard, John Levi, 52
Bataille, Georges, 128
Bead Eye, 65
Beche, Henry de la, 2
Bennett, Jane, 14, 17, 20, 117, 126, 135, 183n57
Berlant, Lauren, 6
Bible: and age of earth, 3-4, 11, 34, 91, 182n28, 188n13; and biblical literalism, 21, 128, 182n28; and earthquakes, 57-58, 66, 68, 76; in geological writing, 97, 99-100. *See also* Christianity

Big Bear, 66–67
Big Warrior, 74
biopolitics: and Christianity, 69; of colonialism, 24, 27, 32, 69, 79, 86, 190n68; Deleuze on, 4; Foucault on, 174, 209n11; and geological fantasy, 56; and plasticity, 207n89; of race, 46, 125; of sexuality, 134; and species extinction, 23, 404–4, 179
biopower: Foucault on, 4, 21, 25, 404–4, 46, 174; and gender, 116; and geochronology, 27, 40–46; and geological fantasy, 28; and geology, 21–26, 424–4, 85; and Indigenous peoples, 43, 190n68; and race, 111, 118, 207n89
Bjornerud, Marcia, 15, 17, 178
Black geographies (McKittrick), 158–59
Blackness, 30, 206n84; and anti-slavery volcano trope, 30, 140–58, 165, 167, 169–70, 204n21, 206n69; and coral, 165–69; and counterecologies, 156–57, 170; and gender, 30, 140, 147, 152–55, 169–70, 187n109; and geology, 30, 116, 137–70; and impressibility, 116, 161; and land, 23, 25, 164, 186-86n94; and revolutionary masculinity, 147, 152–55. *See also* antiblackness
bodies: Asian, 132–33; and biopower, 21–23; Black, 23–24, 116, 158, 164, 170, 179; and the fossil record, 94, 109; Indigenous, 43–44, 63, 126, 164; as matter, 1, 4, 117–19, 125, 135, 178, 196n6; and race, 158, 161, 168, 189n45; and slavery, 163, 170; white women's, 29–30, 116, 121–22, 131. *See also* biopolitics
Bowler, Peter J., 11, 39, 41, 182n33
Bringier, Louis, 76–79, 83, 195n80
Brown, Jayna, 20, 179
Brown, John, 155–58
Bryan, Eliza, 67–68
Buchanan, Joseph, 121–22
Buchanan's Journal of Man, 121
Buckland, Adelene, 9, 28, 38, 94
Buckland, William, 8, 88, 107–08, 115
burial mounds (Indigenous), 78, 83–84, 103, 198n36
Burnet, Thomas, 10, 97–98
Burnett, Peter, 50, 190n82
Byrd, Jodi A., 17–18, 25, 164, 168, 186n102

Cadava, Eduardo, 27, 187n9
California, 48–51, 120, 190n82
capitalism, 55, 80, 175, 183. *See also* petrocapitalism
Capitalocene (Moore), 175
Carboniferous period, 48–49, 122
Caribbean islands, 32, 130, 132, 142–43
Cass, Lewis, 79, 82, 194n56
Chakrabarty, Dipesh, 13–16, 176
Chen, Mel Y., 185n80

Cherokee, 58, 61, 65–66, 77–78
Chickasaw, 17, 61, 64, 164
Choi, Tina Young, 107
Chow, Juliana, 166
Christianity: and the Connecticut Valley fossil tracks, 99–100, 110; and the coral insect trope, 167; missionaries of, 65–66, 193n38; and the New Madrid earthquakes, 57–60, 62, 68–69, 71, 76; and planetary time, 34–35, 37–38, 49; and sacred time, 128; and Spiritualism, 29, 118, 120, 126, 182n33. *See also* Bible; Gnosticism; Moravians
Christian Recorder: "The Force of Volcanos," 145; "The Use of Earthquakes," 145–46; "What a Volcano Can Do," 145
Cinqué, Joseph, 153
Civil War (U.S.), 145–46
Clark, Nigel, 129, 140–41, 152
climate change, 12, 16, 104, 171, 174–77, 183n57
Clytus, Radiclani, 169–70
Cohen, Jeffrey Jerome, 117
Cole, Thomas, 55–56
colonialism: in "The Amber Gods" (Spofford), 132, 134; and the Anthropocene, 175, 177; and antiblackness, 45; and biopower, 21–25, 27, 41; Deleuzoguattarian, 17–19; and geological knowledge, 25, 37, 43, 45, 47, 51, 112; and geological time, 5, 34, 43–44; and the New Madrid earthquakes, 28, 58–61, 67, 76, 86; and the overrepresentation of Man, 15, 22, 41. *See also* anticolonial resistance; Indigenous peoples; settler geology; settler time
Colored American: "Family Cabinets of Nature and Art," 11–12, 143; "Letters from the West Indies," 142–43, 204n19
Columbus, Christopher, 4, 34
Comte de Buffon, 97
Comte de Mirabeau, 142, 148
Conde de Lemos, 22
Connecticut Valley fossil tracks: discovery of, 87–88, 198n40; Hitchcock's writing on, 94–100, 106–12; and ichnology, 91–94; Longfellow's writing on, 100–106, 197–98n30, 198n42; writing on, 28–29, 88–90, 112–13
Cook, James, 4, 34
Coole, Diana, 17
Cooper, James Fenimore: *The Crater, or, Vulcan's Peak*, 28, 51–56, 191n87; *The Prairie*, 191n87
Cope, Edward Drinker, 26
coral: insects, trope of, 165–70; material of, 165–66, 167, 208n112
Cordis, Shanya, 165, 170
Coulthard, Glen Sean, 19, 24, 59, 63
counterecologies (Sharpe), 156–57, 170
Coviello, Peter, 38

236   Index

craniology, 46, 166
Cree, 103
Creek, 61, 64, 72-75
Cridge, Annie Denton, 29, 118-20, 125-26, 182n24, 202n51. *See also The Soul of Things*
Cuvier, Georges, 10, 24, 28, 33, 36, 40-46, 88, 98, 128, 162, 182n28, 189n40. *See also* extinction (species)

Daggett, Cara New, 184-85n74
Dana, James D., 47
Darwin, Charles, 9, 42, 46, 119, 166
Davis, Andrew Jackson, 39, 120
Davis, Heather, 177-78
Day, Iyko, 131
Deane, James, 87, 89, 94, 196n5
deep time, 3, 7, 13, 172
de Landa, Manuel, 1, 17, 117
Delaware (people), 58, 103
Deleuze, Gilles, 4, 17-18, 119, 131, 196n6
Deleuzoguattarianism, 17-18, 183-84n59
democracy, 11-12, 56, 163
Denton, Elizabeth M. Foote, 29, 118-19, 122-26, 135, 182n24. See also *The Soul of Things*
Denton, Sherman, 119, 202n51
Denton, William, 1-3, 8-10, 29, 118-26, 135, 182n24, 182n33. See also *The Soul of Things*
Derrida, Jacques, 93, 133-34
Dickinson, Emily, 112, 116-17
Dimock, Wai Chee, 27
dinosaurs, 14, 16, 26, 89, 112, 199n61
dirt determinism (Adams), 23, 25
Douglass, Frederick: and Martin, 157, 164; and volcano trope, 30, 140, 142, 144, 147, 165, 169; *The Heroic Slave*, 153; *My Bondage and My Freedom*, 137-39, 203n2; "The Revolution of 1848," 147; "Slavery, the Slumbering Volcano," 148-50, 152-55; "The Tyrants' Jubilee!," 149-51; "What of the Night?," 147; "What to the Slave Is the Fourth of July?," 147
Dowd, Gregory 61, 193n41
Drake, Benjamin, 75
Draper, W. W., 87, 91

earth, antiquity of, 3, 5-7, 10-12, 23-24, 33-40, 42-43, 88-89, 91, 119-20, 182n28. *See also* deep time; planetary time
earthquakes: in *The Crater* (Cooper), 52, 54; geologic theories of, 55-56, 76-84, 106, 121, 197n104; as metaphor, 145-47, 152, 177, 206n69; prophecy-based understandings of, 59-67, 71-72, 75-76, 84-86; settler responses to, 67-76. *See also* New Madrid earthquakes

ecological personhood (Allawaert), 23
Edmunds, R. David, 61, 63
Elleray, Michelle, 166-67, 169
Ellsworth, Elizabeth, 12-13, 19, 179, 184n70
Emerson, Ralph Waldo, 27, 53, 89, 187n9, 198n33; "Fate," 32-33; "The Poet," 31-32
evolution: ceaseless, 32; Darwinian, 42; disbelief in, 41, 46, 98, 189n40, 207n88; and extinction, 21; and fossil record, 24-25; and human beings, 10; McCune Smith on, 138, 160; and race, 44, 111, 161
exomodernity, 7, 14-15, 21, 43-44, 177, 189n44. *See also* modernity
exploration (trope of), 343-5, 201n50
extinction (species): and the Anthropocene, 12, 172, 174, 176; and biopolitics, 23, 179; Cuvier on, 10, 24, 36, 40-42, 88, 98, 174; and the fossil record, 14, 31, 93; and geological fantasy, 5; and Indigenous peoples, 43, 84; in literature, 104; and modernity, 209n11

fantasy (Berlant), 6
Farrier, David, 172
femininity, 112, 118, 169-70
feminism: Black, 20, 170, 187n109; Indigenous, 20; and Spiritualism, 118, 120, 126; white, 135
Ferreira da Silva, Denise, 151
Ficklin, Joseph, 70, 80
Fixico, Donald L., 72
Flint, Timothy, 57-58, 68
fort/da game, 7-8, 39, 90, 173, 178
fossil fuels, 16, 183n56, 201n29
fossil other (Pandian), 24-25, 29, 43-44, 60, 79, 90, 179
fossil poetry (Emerson), 31-32
fossil record: of animal tracks, 87-90; and the Anthropocene, 173, 178-79; and biopower, 41-42; and the Dentons, 123-24; as freedom metaphor, 137-38, 167; gaps in, 38-39, 121; and geological time, 2, 10-11, 14, 36-39, 83; and Indigenous peoples, 25, 43-44, 59, 78, 91, 197n9; in literature, 31-32, 115, 128, 133, 171-72; and race, 46, 139. *See also* ammonite; Connecticut Valley fossil tracks; ichnology; rock record
Foucault, Michel: on biopower, 4, 21, 25, 40-44, 46, 174; on Cuvier, 38, 41, 189n40; *History of Sexuality*, 40, 209n11; on modernity, 189n43-45, 209n11; *The Order of Things*, 40-42, 118, 189n40, 189n43-44, 209n11; *Society Must Be Defended*, 41. *See also* biopower
Fraser, Gordon, 140, 143, 158
Frederick Douglass' Paper: "Is the Center of the Earth a Mass of Fire?," 144; "The Schoolmaster," 159; "The Tyrants' Jubilee!," 149

Index 237

Freeman, Elizabeth, 135, 178
Freud, Sigmund, 7. *See also* fort/da game
Friends of the Pleistocene, 184n70. *See also* Ellsworth, Elizabeth; Kruse, Jamie
Frost, Samantha, 17
fugitive geology, 139, 144, 165, 170
fugitive science (Rusert), 30, 139

Gambold, John, 65
Garrison, William Lloyd, 142
geochronology: and the Anthropocene, 1, 13, 171–73, 178; and biopower, 21, 40, 42–46; and colonialism, 59–60, 83–84; and earth's antiquity, 33, 36; and the fossil record, 10; and racialization, 28, 38, 48–49, 113
geological fantasy, 26, 30, 47, 51, 89–90, 112, 189n45; and the antebellum period, 26–30; in the Anthropocene, 12–21; Anthropocene as, 30, 173–74; and biopolitics, 56; and biopower, 21, 28, 85; and Blackness, 30, 139–43, 151, 156, 162, 167, 169; definition, 5–12; and earthquakes, 28–29, 57–86; and extinction, 5; and Man, 15, 26, 60, 75, 85, 112, 139, 170, 176; and new materialism, 17, 20; and the nonhuman turn, 141–7; and the rock record, 16, 21, 121, 172
geological machine (Schuller), 78–79
Geological Society of Britain, 33
geological time. *See* deep time; earth, antiquity of; geochronology; planetary time
geologic turn (Ellsworth and Kruse), 12–13, 19–20, 135, 179
geontopower (Povinelli), 21, 23, 25, 179
geophilia (Cohen), 30, 117–18, 123, 126, 129, 131, 135
Georgia Journal, 72
Gleason, William, 142–43
Glissant, Édouard, 161, 207n93
Gnosticism, 130
Goeman, Mishuana, 19, 62
Goffe, Tao Leigh, 32, 53
gold, 48–50
Gómez-Barris, Macarena, 21, 175
Goodrich, Samuel, 51
Gormally, Alexandra, 140–41, 152
Gould, Steven Jay, 13, 119
Graham Island, 53–54
Great Acceleration, 173–74
Greyser, Naomi, 102
Grimes, J. Stanley, 39, 201n28
Grusin, Richard, 14
guano, 32, 52–53, 55, 191n92
Guattari, Félix, 17–18, 119, 131, 196n6
Gunn, Robert Lawrence, 73–74

Haiti, 142
Hancock, Jonathan, 64–65
Haraway, Donna, 175
Harrison, William, 64
Hartman, Saidiya, 148, 153–54, 170
Haudenosaunee, 62–63, 91
Hayden, Ferdinand, 26
Herculaneum. *See* Mount Vesuvius
Heringman, Noah, 28, 89–90, 100
Hicks, Charles, 66
Higginson, Thomas Wentworth, 88, 112
Hitchcock, Edward, 10, 29, 106, 113, 122, 175–76, 179, 196n8, 198n40; *Elementary Geology*, 98–99, 116; *Geological Survey of Massachusetts*, 88–89; *Ichnology of New England*, 108–10; "Ornithichnites Giganteus, *Redivivus*" (poem), 90, 96–100; "Ornithichnology" (article), 87, 90, 95–96, 98; *The Religion of Geology and Its Connected Sciences*, 11, 110–12, 128, 199n56; *Reminiscences of Amherst College*, 94–95; "Report on Ichnolithology . . . ," 107–08; *Report on the Geology of Massachusetts*, 90–92
hoarding (Bennett), 126, 135
Holbrook, Josiah, 11–12, 143
Holmes, Oliver Wendell, 88
Holocene epoch, 176
Hooley, Matt, 176
Howe, Henry, 85
Humboldt, Alexander von, 50
Hunter, John Dunn, 72, 75, 194n56
Hutton, James, 3, 6, 9–10, 34, 36, 88, 98, 182n28, 188n13
Huxley, Thomas Henry, 112

ichnology, 88, 93–95, 107–08, 112
ichnopoesis, 90
impressibility, corporeal 102, 116, 121–22, 161
Indian Confederacy, 192n14
Indian Removal Act (1830), 65
Indigenous extinction (trope of), 24–25, 43–44, 50–51, 84, 90, 101–5, 184n68
Indigenous peoples: and the Anthropocene, 175–76, 179, 198n37; and biopower, 190n68; Deleuze on, 18–19; and the fossil record, 88, 196–97n9; and the geologic turn, 19–20; as guides for geologists, 76, 83; and land, 23, 47–48, 164–65, 168, 184n66; in literature, 53, 100–105; lithification of, 18, 22; and the Mississippi Valley earthquakes, 28–29, 57–67, 70–86, 196n104; and psychometric geology, 125–26; and psychometry, 125–26. *See also* anticolonial resistance; Indigenous revival movement; pan-Indigenous movements; *individual tribes and nations*

Indigenous place-thought, 62
Indigenous revival movement, 57, 59, 66, 68, 73, 192n14
Insko, Jeffrey, 152
International Chronostratigraphic Chart, 171
International Commission on Stratigraphy. *See* Anthropocene Working Group
Iovino, Serenella, 110

Jackson, Andrew: *Annual Message to Congress*, 101–2, 104, 112
Jackson, Virginia, 105, 112, 195n91
Jackson, Zakiyyah Iman, 15, 151, 153, 185n80, 207n89
James, Jennifer C., 53, 191n92
Jefferson, Thomas, 103, 160, 163, 206n84
Johnston, Jane. *See* Bamewawagezhikaquay
Journal of American Science (prev. *American Journal of Science and Arts*), 76–77, 87, 90, 95–96, 98
Jurassic era, 160

King, Clarence, 26
King, Tiffany Lethabo, 20, 168, 170
Knickerbocker (magazine), 2, 4, 32, 88, 96, 98
Kolbert, Elizabeth, 173
Kruse, Jamie, 12–13, 19, 179, 184n70

La Brea Tar Pits (California), 119–20
LaFleur, Greta, 161
Lakomäki, Sami, 192n14
Lalawethika. *See* Tenskwatawa
land as pedagogy, 23, 60, 185–86n94
land lines (Cram), 20
Latour, Bruno, 18
LeMenager, Stephanie, 33, 191n87
Lenape, 91, 198n35
Lewis, Simon, 175, 179
Lexington Reporter, 57–58, 67
Liberator, 143, 155, 204n21; letter from a "New York philanthropist," 147–48, 150–51
Lincoln, Abraham, 142
Longfellow, Henry Wadsworth, 29, 87–88, 198n32-33; "A Psalm of Life," 105, 198n42; *The Song of Hiawatha*, 79, 101; "To the Driving Cloud," 90, 100–107, 113, 197–98n30, 198n42
Louisiana Gazette, 64, 69, 72
Louisiana Territory. *See* New Madrid earthquakes
Lyell, Charles: and the Connecticut Valley fossil tracks, 87, 97; influence in literature, 51, 53–54, 188n30; on earth's antiquity, 35; on evolution, 46, 166, 207n88; on the New Madrid earthquakes, 83–84, 196n104; *Principles of Geology*, 38, 43, 91, 141, 166, 202–3n78; on progress, 10, 39, 42–44, 97; *A Second Visit to the United States*, 83, 159–60; on slavery, 159–60, 206n79; *Travels in North America*, 159–60
lyric reading (Jackson), 105

Mader, Mary Beth, 41
malleability, racial, 1596-5, 207n89. *See also* impressibility, corporeal; plasticity
Man: and the Anthropocene, 172, 179; and biopower, 25–26, 56; Foucault on, 40–43; and geological fantasy, 112, 170, 176; and Indigenous-extinction trope, 44; in literature, 75, 81, 96; and matter, 117–18; overrepresentation of (Wynter), 15, 20, 22, 28–30, 60, 79, 122, 126, 136, 139, 174; and planetary time, 7–8, 334–0, 49, 113, 119, 131; and the specter, 134; Wynter on, 41, 161, 174, 186n102, 199n58
manifest geology, 28, 30, 47–52. *See also* colonialism
Man's geographies (McKittrick), 1616-2
mapping (geological), 3, 23, 27, 42, 47, 56, 93, 113, 187n94
Marché, Jordan D., II, 97–98
Marsh, Othniel Charles, 26
Martin, Anthony J., 94, 147
Martin, J. Sella, 30, 140, 147, 155–58, 165, 169, 206n69
masculinity, 29–30, 94, 100, 147, 153–54, 169–70
Maslin, Mark, 175, 179
Massachusetts, 10, 29, 87–88, 91–92, 95, 105
Massachusetts Geological Survey, 87
mastodons, 49, 78, 103–04, 123–24
materialism: historical, 16, 183n57; new, 17–20, 29, 90, 110, 117, 125–26, 135, 183n57
Mathews, Cornelius, 103–4, 198n36
matter (Deleuze and Guattari), 196n6
matter-energy, 17, 117
Mayor, Adrienne, 91, 196–97n9
Mbembe, Achille, 25, 44
McBride, James, 68, 71
McCune Smith, James. *See* Smith, James McCune.
McGurl, Mark, 7, 15
McHenry, Francis, 72–73
McKenney, Thomas L., 74–75, 84
McKittrick, Katherine, 22–23, 158, 161, 170, 175, 185–86n94
McPhee, John, 3, 7, 13, 172
mediumship. *See* psychometry
Meillassoux, Quentin, 14–15
Melville, Herman, 27, 88; *Moby-Dick*, 30, 171–73
Mesozoic period, 16, 112
Metcalf, Samuel L., 4, 32, 56, 88, 139
meteor (trope of), 156–58
meteorites, 123, 125, 182n24

Index 239

Mexico, 48
Miller, Hugh, 137–38, 203n2
Miller, Mary Ashburn, 141, 150–51
mining, 22, 60, 82, 185n88, 191n92. *See also* gold; silver
minor geologies, 29, 176, 187n109
Mississippi River, 22, 58, 68, 70–72, 77–79
Mississippi Valley, 28, 59, 76, 84
Mitchill, Samuel L., 80
modernity, 4–12, 21, 23–26, 36, 38, 43–44, 59, 76–77, 79, 96, 134, 173–77, 197n9, 209n11. *See also* exomodernity
molecular sexuality (Deleuze and Guattari), 131
molten core theory, 144–45
Montserrat, 142, 204n19
Mooney, James, 75
Moore, Jason W., 175
Moravians, 65–66, 193n38
Morton, Samuel, 46
Morton, Timothy, 14, 16, 125, 183n57
Mount Vesuvius, 3, 145, 204–5n21; as metaphor, 142, 144, 147–48

nationalism, 26–28, 51, 58–60, 67, 70–71, 75–76
National Magazine, 82
Navakas, Michelle Currie, 167
necropolitics, 25, 42, 176, 180
Neimanis, Astrida, 158
"new cultural geology" (McGurl), 15
New Madrid earthquakes: geologic responses to, 76–84, 197n104; Indigenous responses to, 61–67, 193n38; legacy of, 84–86; overview of, 28–29, 57–61; settler responses to, 67–76
New Madrid Federal Relief Act, 59, 70
new materialism, 14, 29, 90, 110, 135, 183n52, 183n57, 183n59; and geological fantasy, 17, 20; and Indigeneity, 17–20; and matter-energy, 17, 29, 117, 125–26
Nichols, Robert, 64
nonhuman turn, 14–16, 18, 183n57
North American continent, 9, 26, 33, 47–49, 58, 62, 69, 80, 158, 164, 207n98. *See also* Indigenous peoples
North American Review, 51, 91–92, 95
North Star: "Terrific Theory," 144
Norton-Smith, Thomas M., 62

objectivity, 9–10, 17, 125, 150, 178
O'Brien, Jean M., 18, 24, 184n68, 186n97
O'Connor, Ralph, 2, 8, 28
Ogden, Emily, 11, 38
Ojibwe, 18, 101

Omaha (people), 101–5, 197–98n30
ontological turn, 14–19
Oppermann, Serpil, 110
Orbis hypothesis, 175–76, 198n37, 210n17
Osage, 61, 72, 78, 194n56, 195n80
Owen, Richard, 87, 89, 161

Pacific islands, 32, 51–53
paleontology, 16, 26, 44, 46, 88, 94, 97–98, 171
Pandian, Jacob, 24, 43
pan-Indigenous movements, 58–59, 61–62, 64, 72–73, 76, 80–82, 193n41
Parikka, Jussi, 183n51
Penn, Granville, 115–16
Peterson, Carla L., 159
petrocapitalism, 60, 177. *See also* capitalism
Phelps, Almira Hart Lincoln, 115, 135
phrenology, 39, 201n28
Pierce, William Leigh, 68, 71–72
Pinto, Samantha, 45, 187n109
planetary time, 3, 7, 14, 33–35, 37–38, 128, 159, 172, 178, 188n13. *See also* deep time; earth, antiquity of
plantation geographies (McKittrick), 23
Plantationocene (Haraway and Tsing), 175
plasticity, 160, 207n89
Playfair, John, 6, 8, 13, 34, 119, 199
poetics of landscape (Glissant), 161–62
polygenesis, 46
Pompeii. *See* Mount Vesuvius
Pope, Alexander, 81
posthumanism, 15
Povinelli, Elizabeth A., 15, 21, 23, 78
Powell, John Wesley, 26
Precambrian era, 9
Prince, Thomas, 55–56
Prophetstown, IN, 61, 62
psychometry, 118, 120–26, 135, 182n24, 201–2n51, 201n29, 201n50
Puar, Jasbir K., 4

queerness, 29, 115, 117, 124–25, 135, 138–40, 168–69. *See also* geophilia

racial hierarchies, 28, 30, 39, 46–47, 113, 135–36, 139, 160, 162, 201n51
racialization, 20–21, 24–25, 28, 39, 44–46, 111, 132, 153, 161, 186n102, 189n45, 201n51
racial uplift, 143, 159, 166
racism, 32, 41, 45–46, 139, 160, 162, 166–67, 187n9. *See also* antiblackness; racial hierarchies; racialization; white supremacy
Rifkin, Mark, 19–20, 67, 190n68

rock record: and the Anthropocene, 173, 175, 177, 179; and extinction, 42, 44; and geological fantasy, 16, 21, 121, 172; and geological knowledge, 2, 9–10, 51, 117; and moral education, 105, 108, 112; and psychometry, 122, 201n28; and white supremacy, 45–46, 49. *See also* fossil record
Romanticism, 19, 28–29, 59, 77, 848–6, 100, 196n8
Rozet, Claude Antoine, 4
Rudwick, Martin, 36, 39, 45
Rusert, Britt, 30, 138–40, 206n84

sacred time, 35, 128
Sale, Maggie Montesinos, 142, 152–54
Sayre, Gordon, 75
Schoolcraft, Henry Rowe, 22–24, 27, 83; *Algic Researches*, 79, 100–101; *Journal of a Tour into the Interior of Missouri and Arkansaw*, 80, 82; *Transallegania*, 80–82, 195n91; *A View of the Lead Mines of Missouri*, 79
Schuller, Kyla, 24, 42, 78, 116, 118, 207n89
Scientific American, 13, 144, 200n20
Scrope, Georges Poulett, 34–35
sense-methods (Freeman), 135
settler geology, 20, 22, 29, 48–49, 51, 64, 90, 184n66. *See also* colonialism
settler time, 51, 59, 67–68, 86. *See also* colonialism
sexual violence, 132–33, 170
Sharpe, Christina, 156, 158, 170, 179
Shaviro, Steven, 93, 113, 133
Shawnee, 58–59, 61–62, 65, 72, 86, 192n14
shoals (King), 20, 168, 170
Siccar Point, Scotland, 6
Silliman, Benjamin, 87, 98, 107, 144
Silver mining, 22, 185n88
Simpson, Leanne Betasamosake, 19, 23, 60, 185–86n94
Skaquaw, 77
slavery: in "The Amber Gods" (Spofford), 131–34; and the Connecticut Valley fossil tracks, 110–12, 199n56; and geological timescale, 137–39; William Denton on, 121; 66; Lyell on, 159–60, 206n79; and mapping practices, 1858–6n94; and mining, 185n88, 191n92; and soil exhaustion, 191n92; and overrepresentation of Man, 15, 22. *See also* antislavery volcano trope
Smith, Gerrit, 163–64, 168–69
Smith, James McCune, 30, 116, 140, 158–59, 169–70, 207n89, 208n104; "Civilization: Its Dependence on Physical Circumstances," 160–63, 165–68, 208n122; "Heads of the Colored People," 159; introduction to *My Bondage and My Freedom*, 137–39, 204n2; "Lecture on the Haytien Revolutions,"

142, 148; "On the Fourteenth Query . . . ," 160, 162–64, 206n84, 207n98, 208n122; "The Schoolmaster," 159–60
Smith, John Augustine, 166
Smith, William, 36–37, 93
Soul of Things The (Denton), 119–26, 135, 201–2n50–51
specter (Derrida), 133–34
speculative geology, 27, 30, 54, 89, 91, 93, 95, 112, 115, 139–41, 180
Spillers, Hortense J., 133, 163, 170
Spires, Derrick R., 160, 169–70
Spiritualism, 29, 39, 118, 120–21, 124, 126, 182n33, 202n51. *See also* psychometry
Spivak, Gayatri Chakravorty, 93
Spofford, Harriet Prescott: "The Amber Gods," 29–30, 114–15, 118–19, 126–35
Steffen, Will, 173
Stiggins, George, 73–75
Stoddard, Elizabeth, 115, 117
Stoddard, R. H., 82
stratigraphy, 29, 36–37, 39, 47–48, 50, 76, 83, 93, 123, 172–78
subterranean practices (Hartman), 154, 165, 170
surveys (geological), 26–27, 64, 80, 83, 91
Swedenborg, Emmanuel, 120

Tecumseh, 58–59, 61–64, 72–76, 82, 84–85, 193n41, 194n56
Tenskwatawa, 58–59, 61–65, 72–73, 75, 193n41, 194n59
Thoreau, Henry David, 27, 89, 188n30
Todd, Zoe, 18–19, 177–80, 184n66
trace fossils, 93. *See also* ichnology
Train, George Francis, 39
Treatises on the Power, Wisdom and Goodness of God (Babbage), 106
Trench, Richard Chenevix, 187n4
Tsing, Anna, 175
Tuffen, Hugh, 140–41, 152
Tugalo (Cherokee site), 66–67
Turner, Nat, 155, 157–58
Type of the Times, The (newpaper), 120
Types of Mankind: Or, Ethnological Researches (Nott et al.), 46

United States Geological Survey (USGS): 1912 report on New Madrid, 196n104; formation of, 26; *Tecumseh's Prophecy* (1990 New Madrid plan), 84–86, 196n9
Universal Lyceum movement, 11–12
Usher, William, 46

Vanguard, The (newspaper), 120
Vann, Peggy, 65–66
Virginia, 67, 143, 153, 155, 162
volcanos, 52–54, 83, 121, 166; anti-slavery volcano trope, 30, 140–58, 165, 167, 169–70, 204n21, 206n69. *See also* Mount Vesuvius
Volney, Constantin-François, 83

Washington, Madison, 153–54
Watts, Vanessa, 62, 184n72
weather (Sharpe), 156–58, 206n69
Wheeler, George, 26
Whewell, William, 33–34, 37–38, 56, 106
whiteness: in "The Amber Gods" (Spofford), 133; and antislavery movements, 157; and biopower, 116, 125; and gender, 30, 118; and geochronology, 49–51; and geological knowledge, 20–21, 33; and the geologic turn, 135; and land, 47–48; and Man, 25, 29, 37; and plasticity, 207n89; and psychometry, 126

white supremacy, 45–46, 139, 161, 179, 201–2n51
Whitman, Walt, 32, 198n32–33
Whyte, Kyle Powys, 86, 178
Willis, Lloyd, 102, 104, 198n32–33
Wilson, William J., 160
Winnebago, 22–23, 79
Winslow, Charles F., 48–51
women and girls: Asian, 131–34; Black, 169–70, 187n109; and geological knowledge, 38, 115–16; and Spiritualism, 121–22; white, 29–30, 118, 121–22. *See also* femininity; feminism
wonder (Heringman), 89–90, 100
Wood, Norman Barton, 75
Wynter, Sylvia, 15, 20, 22–25, 38, 41, 122, 161, 174, 186n201, 199n58, 206n73

Yusoff, Kathryn, 17, 20, 129

Zalasiewicz, Jan, 173